Machzor:
Challenge and Change

RESOURCE PACK FOR
INDIVIDUAL AND GROUP
STUDY

Central Conference of American Rabbis
5769   New York   2010

Edited by Hara E. Person and Sara Newman

Discussion Questions by Sara Newman

The Central Conference of American Rabbis would like to thank everyone who participated in the Machzor: Challenge and Change conference calls and allowed their presentations to be used in this format.

"Kol Nidre" appears in the forthcoming *Siddur Lev Shalom*, RA Press, © by Merle Feld. Used with permission of Merle Feld.

10 9 8 7 6 5 4 3 2 1

CCAR Press, 355 Lexington Avenue, New York, NY 10017
(212) 972-3636
www. ccarpress.org

CONTENTS

Preface

As the months of Tammuz and Av come and go this summer, and as we prepare to watch the moon of Elul wax and wane, our attention turns to how we will engage in the preparation of Rosh HaShanah and Yom Kippur. At every congregation, at each gathering, we want to ensure that the experience is meaningful and transformative. And we know that none of this will happen if we mindlessly go through the motions of singing, saying, chanting our liturgical script. Rather, we want to re-create our yearly sacred time with intention. We know that the High Holy Days is more than the *machzor*, greater than the sermons, more involved than what melodies we sing. It is the entire moment. And yet, content does play a key role in what we do. As people open up the *machzor* each year, where will they find meaning? Where will they find resonance in its words? No matter what we do, they do come, but when they do come, what is the experience they have?

There is the old story of the congregant who admitted that he stopped coming to synagogue because every time he came, he heard the same story of Abraham taking his son Isaac up the mountain. What does this story tell us? This particular individual appears to have attended Rosh HaShanah morning services on a "regular" basis. We all know that there is more to the calendar year than Rosh HaShanah and Yom Kippur, and yet these holidays carry great significance and add great richness to the calendar year. We may not be able to alter the experience of someone who comes only once a year, but we should try. Similarly, those who are actual regulars who attend throughout the year should also find their High Holy Day experience to be moving and meaningful. Unfortunately, many find a dissonance between what happens during the rest of the year in services and what happens on these two days. Their synagogue turns formal in an unfamiliar way.

It is fair to ask what the goal of the prayer experience should be for those worshiping. We need to take the time to ponder the possibilities. We want those who come to find meaning in their presence and their participation. We want them to be uplifted by the majesty of the moment and the reaching out to a transcendent God. At the same time, we also want them to be moved by the imminence of the community and the sacred nature of the events unfolding before them.

We need time to ease into these sacred days, having given ourselves the chance to reflect and to prepare. The Central Conference of American Rabbis is pleased to assist in this process with the enclosed material. This resource pack of material brings together transcripts of presentations of learned colleagues discussing key prayers, recent articles from the *CCAR Journal* focusing on some of the theological issues of the *machzor*, as well as essays from back issues of the *CCAR Journal* and the *Journal of Reform Judaism* on High Holy Day–related topics. Discussion questions and additional information have been added as further resources for you. As we begin our journey toward the creation of a new CCAR *machzor*, we will be looking for different ways to engage the Reform Movement as a whole in meaningful discussions about important content components of the High Holy Day liturgical experience. Our hope is that this pack of material, presented here in an easy-to-access format, will help to foster those thoughtful congregational or institutional discussions, as well as helping you in your own preparations for Rosh HaShanah and Yom Kippur.

Rabbi Elaine Zecher,
Chair, Worship and Practice Committee

Opening Questions

What do you value about the Yamim Noraim? What do you hope to experience on a personal, spiritual level during these days? What impact would you like these days to have on the community?

How do our actions on these days, including preparation during Elul, services, study sessions, and sermons, help to achieve these goals? What, if anything, are the shortcomings of these actions?

How might our values of preserving tradition and acting as part of *K'lal Yisrael* on these holy days come in conflict with our personal search for meaning and spiritual elevation?

On what different levels do you experience prayer? How would you define those levels? How can you make the best use of these different entry points?

What are your personal boundaries concerning making changes to the liturgical text? How do we best communally set boundaries?

How important is it to follow the "traditional" liturgy?

How do we define "traditional," in light of the complex process of liturgical change that occurs over time?

What options do we use to deal with difficult text?

What changes do we permit ourselves to make in order to pray using liturgy that is in line with our values and/or our theology?

What is the process for making change?

How do we balance individual and communal needs in prayer?

What is the role of the rabbi in making decisions, changes, explanations, *kavanot*, teaching, and so on?

What is the value of adding new voices to this process, and how can they take a part?

Machzor:
Challenge and Change

PRESENTATIONS

Editor's Note

The following are transcripts of oral presentations made during a series of three professional development conference calls offered by the Central Conference of American Rabbis.

Each set of presentations covers some of the following:

1. The origin of the text and its development over time
2. The Reform Jewish approach to this text, both in content and form
3. The theological contributions of each text
4. Ways to reframe the text to highlight its various dimensions of meaning
5. Questions, *d'rashot*, *kavanot*, and creative ways to experience the liturgy in preparation for the Yamim Noraim and during services

In the sidebars there are discussion questions and additional background information where relevant.

Introduction: Historical Overview

Rabbi Lance Sussman, Ph.D.

I'm told I have five minutes to cover this topic so I will try to be as judicious as possible.

What I want to concentrate primarily on is the history of the *machzor* within the CCAR, but I have to, of course, acknowledge that before there was a CCAR, there was a *machzor* and there was a whole tradition of Reform liturgies for the High Holy Days that had already molded the way that Reform Judaism was experiencing the High Holy Days before the Conference was formed in 1889. Many of the basic decisions had been made already by the Movement in terms of defining itself at the point where it became a national body here in the United States. So, for example, already in Germany and England and other places, the decision had been made not to recite *Kol Nidrei* and not to sound the shofar. Questions such as the *Musaf* service on Yom Kippur proved to be much more complicated. The tradition of dropping the second day of Rosh HaShanah seemed stronger in England than in other places.

Here in the United States, before there was a *UPB-2*, there were all types of prayer books that handled different parts of the liturgy in different ways. The Conference met for the first time in 1889, and immediately there was a question of a uniform liturgy. A plan of prayer was put forward by a committee in 1891 for the first *UPB-1*, and to everyone's surprise, someone, Rabbi Moses, had already written a prayer book. Apparently, nobody was happy about it. When his book came out in 1892, it was withdrawn because of objections by the radical Einhornians. The following year the committee's *UPB-2* came out, and that stood the test of time. So *UPB-2*, which came out second chronologically was actually the first uniform liturgy of the Movement. Then in 1894, a new *UPB-1* came out, and that became the standard.

No *Kol Nidrei* was included in *UPB-2*. Instead, a hymn sung to the melody of *Kol Nidrei* appeared at the beginning of the service. The book proved popular, and three hundred synagogues adopted it. One hundred thousand copies were distributed; however it was not universally accepted. In my own synagogue at KI (Reform Congregation Knesset Israel in Elkins Park, Pennsylvania), they had their own prayer book, which they felt was more in line with

Machzor: the prayer book for the High Holy Days.

What do you think were the reasons for the opposition to *Kol Nidrei* and the shofar for the early Reformers?

Does your synagogue observe one or two days of Rosh HaShanah? What is the reason for that practice?

The Union Prayer Book, volume 2 (*UPB-2*) was the first High Holy Day prayer book (*machzor*) published by the CCAR.

The Union Prayer Book, volume 1 (*UPB-1*) was published in 1895, after having been recalled from publication in 1892 for being too centrist. This was the first prayer book published by the CCAR and was meant to be suitable for all American Jews.

The early Reformers were able to reach a compromise regarding *Kol Nidrei*. Does this sound like a workable or satisfying compromise? Why or why not?

The goal of creating a unified prayer book was clearly important to the early American

Reform rabbis, even if it was not wholly successful. Why do you think this was important to them? What do you see as the importance or value of this goal? Do you agree or disagree with this goal, and why?

The *Union Hymnal* was a book of songs and hymns published in 1932 and served as a supplement to the *Union Prayer Book*.

The Columbus Platform: http://ccarnet.org/Articles/index.cfm?id=40&pge_prg_id=4687&pge_id=1656

How much do you think that design issues, from the color of the cover to the design of the interior pages, shape our relationship with the content of a prayer book? How much do the design decisions matter? Explain your response.

Gates of Forgiveness: Shaarei Selicha was published in 1993. This publication was meant to be used for *S'lichot* services and provided a reintroduction of this practice for Reform Jews.

High Holy Day prayer books for children included *Gates of Repentance for Young People*, which included services for young children and those in primary grades.

The Sinai editions were published by Chicago Sinai Congregation for those who wanted to go back to an earlier style of Reform worship more in keeping with the values of Classical Reform.

their radical approach to Reform Judaism. *UPB-1* and *UPB-2* were revised right after World War I, but again, nobody was really happy with the new texts. They were further challenged in the beginning of the 1930s, but the Movement had a mechanism at that point to make adjustments. The suggestion was made in 1930 that *Kol Nidrei* be reentered into the liturgy, but through the *Union Hymnal*, not through the *UPB-2*. That "reform" became part of a greater debate during the course of the 1930s that, of course, led to the Columbus Platform. Then in 1940 the revised *UPB-1* was issued. Five years later, delayed by World War II, a revised *UPB-2* was published, and again, a big fight over *Kol Nidrei* took place. First it was in, then it was out, then it was back in. The Conference also did something very interesting, with respect to holiday practice. I don't know if we'll return to this practice or not, but the CCAR sold shofarot that had metal mouthpieces on them as a way of reintroducing the shofar to our services.

When *Gates of Prayer* first came out in 1975, in part stimulated by liturgical developments in England, it added something else brand-new to the holiday liturgical debate—it added color to the cover. So when *Gates of Repentance* was published, instead of all the subdued Protestant tones, now we had a red *machzor*, making it easier to distinguish from the blue Shabbat book.

Following the publishing of *Gates of Repentance* in 1978, all types of additional liturgies were developed by the CCAR that had not been part of the Movement for approximately one hundred years, including *S'lichot*. Several prayer books were offered by the CCAR for the High Holy Day experience for young people of different ages. The issue of gender finally came forward, resulting in a revised, gender-sensitive edition of *Gates of Prayer* in 1994 and *Gates of Repentance* in 1996. Given the rapid evolution of Reform liturgy in the twentieth century, it was not entirely surprising that a return to the *UPB-2* style was longed for in some quantity. The Sinai editions of the *UPB-1* and 2 (which appeared in 2000 and 2001) are one example of looking to the past. And this brings us up to *Mishkan T'filah*, now in circulation as of 2007. The first question before us, of course, is to what extent *Mishkan T'filah* will be the paradigm for our new High Holy Day book. Given our tradition of liturgical adaptability, this will be only one of many discussions and opportunities to meet the contemporary spiritual challenges of the High Holy Days.

Avinu Malkeinu:
Historical Background

Rabbi Edward Feld

I was asked to speak about the history of *Avinu Malkeinu*. The source for *Avinu Malkeinu* is the Babylonian Talmud, *Taanit* 25a, which reports:

שוב מעשה ברבי אליעזר שירד לפני התיבה ואמר עשרים וארבע ברכות
ולא נענה. ירד רבי עקיבא אחריו, ואמר: אבינו מלכנו אין לנו מלך אלא
אתה. אבינו מלכנו למענך רחם עלינו, וירדו גשמים. הוו מרנני רבנן. צתה
צתה בת קול ואמרה: לא מפני שזה גדול מזה, אלא שזה מעביר על
ימידותיו, וזה אינו מעביר על מדותיו

Another incident that occurred to Rabbi Eliezer: He went down to lead services at the ark and recited twenty-four blessings, but no response came. Rabbi Akiva then followed him and went down to the ark and prayed, "Avinu Malkeinu, we have no sovereign save You. Avinu Malkeinu, for Your sake show us kindness." And the rains came. The Rabbis sang his praises, but a voice came from heaven saying, "It did not happen because he was greater than the other, but because he is humble."

It is a strange source for the development of *Avinu Malkeinu* because the source itself seems to be honoring the qualities of the person who leads the prayers of the congregation rather than the specific wording of the individual prayers. Nevertheless the thought that these words are to be honored and that our prayers should imitate that of Rabbi Akiva become an accepted tradition.

Note, too, that the source for *Avinu Malkeinu* is in Tractate *Taanit*, a tractate devoted to the declaration of fast days proclaimed because of the lack of rain. If you look at the traditional list of verses within *Avinu Malkeinu*, many of them stress prosperity, making a good living, or keeping plagues and other afflictions away from the community. Thus the original development of *Avinu Malkeinu* as a synagogue prayer was in the context of prayers averting natural disaster. From this setting, of congregational prayers on fast days in the face of natural disaster, the prayer moved to the penitential days for Yom Kippur. In the community of Babylonia, the immediate week before Rosh HaShanah and all the days of *Aseret Y'mei*

How does *Avinu Malkeinu* function in the Talmud as a formula?

What was the original context for the use of *Avinu Malkeinu* in the synagogue? How did it move to the High Holy Days?

Based on these origins of *Avinu Malkeinu*, what insights can we glean about how these congregations viewed God? What role did God play in their daily lives and in the life of the community?

T'shuvah between Rosh HaShanah and Yom Kippur were observed as fast days and days of penitence, and so it was natural to move a prayer associated with other fast days to this fixed part of the calendar. Verses specific to the season were added, most notably, "Write us in the book of life," etc. In a later time, communities no longer observing these days as fast days continued to recite *Avinu Malkeinu* at this season of the year.

In Early Siddurim

Seder Rav Amram, created by Rav Amram Gaon, ninth century.

Machzor Vitry, created by Simcha ben Shmuel of Vitry, eleventh century.

The Talmudic source quoted above has only the two lines of *Avinu Malkeinu*. Obviously these lines got expanded in different communities. The earliest records we have of the *Avinu Malkeinu* are in *Seder Rav Avram* and in *Machzor Vitry*, and those sources already include a multiplicity of verses beginning with *Avinu Malkeinu*. In *Seder Rav Avram*, we have in different versions twenty-two to twenty-five verses; in *Machzor Vitry*, there are a little over thirty verses, some of which have dropped out and are no longer recited in any extant rite. In the standard Polish rite, forty-four verses are recited.

In the Medieval Period

At the time of the Crusades, verses mentioning the martyrs were added, and these are expanded in the Polish rite. As one can see, different parts of *Avinu Malkeinu* originate in different eras and are recited in different collections.

On what basis were verses added over time? How does this clarify our understanding of the function of this prayer?

It is the phrase repeated in each verse, *Avinu Malkeinu*, though, more than any singular content, that is what made the prayer so popular and, for us, both attractive and problematic. The prayer combines two opposite qualities of God, two qualities that are in tension, and that is typical of much of Jewish prayer. The standardized form of the *b'rachah* begins with an assertion of God's closeness—we begin with saying "You"—but then moves on to talk of God's transcendence, God's sovereignty and rule over the world. The same is true here. The word *Avinu* is meant to refer to God's kindness. I know that that is not our modern association with the word—our sense of fatherhood is more fraught in a post-Freudian world—but in the liturgy *Av* is frequently modified as *Av HaRachaman*, "the Compassionate Father." You may recall that on Rosh HaShanah after the blowing of the shofar we recite a prayer that says, "Remember us as servants or as children." In this second image, we are considered the children of God—an image that evokes a loving relationship.

What are your reactions to the *Avinu Malkeinu* formula, which is used to "invoke both God's imminence and transcendence"? In your experience or understanding,

To see God as Father is to see God as being close, kind, caring, and merciful. Thus, to see God as *Melech* is to see ourselves as servants of God, but to relate to God as Father is to see ourselves in intimate relationship with God. God as Sovereign induces fear, *yirah*; God as Father induces love, *ahavah*. God the Sovereign is judgmental; God the Father is forgiving. Note that Akiva's original prayer of two lines talked of God being our sole Ruler and then of God as having compassion, thus spelling out these two ideas. To recite the words *Avinu Malkeinu* is to assert both that we accept God as the One who is kind and close to us and also the One who establishes a just rule in the world and whose justice will ultimately reign. To put the two together is to invoke both God's imminence and transcendence in one prayer. It was the combination of the two that was the attractiveness of the formula and explains its popularity.

In ending, I note that most Orthodox prayer books continue the Polish practice and include forty-four verses. The Conservative *machzor*, the Harlow edition, leaves out some of the verses that are in *Seder Amram*, but some others are added—there is no apparent consistency in what was selected. *Gates of Repentance* made a decision to divide many of the verses of *Avinu Malkeinu* and place them in different services. The verses on Rosh HaShanah are not the same as those on Yom Kippur, and even on the latter holiday they are different at different times of the day. These contemporary changes accord with the history of *Avinu Malkeinu*, which, as we have seen, was always an evolving text.

how do these two qualities of God interact with one another? Do you identify more strongly with a God that is more imminent than transcendent, or more transcendent than imminent?

In Modern Siddurim and *Machzorim*

Jules Harlow, ed., *Mahzor for Rosh Hashanah and Yom Kippur* (New York: United Synagogue of Conservative Judaism, 1988).

Chaim Stern, ed., *Gates of Repentance* (New York: CCAR Press, 1999).

Avinu Malkeinu: Contemporary Linguistic Challenges and Innovation

Rabbi David Teutsch

Avinu Malkeinu is one of the extraordinarily beloved high points of the High Holy Day liturgy. A question worth contemplating is what has made *Avinu Malkeinu* so beloved—the melody, or the content, or both. The answer to that question is critical as we think about how to place *Avinu Malkeinu* in the service and how to view it.

The *Avinu Malkeinu's* location is normally right after the *Amidah*. While *bakashah* (petitionary prayer) is at the very heart of the weekday *Amidah*, there is comparatively little *bakashah* in the High Holy Day *Amidah*. The many requests in *Avinu Malkeinu* can be understood to some extent as substitutes that express the longings and concerns that emerge during the Yamim Noraim. Those concerns are on people's minds particularly strongly because *Avinu Malkeinu* follows the meditative time of the *Amidah*. People's worries and regrets about the year past and their fears and hopes about what the new year will bring are very much on their minds as they turn to the recitation of *Avinu Malkeinu*. So it may be a combination of the melody, the placement, and the requesting nature of *Avinu Malkeinu* that gives it the power it has for so many people.

We certainly bring our longing, our wants, and our needs to this recitation, but no less we bring our sense of who we are in the world. For some people, that also means bringing a sense of what is going on in their relationships with God as they confront this prayer. That aspect of the *Avinu Malkeinu* is powerful and challenging. While many people of an earlier generation may have been sufficiently learned to pick up on the nuances that Rabbi Feld has discussed, for more liberal Jews in our time, the image of Father and King, while in some ways comforting, is in other ways quite challenging and even troubling. I will come back to that below.

The version of *Avinu Malkeinu* that appears in the Reconstructionist *Kol Haneshamah Machzor* is nineteen lines; it is short compared to the forty-four-line version found in many traditional *machzorim*. Obviously picking and choosing were necessary to reach nineteen lines. I don't know of any liberal version of the *machzor* in current use that includes the traditional forty-four lines all in one setting.

Rabbi Teutsch discusses the difference between the cognitive and affective experiences of prayer. The cognitive aspect concerns the text of the prayer, and the affective aspect is how the prayer is "performed." Is one of these aspects more important to you in a worship experience than the other? Why?

David Teutsch, *Kol Haneshamah: Mahzor Leyamim Nora'im* (Jenkintown, PA: The Reconstructionist Press, 1999).

11

The reduction to nineteen lines reduces the specificity and vividness of the *bakashah,* thereby solving part of the problem for many liberals.

But that doesn't resolve the problem of the words *Avinu Malkeinu* themselves. They raise questions about both gender and imagery. One approach to dealing with that is to point out that our tradition has always said that all imagery is by itself reductive of God and is meant to invoke, not to attribute. That is the point made brilliantly in *Shir HaKavod* (also known by its opening words as *Anim Z'mirot*), for example. Most Jews don't approach *Avinu Malkeinu* with that kind of sophistication. For them, the image of "Father and King" is the central one of the High Holy Day liturgy. It is the image of God sitting in judgment while they offer their plea. Some are comfortable invoking that imagery, but many others are uncomfortable with the theology it represents. Do we want to support the notion of God as King and Judge? It has problems not only because it seems antiquated to residents of democratic countries but also because it raises theological issues that many people avoid most of the year but must confront on the High Holy Days; they are only too pleased to put those issues back on the shelf for the rest of the year.

Of course, the maleness of "Father and King" also stands out. There are several options for dealing with that, including poetry and commentary. There is one interpretation in *Kol Haneshamah* that talks about hearing this as standards and norms rather than kingship, but I don't think that fully solves the problem. It does, however, get at themes that I think every Jew feels during the High Holy Day season, such as our fragility and our dependence. The supplementary prayers surrounding *Avinu Malkeinu* and commentary on it can help explicate those connections. Even if we have those resources, though, they won't fully solve the maleness and imagery problem. So, some of that gets done by how we translate. Joel Rosenberg, for example, translated *Avinu Malkeinu* as "our Creator, our Sovereign" in the *machzor* I edited. But someone who is attentive to the Hebrew knows that *Avinu Malkeinu* is only very creatively interpreted as "our Creator, our Sovereign," and the "our Father, our King" piece of it stays there for most people regardless of the translation.

The right kind of poetry helps. Ruth Brin has an excellent piece found in her collection of poetry *Harvest,* which is included in the *Kol Haneshamah Machzor.* That helps, but the only full way to resolve the issue is to change the Hebrew. An alternative version of the prayer that appears in *Kol Haneshamah* is "*Mekorenu Eloheynu,* our source, our God." It alters the imagery, interprets the prayer in a different way, and solves the "Father and King" issue. But of course that change is a problem for people with a lifelong attachment to singing the traditional Hebrew refrain.

Attributing imagery takes human terms, such as "father" and "king," and ascribes them to God, based on our beliefs about God's nature. Reductive images of God are metaphors that depict certain aspects of God but are not intended to be all-encompassing descriptions of God's true nature. What are other examples of reductive imagery in our liturgy?

How do you feel about a God who sits in judgment as you offer your plea? What theological problems does this bring up for you? Once this image of God is placed "back on the shelf" for the year, what image do you return back to? What values of yours does this God-concept represent?

What are your thoughts on the question of gender and prayer? How does gender in language affect your prayer experience? Does the language of prayer as it relates to gender ever get in the way for you? Why or why not?

What are your reactions to these various linguistic innovations? Which parts of the formula do they retain or expand upon while using different words?

Ruth F. Brin, *Harvest: Collected Poems and Prayers* (Duluth: Holy Cow! Press, 1999).

There is also a version that has been used in several places that alternates lines between *Avinu Malkeinu,* "our Father, our King," and *Imeinu Malkateinu,* "our Mother, our Queen," or you could translate that "our Father, our Sovereign," and "our Mother, our Sovereign." I don't believe that is an adequate solution for a number of reasons. First, I think solving the problem of gender by multiple gendering just muddies the waters further. Second, the image of queen in biblical usage raises problematical connotations, particularly when we use that image as the name for Divinity; I believe invoking those connotations is not helpful.

It seems to me that there is no way to excise the words *Avinu Malkeinu* from the liturgy of the High Holy Day season without doing horrendous damage to the liturgy as well as to the expectations of the people who come to our congregations on the High Holy Days. Retaining that Hebrew makes the inclusion of interpretive commentary and poetry particularly important. The core of the challenge that rabbis face around *Avinu Malkeinu* is how we help people think through this matter theologically in a deeper and richer way so that when particular images of the Divine are invoked they are understood to be evocative rather than explicit theological statements. Jews need to understand that this imagery is not meant to address the absolute nature of God. It comments on how we humans relate to the Divine. *Avinu Malkeinu* thus opens the way to central issues not only in the High Holy Day season, but in our daily lives.

What do you think about Teutsch's assertion that simply adding female imagery to *Avinu Malkeinu* is not an adequate solution? Do you agree or disagree? Explain.

What other solutions have you come across that appeal to you? What other suggestions might you propose?

Do you agree with this statement about removing the words *Avinu Malkeinu*? How do our expectations and memories factor into our worship experience? What affective power does the familiarity of the words and music of the prayer have in our worship experience?

How much does language impact on the ways that we relate to the Divine? How might we expand upon these ways of relating to/ understanding God? How can innovations, adaptations, *kavanot*, and so on contribute not only to our understanding of God, but to our understanding of our own relationship with God?

Avinu Malkeinu: Contemporary Thematic Challenges and Innovation

Rabbi Ron Aigen

In order to gain some perspective on how *Avinu Malkeinu* can have contemporary relevance, it might be helpful to remember the larger context in which this prayer occurs. In the introduction to the *Hadesh Yameinu* machzor, I described the broad perspective of the prayers of this day in this way:

Ron Aigen, *Hadesh Yameinu (Renew Our Days): A Prayer-Cycle for Days of Awe* (Montreal: Congregation Dorshei Emet, 2001).

> The prayers that we say on these days reflect our heightened awareness of the fragility of human life, our shortcomings and imperfections, regrets and failures. Still the overall message is a positive one.
>
> Our prayers tell us God does not want the death of a sinner, but rather that one turn from one's evil ways and live. The message of the Days of Awe is ultimately one of hope and confidence. These days reassure us above all that we have within us the ability to change our lives for the better and that the possibility of change is always open to us. This empowering concept of change is the meaning of t'shuvah, *the main purpose and focus of the Days of Awe.*

With this context in mind, I've attempted to convey the contemporary significance of the individual prayer in a variety of ways. Through introductory *kavanot,* readings, and commentary, I've tried to give some understanding of the issue that the prayer is addressing. So, for example, prior to *Avinu Malkeinu,* I place two *kavanot.* The first is the Chasidic tale of Reb Zusya, which begins with a Martin Buber kind of introduction to this well-known story. Every person born into this world represents something new, something that never existed before, something original and unique. Everyone's foremost task is the actualization of his or her unique and unprecedented and never recurrent specialties and not the repetition of another, even though the greatest may have been achieved. But as Zusya said a short while before his death, "In the world-to-come I shall not be asked why were you not Moses, I shall be asked why were you not Zusya."

What statement does Zusya make about personal standards and accountability? How does this mitigate the harshness of the *Avinu Malkeinu* imagery?

According to the Talmud, the frame of mind of the worshipers, their *kavanah, or* intentionality, had a real influence upon whether their prayers were answered. What frame of mind is most conducive for us to enter the High Holy Days with? How can *Avinu Malkeinu* help us to enter this mindset?

What does it mean, on the High Holy Days, for our prayers to be "effective"? How does the text of the *machzor* contribute to the effectiveness of prayer?

What can we do to infuse our prayers with humility?

Harold Schulweis, *Evil and the Morality of God* (Jersey City: KTAV Publishing House, 1984).

The message of Zusya resonates deeply, I think, with this sense of never being good enough—the sense of unworthiness that is actually found in the climax of *Avinu Malkeinu, ki ein banu maasim.* But the overall message of Zusya is this: in our desire for *t'shuvah,* expressed in a variety of ways throughout *Avinu Malkeinu,* we should remember that the ideal we are striving for is to be ourselves in the form of the best self that we are capable of being or becoming.

The second *kavanah* that I've offered is the story of Rabbi Eliezar from Tractate *Taanit,* which Rabbi Feld taught, so I won't repeat it here. But I want to make two comments on this piece of *Taanit.* The first is that the first part of the story in which he gets people together to fast and nothing happens until he asks them, "Have you prepared grace for yourselves?" and they break out crying, and then the rains fall. This part of the story points to the fact that it's only the real recognition, not in an intellectual way, but an emotionally real recognition of our mortality, that is the key to real prayer or power of prayer. Only in that frame of mind can prayers be effective, and that's what this story is about.

Then there's the second part of the story in which Akiva seems to be better at praying than Eliezer. Again—I think it's the conclusion of the rabbis or the *Bat Kol*—"it's not that Akiva is greater than Eliezer, but that Akiva is more conciliatory and less demanding of his rights than Eliezer." Here the message is that we need to have some sense of humility in our attitude toward prayer. Whatever it is we're asking for, it cannot be demanded.

Again, this seems to tie in with the climactic verse of *Avinu Malkeinu,* which is attributed to Akiva, the one we all sing with real feeling. It's not just accidental that this melody is so engaging and so powerful—it creates a sense of a true moment of prayer because it combines a gripping melody, a melody that's mesmerizing and powerful, with a real feeling that *ein banu maasim,* that there is some sense that we're not what we think we are or ought to be. That's one way of looking at *Avinu Malkeinu* in terms of what the contemporary issue is for us.

In addition to the *kavanot* or the *d'var t'filah* that might set the stage for prayer, the translation itself is tremendously important for conveying some resonance for today's pray-er. In doing my translations, I've been guided by this simple teaching of my teacher Ira Eisenstein *zichrono l'vracha,* who said, "It's not so much who you're praying **to**, it's what we're praying **for** that matters." In addition, my translations have been influenced by the predicate theology of Harold Schulweis. In the case of *Avinu Malkeinu,* it's the object of prayer that I've focused on, which is, of course, *t'shuvah,* for change, for creating a better life. And so the address of our prayer combines an appeal to both the imminent power for change as well as the transcended authority that will enact change. Therefore, I translated

Avinu Malkeinu as "Our Source, Our Sovereign," alternating with the untranslated *Avinu Malkeinu*, since this term is so well-known and becomes a kind of mantra of sorts, conveying the power of the prayer as a kind of mantra.

In the concluding stanza, the one that we all sing with great passion, my focus was on *asei imanu tzedakah vachesed*, which I saw as a prescription for how we ought to seek the change for ourselves. I translated it this way: *Avinu Malkeinu chaneinu vaaneinu ki ein banu maasim*, "Our Source, our Sovereign, be gracious and answer us though we be undeserving." *Asei imanu tzedakah vachesed*, "Temper justice with mercy," *v'hoshi-einu*, "and deliver us." As such, this is not just a last-ditch effort to ask for two more things, *tzedakah vachesed*, that we want because we're so devoid of anything good. Rather, though we are undeserving, again expressing the sense of humility, *asei imanu tzedakah vachesed*, we must seek the balance of *tzedakah* together with *chesed*. We temper justice with mercy, and perhaps that balance, or pursuing that balance, in our lives is what will deliver us.

This *kavanah* encourages us to be mindful of our need for God to temper God's judgment of us with mercy. It teaches us to mimic God in our treatment of others. What situations in our lives call us to balance justice and mercy, and how can we do so in the year to come?

Avinu Malkeinu Wrap-Up

1. According to Rabbi Feld's history of *Avinu Malkeinu*, the prayer developed as a way for the community to cry out to God in times of great material need. How did the imagery of "Father and King" help them to connect to God? What larger need did the communities express through their *bakashot*?

2. Refer back to your discussion of your communal and individual goals for High Holy Day prayer. To what extent do the "Father and King" images still help you to connect to God? What images might work better? To what extent do the *bakashot* in the *machzor* that you use express your needs? In keeping with the history of the expansion of *Avinu Malkeinu*, what *bakashot* might you add?

3. Using Rabbi Aigen's final example of the last stanza of *Avinu Malkeinu*, how can *kavanah* and translation work together to bring meaning to the prayer and pray-er experience?

Un'taneh Tokef:
Historical Background

Dr. Richard Sarason

Un'taneh Tokef is probably the most well-known of all of the *pi-yutim*—the liturgical poems—that appear in the Ashkenazic rite on the High Holy Days. Everybody has their own memories and their own thoughts and sometimes their own problems with *Un'taneh Tokef*. There is no question that from a literary and performative point of view, this is a very, very vivid and dramatic poem. In the premodern period, and among traditional Jews today, it was (is) not uncommon as this poem was (is) being recited at services for people to weep out loud when contemplating the enormity of the things that could happen to them over the coming year.

What memories or associations do you have with *Un'taneh Tokef*?

The *piyut* appears in the Ashkenazic rite. It does not appear in the Sephardic or any of the other rites, except sometimes very late under Ashkenazic influence. In the Ashkenazic rite, traditionally this is recited during the *Musaf Amidah* on Rosh HaShanah, and in the eastern Ashkenazic rite—that is, the Polish as opposed to the German rite—it is also recited in the *Musaf Amidah* on Yom Kippur. It is certainly, as I said, one of the dramatic and musical highlights of the service.

Placement in the *Machzor*

Technically, the poem is a *siluk*, that is, it is a poem that leads directly into the recitation of the *K'dushah*. It is the last of a series of poems. Notwithstanding the well-known medieval Ashkenazic legend that connect this *piyut* to the martyrdom of a certain Rabbi Amnon of Mayence (Mainz), the *piyut* is, in fact, much older than that. It was written in the Land of Israel in the Byzantine period (sometime between the fourth and sixth centuries c.e.; we don't know the exact date). All of the Rabbinic allusions in this *piyut* are to tannaitic literature or to the Talmud of the Land of Israel; there are no allusions at all to sources in the Babylonian Talmud. The earliest manuscripts that we have of this *piyut* are three fragments from the Cairo Genizah—one of these is at Cambridge, one is at the Jewish Theological Seminary, and one is at the British Library in London. I have had the opportunity to see plates or digital images of two of the three fragments, the ones from the British Library and JTS. There is not a lot of difference verbally between the form of the *piyut* that we know from the *machzor* today and what exists in the Genizah fragments—a few differences but nothing that is terribly

Origin

Early Manuscripts

19

significant. These fragments probably date from somewhere between the eleventh and the thirteenth centuries—this is the period during which most of the Genizah materials were copied or written. Israeli scholar of Hebrew poetry Joseph Yahalom has suggested that the author of the *piyut* was Yannai (sixth to seventh century), since in at least one of those fragments the poem appears following some of Yannai's poetry. I would say, however, that this attribution is doubtful, because *Un'taneh Tokef* doesn't display the same kind of *recherché* literary quality that appears in most of Yannai's poetry.

Structure

The poem itself is unrhymed, although it does have scattered rhymes and is more or less metrical. It subdivides into several sections. In its present form, it might even possibly be composite, because we're not sure exactly where it ends or whether something has been added at the end to make it formally into a *siluk*, that is, to lead into the recitation of the *K'dushah*. We'll talk about each of the several sections of the poem momentarily.

Connection to the Mishnah

It's worth pointing out at the very outset that the seed of the poem is a Mishnah text. The poem is based, at least in part, on *Mishnah Rosh HaShanah* 1:2, which reads as follows:

> *B'arbaah p'rakim haolam nidon: b'Pesach al hat'vuah, b'Atseret al peirot ha-ilan, b'Rosh HaShanah kol ba-ei haolam ovrin l'fanav kivnei maron, shene-emar, "Hayotzeir yachad libam, hameivin el kol maaseihem."*

Why might the world be judged at different times for different aspects?

At four times during the year the world is judged: on Pesach with respect to produce; on Atseret [Shavuot] with respect to the fruit of the tree; on Rosh HaShanah all creatures pass before Him like b'nei maron [we'll leave that untranslated for the moment], as it is written, "The One who fashions all of their hearts together, the One who discerns all of their deeds" [Psalm 33:14].

The text concludes, *Uvehag nidonim al hamayim*, "And on Sukkot the world is judged with respect to water." Now, the Mishnaic phrase *v'chol ba-ei olam yaavrun l'fanecha kivnei maron* occurs in the poem itself. *B'nei maron*, which looks like *b'nei* **marom**, "the dwellers on high," is in fact a corruption of the Greek word *numeron*, which becomes the Latin *numerus*, and refers to a cohort of troops in a military muster. The word appears correctly in the better Mishnah manuscripts as well as in some of the manuscripts of the *piyut Un'taneh Tokef* itself. So, the image here is of all creatures passing before God on the reviewing stand, as it were, as if they were passing in a military parade or a military muster.

How does this linguistic discovery change the meaning of the piyut? What role does liturgical scholarship play in our understanding and appreciation of our prayers, and how can we incorporate these findings into our prayers?

Content

The entirety of the *piyut* is a very, very powerful, dramatic, vivid, mythic picture of Rosh HaShanah as Yom HaDin, the Day of Judgment. It begins by invoking the awesome nature of the Day of

Judgment and the image of God seated on the throne of judgment. God judges and bears witness and writes and seals and counts. The Book of Judgment in which all deeds are recorded (a very old image in the ancient Near East) is opened up, and everyone's deeds are sealed in the book.

Following this is the dramatic image of the great shofar being blown and everyone trembling with fear. The angels also tremble for they too—the *tz'va marom*—are not exempt from judgment. I've often wondered in reading this poem whether the line *lifkod al tz'va marom badin*, "to pass judgment on the heavenly hosts," is already based on a misreading of *banumeron* as *b'nei maron/marom*. That is, the idea that both the dwellers on high and the dwellers on earth are judged on this day might indicate that the reading of *kivnumaron* as *kivnei marom* is already embedded in the *piyut*—but this is not entirely clear because, as I have indicated, we do have Genizah manuscripts of the *piyut* that give the reading correctly as *numeron*.

At any rate, we now have the image of people passing before the divine throne like sheep passing muster.

This is followed by *B'Rosh HaShanah yikateivun*, "On Rosh Ha-Shanah it is written:" who shall live and who shall die, and a vivid enumeration of the various kinds of death (this, obviously, is when people would weep). Everyone's fate is being decreed for the next year, but we also are told how to avert that fate: repentance, prayer, and charity avert the severity of the decree (or turn back the decree). That statement is based on a tradition in the Jerusalem Talmud, *Taanit* 2:1, which indicates that three things—repentance, prayer, and charity—can avert the evil decree. The parallel tradition in the Babylonian Talmud, *Rosh HaShanah* 16b, lists *four* things that avert the evil decree: charity, prayer (*tzaakah*, literally "crying out"), changing one's name, and changing one's behavior. So, clearly, the *piyut* follows the *Y'rushalmi* tradition rather than the *Bavli* tradition. What follows this terrifying passage is more calm. The poem now appeals to God's attribute of mercy, *Ki k'shimcha kein t'hilatecha*, "For as is your name [= reputation], so is your praise: you are patient, you are merciful toward human error, and you do not desire the death of sinners but rather that they repent, and then you will immediately receive them."

The next section of the text, *Adam y'sodo mei-afar*, contrasts human mortality with God's eternality. Finally, the last portion, *Ein kitzvah lishnotecha*, is, again, a meditation on God's eternality and power that moves into a meditation on God's name and its holiness (*Aseih l'maan sh'mecha*). This transitions into the recitation of the *K'dushah* itself (*v'kadeish et shimcha al **makdishei** sh'mecha baavur k'vod shimcha hanaaratz **v'hanikdash***—those are the transition words into the *K'dushah*). This last part does not appear in most Reform prayer books, as we will note shortly.

What are your reactions to the image of God writing in the Book of Life? How literally do you understand this process, or what figurative meaning might it have?

Have you ever felt so connected to a prayer or melody that you were moved to tears? What was it, and how do you relate to that prayer or melody differently after that experience?

What is the connection between the *piyut* and the legend of Rabbi Amnon? What does the *piyut* say about martyrdom? Why has the attribution of this *piyut* to Rabbi Amnon endured, even though it is not historically accurate?

Shalom Spiegel, *The Last Trial* (Woodstock, VT: Jewish Lights Publishing, 1993).

The legend of Rabbi Amnon, who was martyred on Rosh Ha-Shanah and recited *Un'taneh Tokef* immediately before expiring in the synagogue, first appears in *Sefer Or Zarua* by Rabbi Moses ben Isaac of Vienna (c. 1180–1250). He claimed to have copied this story from a manuscript by Rabbi Ephraim ben Jacob of Bonn (1132–1197). We know that Ephraim of Bonn witnessed the Second Crusade. (He was the author of the *Akeidah piyut* transcribed and published by Shalom Spiegel in *The Last Trial*.) This legend is one of many Ashkenazic martyrological legends, and it is also a "foundation narrative" that justifies the recitation of this *piyut* in Ashkenazic liturgy. (The name Amnon is not an Ashkenazic name; it's an Italian name. There was an Italian Rabbi Amnon who had been martyred years before this.) At the end of the legend, Rabbi Amnon appears in a dream to Rabbi Kalonymos ben Meshullam ben Kalonymos (an Ashkenazic rabbi who died during the First Crusade) and teaches him the poem. Indeed, the poem was disseminated in the Rhineland, and more widely in Ashkenaz, by the Kalonymos family, a prominent Ashenazic rabbinic clan whose origins were in Italy. As I noted, our *piyut* appears only in the Ashkenazic rite. It was not uncommon for literary texts and liturgical customs to move from the east, from the Byzantine world, through Italy up into the Rhineland. That is a very, very common mode of cultural transmission, and it is likely what happened here as well. The poem became very popular in Ashkenaz, and it became connected, again, to Ashkenazic recollections and reflections about martyrdom.

In Reform Liturgies

A few final words now about the use and adaptation of the *piyut Un'taneh Tokef* in Reform liturgies: Because of the popularity of this *piyut* in Ashkenaz, it in fact appears in most Reform liturgies, often in an abbreviated form. The only Reform prayer books among the most historic ones going back to 1819 in which it does not appear are those that essentially follow the western Sephardic (Spanish-Portuguese) rite: the Hamburg Temple prayer book (1819; 2nd edition, 1841; virtually all of the *piyutim* that appear in the Hamburg Temple prayer book are from the Spanish-Portuguese rite) and *Forms of Prayer of the West London Synagogue* (1841). It is also missing from the liturgy of the very radical Berlin *Reformgemeinde*, which was organized in 1845. But, otherwise, it appears in all of the major Reform prayer books.

For more information on the development of liberal High Holy Day liturgy, see additional readings.

In North American Reform liturgies, *Un'taneh Tokef* usually appears in a somewhat abbreviated form. It appears in the first prayer book that was prepared for a Reform congregation in the United States (the Emanuel Tempelverein, which became Temple Emanuel of New York City), Leo Merzbacher's 1855 *Seder Tefillah* (and the 1860 revised edition by Samuel Adler)—but only in the Yom Kippur *Musaf* service. There are no *piyutim* in Rosh HaShanah services in this prayer book. So the tradition of including this *piyut* **only** in Yom

Kippur *Musaf* (which is where it appears in all editions of the *Union Prayer Book*) begins with Merzbacher and Adler. They include the first half of the *piyut*, through *Ut'shuvah ut'filah utzedakah*. In Isaac Mayer Wise's *machzor*, the second volume of *Minhag America*, which was published in 1866, *Un'taneh Tokef* appears in both the Rosh Ha-Shanah and Yom Kippur *Musaf* services, but only the *second* half, beginning with *Ki k'shimcha kein t'hilatecha*, through the very end.

Following Wise's abbreviation, this is also the portion of the *piyut* included by Isaac S. Moses in the unpublished 1893 draft of the original *Union Prayer Book*, volume 2. There it appears in the Yom Kippur afternoon service. In David Einhorn's *Olat Tamid*, first published in 1858, it appears in the Yom Kippur afternoon service before *Aleinu* at the beginning of *Seder HaAvodah*. Einhorn does something very interesting here. He begins with *Ki atah hu dayan umochiach*, the third line of the *piyut*, and continues through *mi yushpal umi yarum*. Then he cites Psalm 8:4, *Mah enosh ki tizk'renu, u'ven adam ki tifk'denu*. Following this, he resumes at *ki lo tachpotz b'mot hameit* and continues through *V'atah hu melech*. In the final published *Union Prayer Book*, volume 2, of 1894 (and its subsequent revisions of 1922 and 1945), *Un'taneh Tokef* appears in the Yom Kippur afternoon service before *Aleinu* at the beginning of *Seder HaAvodah*. Only the first half of the *piyut* appears, from the beginning through *V'atah hu melech*. In *Gates of Repentance* (1978), interestingly enough, the *piyut* is put back into the Rosh HaShanah morning service (since there is, of course, no *Musaf* service). There it takes its appropriate place before the *K'dushah* and is introduced with a meditation by Chaim Stern that relates the Rabbi Amnon story.

The text of the *piyut* in *Gates of Repentance* is identical with the text that is in the *Union Prayer Book*: the beginning of the *piyut* through *V'atah hu melech*. While we are dealing with Reform prayer books, there is a very interesting adaptation of the text of *Un'taneh Tokef* in Israel Mattuck's first prayer book for British Liberal Jewry, the *Liberal Prayer Book*, volume 2 (1923), where it also appears in the Yom Kippur afternoon service. Mattuck begins with the verse from Ezekiel 18:32, *Ki lo echpotz b'mot hameit*, which, of course, is the source of the relevant phrase in the *piyut* itself. He then continues, *Bit'shuvah ut'filah utzedakah nashuvah el Adonai Eloheinu*, adapting that phrase of the *piyut*. This is followed by *Ki lo tachpotz b'mot hameit*, continuing through *V'atah hu melech*, somewhat like Einhorn.

To summarize: Most Reform prayer books have included *Un'taneh Tokef* in some form, but none have included it in its entirety, and none have included the very end of the *piyut*, which is the transition into the *K'dushah*. These prayer books give either the first half or the last half, or they have some mix of the two.

What factors might have influenced these different decisions of how to include *Un'taneh Tokef* in the *machzor*?

Un'taneh Tokef: Contemporary Usage and Innovation

Rabbi Richard N. Levy

Un'taneh Tokef is, of course, one of the most disturbing texts in our tradition. This discussion is a tribute to the growing Reform willingness to take on hard texts, since this prayer was not always present in earlier Reform prayer books. This is a scary text. It says that God—however we understand God—judges us. The Truth judges us. But this text also reflects the confidence that we can subject ourselves to an ultimate judgment, and because it is God who is judging, we can believe it will be done with love.

This prayer is meant to follow the month-long work of *t'shuvah* and self-reflection of the month of Elul, and I think the prayer has its intended effect only if we have encouraged our people to take Elul seriously, if we have helped them to develop a discipline for looking at some of the issues in their lives, perhaps with a different agenda each week; perhaps taking advantage of prayer services during Elul to help them do that. If they have done this work, if we have done it (which we often don't give ourselves the time to do), *Un'taneh Tokef* becomes like a major final exam. We can go in with confidence, with fear, with a rushing adrenaline; but the adrenaline can be interpreted as similar to the rushing angels (second stanza), who are our representatives, our advocates in heaven. These *malachim* (angels) insist that we help people develop a sense of *yirah*, and if we can help them do that during Elul, this prayer offers them a great opportunity to experience *yirah* (fear or awe of God) in all its power.

The music is vital, but it is also important that we engage people with the text, and one of the ways of properly utilizing this text is to offer a study session either just before it appears in the service or a few weeks in advance, so that we push people up against the reality of *yirah* in order that they may grow into a realization that this is the day of *yirah*, a day of awe and fear.

We might remind them in a sermon that fear is an important spiritual value. A lot of people are fearful these days because of the economic situation. When people face serious illness, they know about fear. When our children are not growing in the way that

Many discuss this prayer as "challenging" or "offensive," but it is rarer for people to discuss it as "scary." To what extent do you think people's difficulty with the prayer is this rooted in fear? What are some ways to become aware of and deal with this fear?

How can *yirah* be a feeling that we embrace and utilize, rather than avoid? What are other ways to develop a sense of *yirah* in anticipation of the Yamim Noraim?

What other sources of fear do we face this year?

we wish they would, we know fear. We can help people channel the fear they have been feeling in the past year into a sense of being judged, but also into the confidence that we will ultimately be judged for good.

One of the ways to utilize this text is through the kind of translation that I am suggesting (see translations on pages 28–29). The prayer begins, *Un'taneh tokef k'dushat hayom*, "Let us declare the holy power of this day." As Dr. Sarason mentioned, this leads into the *K'dushah*, and so there is a double sense of *k'dushah* because that is the prayer we are soon going to proclaim. *Uvo tinasei malchutecha*, Your *malchut*, Your sovereignty, Your majesty is raised up even higher today. Remember that in the *Kaddishes* we say *l'eila ul'eila*— God is in some ways more distant, more sovereign on the High Holy Days, and the sense of *yirah*, which should be always present in prayer, is even more so on these days. *V'teisheiv alav be-emet*, "for now You take Your place on the throne in truth," but the throne itself is established *b'chesed*. That's a very interesting pairing: God takes God's place with truth, but the throne is based, rooted, set in the concrete of *chesed*, a love that is sealed into the covenant made with those who came before us. That is part of the sense of confidence that this prayer is meant to embody: yes, God looks at us honestly, thoroughly, but at the same time the love that infuses the concrete base of God's throne flows up through the Divine as God judges us with truth. When you have made judgments on your children, or on others whom you love, you know that your clear eye is infused with the love of your covenant with them.

Then there follows the legal imagery: We are standing in a court. God plays every role in the court, and so this becomes the ideal court where God is judge, prosecutor, executor, expert witness, and scribe. Then, before God, "all things forgotten present themselves" (*v'tizkor*). The root *z-ch-r* really means "being present," not only remembering, because "remembering" generally implies the ability to forget. God doesn't forget; the sense is that everything, everyone, is present on these days, and as God opens the *Sefer HaZichronot*, "the Book of Recollections," it reads itself aloud. (One of the things you might do in a study session is to have a book in which people have entered some of their own reflections, judgments, or reminiscences of their year and ask some of those people to read them aloud, illustrating how we might experience such a volume.) The prayer suggests a book that is very much alive, with "the seal of every person's hand . . . in it."

Then the text goes on: *Uvashofar gadol yitaka* ("The great shofar is sounded"), and you or your cantor might want to proclaim that sentence in a voice that sounds like a shofar. But then the text becomes very soft: *v'kol d'mamah dakah yishama*. What does that contrast mean? We know *kol d'mamah dakah* is from Elijah, who realizes

---

A similar idea is expressed in the Babylonian Talmud, *B'rachot* 7a. The Rabbis ask, "What does God pray?" Rav Zutra son of Tuvia said in the name of Rav: "Let it be My will that My mercy suppress My anger, and that My mercy prevail over My other attributes, and that I deal with My children with the attribute of mercy, and that I deal with them beyond the letter of the law."

How does this suggestion bring to life the image of *Sefer HaZichronot*? What other ideas might you try?

What contrasting aspects of God are represented by the *shofar gadol* and the *kol d'mamah dakah*? How do they complement one another?

that God was not in the fire but in the "still small voice." How is Elijah's experience present for us? How are we standing on Carmel this day?

Dr. Sarason made reference to the angels rushing about who seem to have no more merit than we at the time of judgment. He mentioned also that, in Hebrew, *kol ba-ei haolam ovrin l'fanav kivnei maron* is the mishnah (*Rosh HaShanah* 1:2) around which this prayer may have been shaped. It's important to remember that this is Judgment Day for all people, and one might even invite individuals from other religions into the synagogue to reflect on what it means to know that Jewish neighbors are praying for them as they enter into judgment along with us.

The word *ovrin* in the verse from the mishnah becomes an important key to the rest of the prayer. Now, rather than people appearing in court, we see ourselves as sheep. We often don't like the notion of sheep, but aren't there times when all we really want to do is to be led, to be guided? God *maavir* (from the same root as *yaavrun*), "moves them on beneath the staff"; steering us, with the repetition of that word "moving us on," leading into a repetition of some of the language of the court in the first stanza. *V'tachtoch kitzvah*, wonderfully crisp words ("appointing the remainder of each creature's life") that are a reminder that the word "decision" in Latin also means, as *tachtoch* does, "to cut off."

Now comes the decision itself, the final paragraph of the main prayer (*B'Rosh HaShanah yikateivun*), and again, the first decision is *kamah yaavrun* ("How many shall move on?" or, as *Gates of Repentance* adds, "Who shall live and who shall die?") Then follow various examples of how we face death ("who by fire and who by water"). The second part of this section details how we face life ("Who shall have rest and who can never be still?"). This part of the prayer forces us to ask: *Can we have any effect on how we die?* Of course we can. How we live helps determine a great deal about the nature of our death. And with all of these modes of facing life, the sense is that God will be bringing us any of these conditions as part of God's judgment of us. That can encourage us to believe that if we are torn apart, God is present in that storm with us.

How is God with us? Where is the truth and where is the covenantal love in times of ease and times of affliction? This text pushes us to see God present with us in the struggle as well as in the rest.

Finally we arrive at the last verse of this section, built around this same word (*maavirin*) that ultimately comes from the text of the mishnah. One of the ways of understanding this verb here is that *t'shuvah*, *t'filah*, and *tzedakah* will help us avert the evil decree, but I think that *maavirin* here conveys something else. *T'shuvah*, prayer, and *tzedakah* move us past the pain, seeing *roa hag'zeirah* as "the pain decree." In a sense, *t'shuvah*, *t'filah*, and *tzedakah* constitute a little

How do you relate to this statement? What relief might we find in the feeling of God "moving us on"?

How does Rabbi Levy connect God's judgment to God's presence in our lives? Can we view judgment in a positive light?

This *d'rash* teaches that our righteous actions, supported by God's kindness, will enhance our appreciation of life in the year to come. How can we remind ourselves of this message throughout the year, so that we do not lose sight of God's *emet* or *chesed*?

boat in which we may sail across the roiling waves of whatever our life will raise up for us. So, even at the end, the sense is that God's *emet* may be the roiling waves, but God's *chesed* is the boat that enables us to do *t'shuvah*, to join in *t'filah*, and to engage in *tzedakah*, all of which will move us past the pain and ultimately help us appreciate the depth and even the beauty of whatever waters it will be our lot to traverse in the year to come.

Un'taneh Tokef
(Translation by Rabbi Richard N. Levy from On Wings of Awe, *revised edition, KTAV, 2010)*

Let us declare the holy power of this day:
It is awe-filled, mighty.
Your sovereignty is raised up even higher today,
For now You take Your place with truth,
Though Your throne is based in love,
Which You sealed into the covenant You made
With those who came before us.
In truth, You are the Court:
Judge and Prosecutor,
Expert witness,
Scribe, Bearer of the Seal, Enumerator,
The One who calls to account.
Before You all things forgotten present themselves
As You open the Book of Recollections
Which reads itself aloud,
For the seal of every person's hand is in it.

THE GREAT SHOFAR IS SOUNDED!
And a still small voice is heard
The angels in heaven rush about, dismayed–
They are seized with fear, with trembling;
They cry out:
Behold, the Day of Judgment!
The hosts of heaven are to be arraigned in judgment,
For in Your eyes even they
Will have no merit at the time of judgment.
All who have come into the world move on before You,
One by one,
Like a flock of sheep.
As a shepherd gathers the sheep,
Moving them on beneath the staff,
So You move and enumerate,
Call to account and visit every living soul,
Appointing the measure of every creature's life,
Inscribing the decree of their judgment.

On Rosh Hashanah it is inscribed
And on the Fast of Atonement it is sealed:
How many shall move on and how many be created,
Who shall live and who shall die—

> Who at the conclusion of their life and who not at the
> conclusion;
> Who by fire and who by water,
> Who by the sword and who by wild beast,
> Who by famine and who by drought,
> Who by earthquake and who by epidemic,
> Who by strangling and who by stoning;

Who shall have rest and who can never be still,
Who shall be serene and who torn apart,
Who shall be at ease and who afflicted,
Who shall be impoverished and who enriched,
Who shall be brought low and who raised high—

> *But Tshuvah, Prayer and Charitable Acts*
> *Will move us past the pain of the decree.*

(for Hebrew of *Ki k'shimcha* see *The Complete
ArtScroll Machzor: Rosh Hashanah*, p. 484)

For Your Name is Your praise:
Adonay, the Source of Compassion,
Hard to anger and easy to appease,
For You do not desire the death of mortal beings,
But that we do *tshuvah,* turn from our path,
That we may live.
Indeed until the day of our death You wait for us,
And if we do *tshuvah,* how quickly You welcome us home!

In truth You are our Creator,
You know our *yetzer,* our temptations,
For we are flesh and blood.
Our origin, we mortals, is the dust,
And our end is the dust.
At the cost of our lives we carry in our daily bread.
We are like a broken shard, a withered reed,
A fading flower, a shadow moving on,
An ephemeral cloud, a passing breeze,
Dust flying up,
A dream that flies away.

(But the clay remains, the stalk remains,
The flower flutters still in the breeze,
And the dream is not forgotten.)

For You are our Majesty, the God of life who lives forever!

Un'taneh Tokef:
Contemporary Challenges

Dr. Rachel S. Mikva

For convenience, I identify three categories of challenge—cognitive, affective, and practical—even though they frequently overlap.

Cognitive challenges stem primarily from the apparent theology of the prayer: words that attribute divine causality to every catastrophe and cast each personal tragedy as God's intention. Since *t'shuvah, t'filah, tzedakah* temper judgment's severe decree, there is also a degree of implied culpability for those who suffer.

In response, we attempt to reinterpret or re-present this *piyut* in ways that make it compelling for our communities, or we protest against the offending words and encourage our members to struggle *k'negdan* (over against them). Paradoxically, we frequently do both at once.

I examined some of the better-known efforts to re-present the prayer in order to explore more carefully the problems they address. Leonard Cohen, for instance, in his haunting musical rendition of "Who by Fire," updates some of the sorry fates to be more contemporary and also inserts the refrain "and who shall I say is calling?" to represent our uncertainty with the theology.

Post 9/11 rewritings mostly tried to give voice to entirely new sets of fears that had come to plague us. And some were careful to assert that human hands, not divine purpose, lay behind the unleashing of this terror.

It appears, however, that another perceived challenge is the prayer's painful emphasis on the negative; even though there is mention of birth and tranquility, strangely we recall the dire fates in the list almost exclusively. Martin Buber, in *The Prophetic Faith*, said that every prediction of impending catastrophe has a concealed alternative. So there are efforts, like Linda Hirschhorn's reshaping of the prayer, that focus on recovering the positive complement to each potential doom:

Who will *live* by fire?—With passion, commitment and purpose that do *not* burn out.

How do you become captain of your own boat, so you do not perish adrift in the seas?

On what aspects of the cognitive meaning of the prayer do these re-presentations focus? How do they deal with these issues?

Martin Buber, *The Prophetic Faith* (New York: Harper Torchbooks, 1960).

Linda Hirschorn, *Unetaneh Tokef* http://www.lindahirschhorn.com/ writings/unetaneh_tokef.html

Can we feel the earthquake, the earth move under our feet in eye-opening, life-changing ways?

Hirschhorn also tries to emphasize the human role in determining our destiny, as do so many of us, emphasizing the complicated truth of our existence: God may record and recount, but we are indisputably the author of our Book of Life.

There are other re-presentations, though compelling, that do not actually address the challenges of the prayer. Instead, they use it for their own purposes. For instance, a rendition entitled "Time of Terror" echoes the prayer's rhythms to make the reader recognize the horrors of torture—a worthy aim, but not truly the purpose of the prayer. It may be used to good effect outside the context of a recitation for the Days of Awe. In a very different tone, there is now an iPhone graphic circulating that has an icon on the face of the phone for every fate: fire, water, sword, etc. Clever, but it would need a good *d'rash* to make it count.

I believe the most powerful response to the cognitive challenge, however, is to teach people how to pray again, to work with prayer as poetry, not theology—sacred drama that can move you, not a systematic presentation of tenets of faith. Heschel (*Man's Quest for God*) talks about words transcending their signified meaning; they are more than beasts of burden, more than train porters lugging a definition behind them. They create a lens for viewing the world and responding to it. "In prayer, as in poetry, we turn to the words, not to use them as signs for things, but to see the things in light of the words."

In this regard, I think our congregants grasp the nature of *Un'taneh Tokef* more than most of *t'filah*. They are drawn to it, compelled by it, moved by it—even though they cannot abide by its theological implications.

I think we *can* teach its sacred power:

Life is fragile; some of us will not be here next year.
Some of us will not be whole next year.
And it is impossible to assert real control over this future.
What *can* we do?
   T'shuvah: We can repair our relationships with God and everybody else.
   T'filah: We can build a spiritual life full of purpose.
   Tzedakah: We can fight for justice and a better world.

These transform our lives, investing them with meaning and purpose, no matter what happens *to* us in the year to come.

Everything we do on Yom Kippur enacts our deathbed: we don't eat, don't drink, don't bathe; we recite confessions again and

Margin notes:

What other causes, besides the movement against the use of torture, might utilize this prayer to teach a lesson?

What does it mean to "work with prayer as poetry, not theology"? How does this approach to prayer serve us when facing challenging text, as well as help us to find meaning in less challenging texts?

Abraham Joshua Heschel, *Man's Quest for God* (New York: Charles Scribner and Sons, 1951).

How does Rabbi Mikva explain the relationship between the prayer and its final line about *t'shuvah*, *t'filah*, and *tzedakah*? Do you agree or see it differently?

again. So even before we get there, we imagine we are there and use that abject terror to reshape our lives. "Reborn," we get another chance to live so that we will be content in our final days. Sacred drama, not theology. As Richard said, God's sovereignty is raised up even higher on that day, even if this image of God is not the one we usually believe in. We imagine—if only for an instant—that we really do stand before the Judge and have to make an accounting . . . and *everything* is at stake. Can this shake us from our complacency, relieve us of our distractions, and enable us to turn? Sacred drama, not theology.

In effect, we blend the cognitive with the affective in order to address the cognitive challenges. But the affective dimensions of the prayer have their own challenge: the seemingly inadequate power of words to fill our soul and effect life change, when we are used to surround-sound and 70-mm just to make us cry. How do we transport ourselves across the threshold? How do we recognize that these are not some abstract ideas, but the real possibilities of our lives?

David Rubin produced (and Daniel Jankovic directed) a video last year that can be viewed on YouTube called "Who Shall Live?" It has powerful images of individuals and communities that endured each fate, with chanting of the prayer as the "soundtrack." Some people responded that it changed the whole experience of the Days of Awe—drawing from its affective power. Others were furious that the film seemed to suggest God ordained the flooding in the Midwest, the fires in California, Hurricane Ike, China's earthquake, violence in Darfur, and so on—the cognitive problems looming larger due to the power of the visual imagery and specificity of the tragic fates.

It is (kind of) tempting, actually, to imagine a video and music meditation before the prayer, with images of world events but also framed by references to the congregation—beginning with the faces of newborn members and those who passed away in the last year; then at the end, the congregation praying, turning, and working for social justice. The sum of events in the past year help us to recognize all that can happen in the span of the year to come, to internalize how much is at stake.

But for those who cannot go this route—whether due to technical or financial constraints, or abject horror at something so Hollywood—the challenge remains: How do we embody this prayer in profoundly moving form? People need not only to understand it, but to be changed by it.

Some congregations have their own members compose music or words, tell a personal story of transformation, or write down how they would spend the next year if they knew it would be their last. These are efforts to make it real by making it personal, in order to strengthen the affective dimensions of the prayer.

What else on Yom Kippur, at the synagogue, in the *machzor*, in our behavior, sets the stage for the "sacred drama"? How can we take part in the drama, rather than just observe?

Watch this video—what is your response? How, or would, you incorporate this video into High Holy Day preparation or the service itself? www.youtube.com/watch?v=fdkDk8xIEXw

Take some time to share these stories and creative works.

What other ideas can you think of to take advantage of the affective power of this prayer? How could the text of the *machzor* contribute to the affective experience of the prayer?

The good news is that the affective challenge is already met to some degree. Music is the most powerful element of this, I think. But the cognitive problem is also part of the affective solution; the horrendous wallop of the words does have an impact. As illustration, I would like to share my experience of the prayer in 2001 in my New York congregation. I was in protest mode. On Rosh Ha-Shanah, I announced we would not recite these words. We played its melody, we sat in turmoil. It was incredibly hard not to sing. The words—we wanted these terrible words; they bubbled up from our hearts to our mouths. By the time Yom Kippur came around and we finally sang it, it was not at all about God's doing, but our profound lament for the fate of people we knew and people we loved. They were the words we used to express our pain.

I do not really need to discuss the practical problems, which are all too evident as we wrestle with how to enhance our experience of this prayer. How do we express in a brief *iyun* the complex encounter with this prayer? Is a sermon the right vehicle at the right time? A *shiur* in advance of the Days of Awe may have the freedom to explore deeply and creatively but will attract only a small percentage of people and may lose its power when the moment of recitation comes. How would we incorporate a creative activity, music, re-presentation, etc., that doesn't seem kitschy and would enhance the experience even for those who resist change?

When our listing of the fates concludes, of course, we must also find a way to help our congregants see themselves in the presence of the Most High. כי כשמך כן תהלתך—At the end of the prayer, we turn directly to our covenantal partner for the "big talk"—who are You and who am I? I am dust and ashes, You are מלך אל חי וקים. What is it that You need from me? Is it something I have in me to give? You know how flawed I am. In the end, we reconcile with our own mortality because we have touched the Eternal.

What other needs of ours do these words express?

What ways can you think of to further study this prayer? What questions are you left with that you would like to explore?

This intimate dialogue is a powerful part of the sacred drama. How do we enter into this conversation during prayer?

Un'taneh Tokef **Wrap-Up**

1. According to Rabbis Sarason, Levy, and Mikva, what details in the *piyut* come together to paint a portrait of Yom HaDin? What themes are expressed?

2. What role does this text play in your overall experience of High Holy Day worship?

3. The themes that are central to Yom HaDin can be sources of anxiety for congregants (see Rabbi Levy's discussion of the fear of judgment and Rabbi Mikva's discussion of the fragility of life). How might *Un'taneh Tokef* serve as a tool for expressing and coping with these anxieties? For ideas, refer to the creative suggestions in the lessons for teachings, *iyunim, divrei Torah,* and performance of the liturgy.

Kol Nidrei:
Historical Background

Rabbi Sheldon (Shelly) Zimmerman

Many of us have studied *Kol Nidrei* over the years. We have learned it from different teachers, from many perspectives, and what I'm going to try to do today is to review all of that material within the fifteen minutes that have been allotted to me. I would also suggest Reuven Hammer's *Entering the High Holy Days*; from my point of view, it is probably the very best book available to us on many of the High Holy Day prayers, and the footnotes in the very back of the book take you to many recent scholarly reviews of much of the materials, and I would recommend it to you. It was very helpful to me in reviewing and preparing for today's phone session as well, because some of the references really are hard to find in other places, and he really gives us a wonderful set of references.

Now, *Kol Nidrei* takes on such importance that the entire evening service of Yom Kippur is called *Kol Nidrei*. But, technically, as we all know, *Kol Nidrei* is not a part of this service, since annulment of vows is a legal act and must be done before the festival day or the holy day begins.

We know we wear a tallit, which is already different, since we begin during the daylight hours, and the commandment is to see the fringes, *uritem*, but originally, only the *chazan* wore a tallit. It is interesting that the practice since then spread out to everyone in the community, in the *kahal*, that was gathered for prayer. Goldschmidt deals with this in his *machzor*, which was published most recently in 1970. But the question there remains: "Why not remove it after you said that prayer and had the vows annulled?" And I think that the only possible answer would be that it helped differentiate Yom Kippur from other holy days and other times. It's almost as if, and Reuven Hammer was very helpful here, the tallit represents the connection between *Kol Nidrei* and the ideas of eternity and separation from the world of history, because technically, as soon as one finished *Kol Nidrei*, one should, and not just by *minhag* but almost by halachic requirements, remove the tallit.

The *Kol Nidrei* prayer or statement really begins with the "*Bishivah shel malah . . . ,*" which was written by Rabbi Meir Ben Boruch of Rothenburg in the thirteenth century. What's interesting here is that this gives us permission to pray with transgressors. But we

Reuven Hammer, *Entering the High Holy Days* (Philadelphia: Jewish Publication Society, 2005).

A Legal Act

In the Reform Movement, we have a less literal understanding of Jewish law. How then do we relate to *Kol Nidrei* as a "legal act"?

The Custom of Wearing a Tallit

For many, Erev Yom Kippur services are one of the few that they attend the entire year. They have not been excommunicated, and yet, they might feel like

37

outsiders in the community. How do we welcome them into the community on this night, and how can this relationship continue throughout the year? How can the *machzor* help them to engage in experience?

Ismar Elbogen, *Jewish Liturgy* (Philadelphia: Jewish Publication Society, 1993).

The Controversy

How would you have reacted to this statement as a German Jew, one hundred years ago? How does this add to your understanding of the motives of the early Reformers regarding prayer?

From Philip Goodman, ed., *The Yom Kippur Anthology* (Philadelphia: Jewish Publication Society of America, 1971), p. 84.

Difficulty in Translation

Reciting Three Times

are permitted to pray with transgressors all year long. We don't say that stanza before we begin our Friday night prayers or our Shabbat morning prayers. We don't use that stanza. And one would think that if we needed permission to pray with transgressors, why would we do it then, and not all the time? And the suggestion has been made, especially by Elbogen in his book *Jewish Liturgy*, that many scholars today believe that the declaration was to lift a ban on those who were actually under *cherem*, who had been excommunicated, but on Yom Kippur were able to rejoin the community in prayer. They had defied particular regulations adopted by the medieval self-governing community and therefore needed permission to come back into the *kahal* or *k'hilah*, particularly for that service. And that would make some sense out of a stanza that really does not make any sense at all given the fact that one could pray with transgressors at any other time without permission.

Now, we all know that the *Kol Nidrei* prayer itself is probably the most controversial in Jewish history.

When Menasseh ben Israel tried to persuade Oliver Cromwell to readmit the Jews to England in the seventeenth century, he had to demonstrate that *Kol Nidrei* did not mean that Jews could not be trusted. You can see that in Herman Kieval's article "The Paradox of *Kol Nidre*." And Hammer points this out for us: in September of 1910, in the Berlin newspaper *Staatsburger-Zeitung*, they called the *Kol Nidrei* prayer an insult to civilization. Listen to his translation of it:

Like the Talmud, it is a culpable deception of the Aryans by the Jews. A Jew can commit perjury in court; his religious convictions allow him to do it. He may brand truth a lie and ruin his fellow man. These moral dues of Judaism are a criminal assault on humanity and civilization.

Now given that reality, and given the reality that it's impossible to translate the *Kol Nidrei* anyway, what is the difference between these oaths and vows that are mentioned? The tenses are bad in the Ashkenazic version of the prayer . . . we speak of what we have done in the past, but then we talk of annulment of vows in the future. It just doesn't make any sense. Now we know in the Sephardic liturgy, it's "from last Yom Kippur to this one"; they changed the tenses as the Rabbis tried to do in the land of Ashkenaz a little later on. But the point is that the statement itself does not make any sense. What are we annulling? Are we talking about the future or the past? It's not clear at all.

Now why is it recited three times? And here we go to *Mishnah M'nachot* 10:3, which claims that it was the traditional way to recite legal formulas. But it also suggests that it makes it possible for latecomers to hear it. I guess it's the kindest reason for not closing the doors during *Kol Nidrei*, which is the practice in many congregations.

But the problem remains with the *Kol Nidrei*. Renunciation of vows, what vows, made when—the biblical *asmachta* for this is in Numbers 30:14, where it talks about *Kol neider, v'chol sh'vuat,* and even though it is dealing with another matter, their aim is the annulment of vows made by a woman, her husband's ability, her father's ability to annul them. That's the only biblical version of any kind of *asmachta* text that we could use. And although *Kol Nidrei* appears to be a legal formula for a nullification of vows, it doesn't meet the criteria for doing so.

The *Shulchan Aruch* in *Yoreh Dei-ah* 228 makes it very clear that there is a specific method for annulling legitimate vows, insisting that they be declared void by an ordained teacher or by three lay-people. This is not the case here. And, it just doesn't meet the criteria, nor does it specify the vows, nor is the court convened for doing so. And to suggest that we take out three Torahs and that is a court, that's a later emendation, originally only two *sifrei Torah* were taken out. You can check Agnon and some other sources on that.

Now most of us like to believe that the *Kol Nidrei* originated, somewhat like a romantic history here, that it originated with the (if you will) Marranos or that it dates to the seventh century when the Visigoths forcibly converted Jews. Those are very romantic and interesting things, but not true. There are two suggestions, and Hammer stresses them, that warrant serious consideration. The first is that *Kol Nidrei* is a later displacement of an ancient custom that is mentioned in the Talmud in *N'darim* 23b—where it says that a person wishing, "*Shelo yitkaymu nedarav kol hashana, yaamod b'Rosh HaShanah v'yomar sh'kol neder sh'ani atid lidor yeheh batel . . .*", that he who wishes that his vows made during the year should not be valid, stand at the New Year and declare every vow that I may make in the future shall be void. And the text then insists that the very time the person says that, those vows, you must be thinking of these vows, and he has to remember and focus his mind on this particular, on the vows that you want to annul and on the statement itself. But on the very same page, the Talmud says that we shouldn't teach this rule publicly, so that vows should not be treated lightly.

So it's very, very possible that there was this tradition on Rosh HaShanah at night, where what you did was you annulled your vows. And that, then, is the source of *Kol Nidrei*.

So that's one possibility.

But there's another possibility (and here I'm very, very grateful to my teacher, Baruch Levine, who spent much of his career at NYU and has written some wonderful things, particularly on *Vayikra* and on some of these other matters). In the book that Jacob Neusner

In the Bible

In the *Shulchan Aruch*

In the Talmud

Whom do you think the Rabbis had in mind when they said that the vows should not be treated lightly? Could they have meant outside of the Jewish community, within the Jewish community, or both?

The Rabbis' Opposition

Jacob Neusner, *A History of the Jews in Babylonia* (Leiden: E.J. Brill, 1970)

published, *A History of the Jews in Babylonia*, Levine wrote about "The Language of the Magical Bowls."

During the geonic period in Babylonia, magic formulas were in common use among Jews and non-Jews alike, and many of these were written on bowls and used as spells for the exorcism of demons and evil spirits. And according to Levine's article, and Hammer make[s] reference to it as well, these formulas contain many of the key words we find in *Kol Nidrei*, "released, abandoned, inoperative, null, and nullified." And one of the suggestions that Levine considers there is that *Kol Nidrei* may have originated as a magical formula to eliminate demons, assuring that no evil spirit could interfere with the sanctity of Yom Kippur itself.

But perhaps this explanation seems to be a little more validated than the other, because what's amazing is that it would explain the tremendous opposition to it that we find in Rabbinic sources. It was the Rabbis who felt that it strayed so far from Judaism itself—it was opposed by the *Tannaim*, it was opposed by the *gaonim*, and it probably was the creation of the masses and *amcha* had its role in all of this. But let me just refer to a few rabbis who opposed it: Amram Gaon cited the Hebrew text of *Kol Nidrei* in 879 but disapproved of it, calling it a foolish custom. Saadyah accepted it, Hai and other *gaonim* approved the revised text, but it had to be understood as a plea for mercy rather than as a statement of legal annulment of vows. Sadly the custom spread, and it eventually was accepted when the son-in-law of Rashi, Rabbi Meir ben Rabbi Samuel, implemented the Talmudic concept and changed the tenses, but the tenses were never changed in the official liturgy we have. The traditional text speaks of annulling vows from now until next Yom Kippur but uses the past tense, and even the final changes made in the thirteenth century by Rabbi Meir of Rothenburg turned the verses at the end, even though we changed the tenses, into some kind of congregational response.

> What is your reaction to this liturgy now, in light of the knowledge that so many major rabbis in our tradition viewed it as foolish, tried to change it, or tried to get rid of it altogether?

So I really think in just summing up the history of it, we had the same thing in the modern time as well, as you well know; in the modern age, it was the old *Union Prayer Book* that just left the melody, or said "*Kol Nidrei* melody," and didn't in fact include the words. And it's always been a problem for the rabbis, because it's not an official formula, it's not an accepted formula. It probably originated in some magical formulas in the eighth and ninth century, as we discovered, and further, somehow diminishes the ability of other human beings to trust us.

So in a short, short time you have an overview of the history of *Kol Nidrei* itself.

Kol Nidrei: Current Usage and Innovation

Rabbi Reena Spicehandler

I want to begin by speaking a bit about the power and the paradox of *Kol Nidrei*. As we've already heard, *Kol Nidrei* is a treasured tradition, yet it is also quite controversial. All the way back to the ninth century, Jews have been objecting to the use of *Kol Nidrei*. I'm not going to go into details at this point; we already have some of that background. On the one hand, we have a deep spiritual connection with *Kol Nidrei*, and on the other, it has been used to denigrate Jews. It's a prayer, in a way, and yet, it's supposed to be based on a judicial formula. It talks about release from vows and yet reminds us of our responsibility. It also goes from daylight into nighttime, as we've heard in regard to the tradition of wearing a tallit. One version looks at the past year, while another looks forward to the year ahead. Finally, it refers to both the heavenly court and the human court.

The questions I'd like to address here are: Where does the power reside in this most complex and contradictory of prayers, and can we add to that power in any way in our use of it on the High Holy Days? Is the power in the music, is it in the words, is it in the drama and visual pageantry that we have? Certainly we know that many Jews and non-Jews have been moved by the music. We know that Tolstoy and Beethoven and Bloch and even lapsed Jews such as Theodore Hertzl and Heinrich Heine and, most famously, Arnold Shoenberg were moved by the melody of *Kol Nidrei*.

Any of us who have spent Yom Kippur in Israel have probably experienced the sight of the streets outside of the synagogue on *Kol Nidrei* night being filled with secular Israelis who just want to hear that melody.

On the other hand, when Mordechai Kaplan tried to do away with the words and only keep the melody, he ran into quite a bit of resistance. At first Mordechai Kaplan wanted to set a poem by Luzzato to the melody of *Kol Nidrei*; afterwards he decided to use a psalm. In both cases, he got quite a bit of resistance, even though he promised to preserve the melody. As a matter of fact, he was told by more than one person that he was destroying Judaism by trying to do away with the words of *Kol Nidrei*. Even Kaplan's mother objected. She wrote to him, "You are destroying Judaism. Do you

What is the affective power of this prayer? How does this power contribute to the overall worship experience?

What memories or associations do you have with this prayer in the synagogue? To what extent do you think about the words, and how do you relate to these words?

Why did Kaplan's mother react so strongly? How is omitting this text

41

"destroying Judaism"? Considering the history of this text, which has been used to spread anti-Jewish messages, how has the role of this liturgy in our tradition developed?

What is the effect of this *kavanah*? What other analogies might you use to bring meaning to the custom of reciting *Kol Nidrei* three times?

What are other possible combinations of three?

A *kavanah* for those who are hiding part of their true identities:

What other parts of our identities do we hide? How does this hurt

understand what you are doing to yourself? I will not tell you what you are doing to me, and maybe to your father in his grave. I am too weak now, I cannot write more. Be well and happy with your family. Signed, Your Mother."

So, first Mordechai Kaplan tried to eliminate *Kol Nidrei* altogether; then he tried to put different words to the *Kol Nidrei* melody. In the end he was convinced to reinstate *Kol Nidrei*. And in a few minutes, I will talk about why he was convinced and what we might learn from that. But before I do that, I want to talk about the actual presentation of *Kol Nidrei*. It is traditional, of course, to read or chant it three times. However, in many Reform congregations this doesn't happen. The *Machzor Vitry* in the thirteenth century says that the first time the reader chants *Kol Nidrei*, he has to chant in a very low voice, like someone who is amazed at entering the palace of the king to ask for a favor and is afraid of coming close to the king, and so the reader speaks softly, like one asking for something. The second time, he has to raise his voice a little higher than the first time, and the third time he has to raise his voice higher and higher, like a man who is at home and is accustomed to being a member of the king's household.

Clearly, increasing the volume does increase the power, and as I've said, in many Reform congregations, *Kol Nidrei* is only done once. I would really like to encourage us to think creatively about how to do *Kol Nidrei* three times. As the result of serving as an interim rabbi over the last eight years, I've led many congregations and seen many ways of doing this. This year, we had a cello do the first rendition, and the cantor did the second rendition, and then I read the English for the third rendition. Another way to do it would be to have an instrumental playing as people are coming in, and then have perhaps a choir sing through one, and then a cantor sing. My point is to encourage us to really think about reinstating this idea of three, and of course the three does have a kind of magical power.

I want to turn back now to this idea of what we can do in modern times to add to the experience of *Kol Nidrei*. I prefer to go in the direction of *kavanot*. One of the associations as we all know for *Kol Nidrei* is that the *avaryanim*, who are related to Iberians, whom in turn have been identified with the Conversos, were people who were required to make oaths that they could not keep, or that they did not want to keep, and who wanted to be absolved of those forced vows. So there is this connection to the Marranos, or Conversos. In this connection I'd like to read here from a *kavanah* by Adina Abramovitz:

This prayer has long been associated with hidden Jews, the Jews in Spain who converted to Christianity during the Inquisition and kept their Jewish life secret in order to survive. This prayer al-

lowed them to pray as Jews by forgiving the vows they had made to another religion, another system of belief. What a deep resonance this interpretation has for gay and lesbian Jews who are living hidden secret lives, for those in the closet about their gay identity in their Jewish communities, and those in the closet about their Jewish lives in the gay community. This prayer recognizes the pain of hidden and secret identities, and offers the hope for integration and healing.

Now, back to Mordechai Kaplan—of course Kaplan always felt that it was very important to say what you mean, and mean what you say in Judaism, and that was his reason for objecting to the words of *Kol Nidrei*. He was finally convinced to reinstate *Kol Nidrei* by a letter from Ira Eisenstein's grandfather. And in this letter, Eisenstein says:

> *As we cannot ask God to pardon our sins until we wipe out all ill feeling toward others, goodwill is the keynote of Yom Kippur. For this reason, the Kol Nidrei was instituted as the prologue before our prayers on Yom Kippur in order to absolve all vows and oaths foolishly and in anger hastily enunciated, vows that would act to break up a relationship with a friend, even to separate a son from a father. As was the case mentioned in the Mishnah.*

And this is what convinced Kaplan to bring back *Kol Nidrei*. He did add some words. Reading this reminded me how in my own family, my grandmother and her sister didn't speak for many years. I'm sure that many of us have heard of similar family situations where people are so estranged that they have said, "I swear I will never speak to that person again" or "I will never let that person in my house again."

If we could create a *kavanah* for *Kol Nidrei* explaining that this is what is meant by absolving of oaths—that any oaths that are really counter to our sense of community, our sense of forgiveness, that prevent us from doing *t'shuvah*, from changing the way that we act in the world, these are the vows that need to be absolved. So I want to suggest that Mordechai Kaplan can inspire us to give renewed meaning to *Kol Nidrei*'s words by creating a *kavanah* in this way. Finally, I want to conclude with a poem by Merle Feld, as another alternative:

Kol Nidre

I am grateful for this,
a moment of truth,
grateful to stand before You
in judgment.

us? How can we use Yom Kippur as a time to not only atone for our actions against others, but to become more true to ourselves?

A *kavanah* of reconciliation:

A *kavanah* for standing in honesty before God:

What other *kavanot* might you create to focus your recitation of these words?

You know me as a liar
and I am flooded with relief
to have my darkest self
exposed at last.

Every day, I break my vows,
to be awake in this moment,
to be a responsible
citizen of the world.

No one sees, no one knows,
how often I become distracted,
lose myself, and then lose hope –
every day, every day.

On this day, this one day,
I stand before You naked,
without disguise, without embellishment,
naked, shivering, ridiculous.

I implore You—
help me to try again.

Merle Feld

Kol Nidrei:
Contemporary Challenges

Rabbi Elaine Zecher

As I was listening to these beautiful teachings from Shelly and Reena, learning about how we can understand *Kol Nidrei* for ourselves as leaders and then how we can convey its depth of meaning to our communities, I began to reflect on its purpose and why we use it in the first place. First, I call *Kol Nidrei* a ritual. It carries significance more than words or the melody. It has a specific role in the liturgical drama of the Yom Kippur evening. Since it is a ritual, it moves us from one place to another spiritually, and we have the potential to be transformed by it.

This leads me to describe two images that *Kol Nidrei* evokes for me. The first is the courtroom. On this sacred night, the entire community sits in a courtroom together. We appear before the Eternal Judge, asking, pleading, beckoning the Holy One to look upon us and examine us with these particular words. What vows will we make? How will our lives be shaped by them? How might we alter the course of our direction by pondering these words in the presence of One who makes judgment for our very existence? The magnificence of the scene places us as vulnerable plaintiffs and, at the same time, protected by being surrounded by our community. The melody (in the Ashkenazic form) like a true courtroom scene enhances the drama, adding its own suspense.

The other image is that of the deathbed. On Yom Kippur, in many ways, we re-create death. We don't eat or drink we don't bathe, we don't have sexual relations, we don't put on perfume. We don't engage in "living" activities. And so, metaphorically we die in some way, only to be resurrected by the end of Yom Kippur. We come back to life again as our first act is the building of the sukkah. On Yom Kippur eve, however, we prepare to recite the confession and *Kol Nidrei* helps us wipe the slate clean in preparation for this moment. We not only have the opportunity to ask for forgiveness, but to forgive ourselves. *Kol Nidrei* calls us into this moment.

In addition to these images, I think we might also consider *how* we offer *Kol Nidrei* within our communities. Is it the cantor alone who stands before the congregation to offer these words and melody? How might we enhance this moment? We heard the idea of starting quietly, building up to a crescendo. Since it is offered three

Rabbi Zecher provides two images for this ritual: the courtroom and the deathbed. How do these resonate with you? What other images does this ritual evoke?

How else does movement enhance prayer? What is the connection between mind, body, and soul, and how can we use these entry points to create a more holistic worship experience?

times, what would it be like if first the melody came from a cello or other musical instrument, then from the entire congregation—they would need to receive the music—and then for the last time, the cantor would sing it? We actually do this in our congregation. Also, how might it be possible to incorporate movement with the *Kol Nidrei*? In our congregation, the clergy start within the congregation at the back of the room, moving closer to the bimah with each time *Kol Nidrei* is sung. By the last time, the cantor and the rabbis are up front, and the cantor faces the congregation, offering *Kol Nidrei*. The movement of the clergy forward serves as a visual metaphor of drawing closer to the Yom Kippur experience.

I hope I have added a complement to our gifted teachers.

Kol Nidrei
End-of-Call Discussion

Rabbis Deborah Prinz, Reena Spicehandler, Elaine Zecher, Shelly Zimmerman

Debbie: Shelly, Reena, Elaine, do you have something you want to say at this point to each other, or questions you would like to address to each other?

Shelly: First of all to thank both Reena and Elaine for this, and Debbie for this wonderful, wonderful thing—Elaine and Reena really have helped us understand things in a wonderful way, and it underlines something very powerful: the ongoing dialectic, the ongoing dialogue between the Jewish people and its religious leadership. It is clear that in the issue of *Kol Nidrei*, the religious leadership, including Mordechai Kaplan, eventually yielded to *amcha*, to God's people, for whatever reason, the power, the majesty of *Kol Nidrei* spoke to them. And I think in the issues that we're talking about, we're seeing that it bonds our people together, even if they don't even understand it, the words don't matter. What matters is this extraordinary power, and the power of the people because the siddur is, as the late Henry Slonimsky pointed out, our people's book, far more than the *Tanach* itself.

Elaine: I agree that Professor Henry Slonimsky gave us a beautiful gift in how he described the siddur. I happen to have it right in front of me: "And if you want to know what Judaism is, the question which has no answer, it's debated on the plane of intellectual argument . . . you can find it by absorbing the siddur. The Jewish soul is mirrored there, there is nowhere else, mirrored or rather embodied there. The individual soul in his or her private sorrows and the people's soul in its historic burden . . . its heroic passion and suffering, its unfaltering space through the ages."

I think that he is exactly right in that we have the opportunity to offer a message, and the message has to have meaning. We certainly found, in putting out *Mishkan T'filah*, that community has a profound influence in how it responds to a prayer book. As we piloted it among many congregations and settings, there was an intentional move to bring the prayer book, unlike the way prayer books have been developed in the past, to the people to receive feedback and reaction. I firmly believe that *Mishkan T'filah*, with Elyse Frishman as an incredible guide and visionary in its development, was enhanced in multiple ways by the people's yearning to be involved in its development.

Debbie: Reena, do you have anything that you would like to add at this point?

Reena: Well, I do want to lend my support to what Elaine has just said, because the prayer book commission that I worked with did have laypeople included, and many of the insights that we had came from those laypeople, because rabbis, to some degree, have blinders on—we don't know how much we actually know, and we don't know how some things appear to the average person in the congregation. So it is very helpful to have that feedback. And I'd also like to suggest in something like *Kol Nidrei* that it might be useful to have input from cantors. One cantor that I spoke to said that the range of *Kol Nidrei* is very difficult for her, which is why she doesn't like to sing it three times. That never would have occurred to me. I'm sure there are other more profound insights than that, but we don't hear them.

Elaine: I would also like to say that people are very attached to the melody of *Kol Nidrei* and that the cantors are very attached to the melody, for very good reason. Whether the range is difficult or not, it is a very wonderful moment to be able to hear a cantor sing these words, offer these words in an interpretative way through music.

Reena: Absolutely.

Shelly: Absolutely. Let me just remind all of us that this is the Ashkenazic motif—the Ashkenazic motif is the primacy of *Kol Nidrei* as a magnificent cantorial piece, and I've been blessed to hear great *chazanim*, male and female, sing it and chant it. But in the Sephardic community, in *Eidut HaMizrach*, it's a very simple annulment language and melody. It lacks the grandeur so that it's a melody—yes, and Reuven Hammer likes to struggle with it—the powers of melody, but there's something else going on here that just grabs the heart and the soul of the Jewish people. And I'm not sure what it is—I mean, I'd like to hear what you think it is, but I'm not sure what it is. What is it that binds us in such extraordinary ways that we even call the whole night *Kol Nidrei*?

Elaine: It also occurs to me that familiarity with the melody is also very attractive. I think that there is much about the High Holy Day experience that in some ways is not as familiar because it's not part of the yearly ritual. It comes into our consciousness for that period of time, and then goes out, and then people are reminded again. But *Kol Nidrei*, particularly in Ashkenazic tradition, is carried with us through the year. And so it's, in a sense, coming back home, coming back to a place of familiarity amidst some things that aren't so familiar.

Debbie: You raised the issue of what it means to us; the melody evokes something. I wonder if each of you might be willing to say something about what *Kol Nidrei* has meant to you personally. Maybe a particular experience, a particular moment, a particular insight, a particular understanding that you have had related to *Kol Nidrei*.

Elaine: Well, I can say that we develop new ways of doing the High Holy Days in our congregation. Because of our size, we hold four *Kol Nidrei* services, two back-to-back running simultaneously. In two of the four, we have congregational participation, and hearing the entire congregation—even the trills—the congregation actually singing, or trying to sing, with the musical score in front of them is incredibly moving to me. To hear that it's not just one person offering *Kol Nidrei* for all three repetitions, but all of the community brings us together.

Shelly: My grandfather, *alav hashalom*, was a great *rav* and *chazan*, and his sons were part of the choir. And I remember as the young child, they dressed me up to look like a young *chazan*. Trouble is, I never had either the voice or the capacity for any of that. But I always remembered the melody and my grandfather and my uncle singing with him. Once I even spoke about it—that my grandfather was able to sing for me, but I was never able to sing for my grandfather. And there was—there is—this sense of being bound by a melody, which somehow is deep within the soul, and even though we may not be able to chant it with the same extraordinary quality as the *chazan*, somehow the music resonates through us and calls us back to worship and to the Jewish people.

Reena: Amen. I would just say that for me, many of the times that have allowed me to feel so moved by *Kol Nidrei* have been the times when I have not been the rabbi at the congregation. And this is something that is very much lacking I think for most rabbis, but it would be wonderful if there was a way for rabbis once every few years to actually just be a congregant at the *Kol Nidrei* service, because I think that because I've had the luxury of that experience, it has just so enhanced my own relationship to *Kol Nidrei*. That's my thought.

Debbie: Thank you. This year people—our congregants and our members—will be coming to services in a very difficult economic milieu, and I wonder if you have any thoughts about how *Kol Nidrei* could be used to comfort them, either liturgically or homiletically. Do you see any *nechemta* (words of consolation) that can be derived from *Kol Nidrei* this year?

Shelly: One of the things that I'm starting to try to do now and build toward that time is the renewal of trust in those who speak to us, and make promises, who say words that in Jewish law, halachah, bind us—I mean most contractual things can be done verbally, and the words are that powerful. And somehow, how do we start communicating with each other in ways that are trustworthy, reliable, that not only come from the heart, but enable us once again to find our way into—not trusting authority—but somehow being able to relate to each other in an environment of care and love in which the words we speak can be taken at face value?

Elaine: When people come in for Yom Kippur, there is an opportunity for reflection unlike any other time. There is a different kind of opening for them. Larry Kushner speaks about what we do on Yom Kippur is like looking at a picture of ourselves when we were younger and wondering, at that point in our lives—well, what were we going to be like, and what was open to us? Then we look back and we wonder if we became what we thought we would become and who we are. This ritual moment of *Kol Nidrei* provides an opportunity for a forgiveness of ourselves. And if we can work at that as the forgiving of ourselves for what we didn't become, for what we might have done that we regret, then it allows us to be open to the forgiveness of others, and/or forgiving others, and to create those bonds of trust that might have been lost during the year.

Debbie: Thank you.

Reena: I would go in a little bit of a different direction. I want to add another approach to the rich insights we have just heard, and that is that the sound of *Kol Nidrei* is very old. It doesn't depend on our economic condition. There are gifts that we have—Jewish community, education, prayer,

Kol Nidrei—that we have from year to year in good times and in bad times. They can't be taken away from us, like a house, when you lose the mortgage, or any other material possession. There are some things that are treasures for us as Jews and that are really not affected by whatever is happening in the economy or the outside world. Even in the concentration camp, people sang *Kol Nidrei*. So, under all sorts of circumstances, Jews have survived with the *Kol Nidrei* experience being part of their lives. So that—I would try to point out—that even though people are feeling that they have lost so much, there are some very important things that they have not in fact lost.

Shelly: That is truly wonderful, Reena. And thank you for that insight. I just want to add that those of us in the greater New York area whose lives especially have been touched by the Madoff scandal and everything else—the losses in the economy are across the board. Very few people have been untouched by all of this. But very much at the same time, there are people that I am working with every day whose children have lost everything, or they had trusts for their children, plans made on the basis of words and commitments that are shattered and broken forever. And yet we have to come back into ourselves to what the *Rav, alav hashalom,* said, the jungle of this whole, as we find *t'shuvah* and meaning on Yom Kippur. I think there also has to be a sense of safe haven, safe community, and here when you come to this synagogue, you can trust and be trusted. Because let us not forget that a lot of the shenanigans occurred at the supposedly safe places of our lives: country clubs, retirement places, even in the synagogue.

Reena: Yes, very important.

Debbie: Thank you so much for your presentations, Shelly, Reena, and Elaine. We extend to you much appreciation. We know you are very busy, and we appreciate the reflections and perspectives about the complexities of *Kol Nidrei*, about the insights you have, and your personal thoughts about it. We thank you for all of it.

Kol Nidrei **Wrap-Up**

1. The ritual of *Kol Nidrei* is one of the most prominent of the entire Yamim Noraim, so much so that the Erev Yom Kippur service is generally referred to as *Kol Nidrei*. Most of this power comes from the affective experience: the melody used, the cantor or choir's voice/s and other instruments that might be used, standing for a long period of time before the open ark, etc. How does the affective experience of this ritual contribute to your experience of the High Holy Day worship?

2. The text of *Kol Nidrei* is not only controversial today, but, as Rabbi Zimmerman teaches, has been criticized within the Jewish community and by non-Jews for many centuries. Each of these three lessons has provided ways to frame the words of *Kol Nidrei* so that the words themselves, and not just the affective experience, add to the meaning of Yom Kippur. Once again thinking of your experience of High Holy Day worship, which theme(s) might you focus on in order to connect to the words of *Kol Nidrei* and the power of the ritual?

3. Unlike most other challenging texts in our liturgy, *Kol Nidrei* has been a source of controversy both in the Jewish community and in non-Jewish circles. What effect does this have on our approach to finding meaning in the text or the consideration of making changes to it?

Biographies of Presenters

Rabbi Ron Aigen has been the spiritual leader of Congregation Dorshei Emet in Montreal since 1976. He is a graduate of the Reconstructionist Rabbinical College (1976) and was awarded a Doctor of Divinity from that institution in 1991. He is the author of *Siddur Hadesh Yameinu / Renew Our Days: A Book of Jewish Prayer and Meditation*, and *Mahzor Hadesh Yameinu / Renew Our Days: A Prayer-Cycle for the Days of Awe*. Rabbi Aigen is a *chaver* of the Spirituality Institute and currently a rabbinic fellow of the Shalom Hartman Institute in Jerusalem.

Rabbi Edward Feld is a noted teacher and author and is currently the editor of the new Rabbinical Assembly High Holy Day *machzor*. For the past seven years he has served as rabbi-in-residence at the Jewish Theological Seminary of America, where he has been an advisor and mentor to rabbinical students, and has just stepped down as educational director of Rabbis for Human Rights–North. He is the author of *Spirit of Renewal: Faith after the Holocaust*. He has published essays on theological and halachic issues, and his book on biblical philosophies of law, *The Book of Revolutions: The Bible and the Formation of Judaism*, will be issued shortly by Aviv Press.

Rabbi Richard N. Levy (HUC-JIR, C, 1964) is the rabbi of the Synagogue at the Los Angeles Campus of HUC-JIR, where he also serves as director of spiritual growth. He has just completed ten years as director of the School of Rabbinic Studies at the Los Angeles campus, where he coordinated the school's transition to an ordination program. Previously he served as president of the CCAR from 1997 to 1999, where he shepherded passage of the 1999 Statement of Principles. He served for thirty-one years as director of Hillel at UCLA and regional director of Hillel for the Greater Los Angeles area. He is the author of *A Vision of Holiness: The Future of Reform Judaism*, published by the URJ Press, and editor of three liturgies published by KTAV and Hillel—The Foundation for Jewish Campus Life: *On Wings of Awe*, a High Holy Day *machzor*; *On Wings of Freedom*, a Haggadah; and *On Wings of Light*, a Shabbat evening siddur. A revised edition of *On Wings of Awe* is scheduled to appear in 2010.

Dr. Rachel S. Mikva (HUC-JIR, C, 1990), a congregational rabbi for thirteen years, is currently the Schaalman Professor of Jewish Studies at Chicago Theological Seminary. She is the editor of *Broken Tablets: Restoring the Ten Commandments and Ourselves* and specializes in the history of biblical interpretation.

Dr. Richard Sarason (HUC-JIR, C, 1974) is professor of Rabbinic Literature and Thought at HUC-JIR, Cincinnati, and associate editor of the *Hebrew Union College Annual.* He writes and teaches in the areas of early rabbinic literature, Jewish liturgy, and the history of Judaism in late antiquity. He is a member of the Joint Commission on Worship, Music, and Religious Living and was a member of the Ad Hoc Siddur Editorial Committee that guided the creation of *Mishkan T'filah.*

Rabbi Reena Spicehandler is a pioneer in the area of the interim rabbinate, having served five URJ congregations in this capacity since 2001. She earned a BA in French Languages and Literature and an MA in General Studies in the Humanities from the University of Chicago, where she also pursued doctoral studies in the Committee on Comparative Studies in Literature. She received an MAHL and ordination from the Reconstructionist Rabbinical College, where she also served as dean of students and admissions. Reena was a member of the Reconstructionist Prayer Book Commission and Assistant Editor for the Kol Haneshamah Prayer Book series. She has published numerous articles in the areas of poetry, prayer, and creative liturgy. Reena resides in Philadelphia with her partner Jeremy Brochin, who is the director of Hillel at the University of Pennsylvania. They have two adult children.

Rabbi Lance J. Sussman, Ph.D. (HUC-JIR, C, 1980) is senior rabbi of Reform Congregation Keneseth Israel in Elkins Park, Pennsylvania, serves as national chair of the CCAR Press, and is the author of many books and articles, including *Isaac Leeser and the Making of American Judaism* and *Sharing Sacred Moments.* He is past chair of the Judaic Studies Department at Binghamton University and has taught American Jewish history at Princeton University and Hunter College, among others. He is involved in community and interfaith activities nationwide and currently serves as a trustee of the Katz Center for Advanced Judaic Studies at the University of Pennsylvania.

Rabbi David Teutsch (HUC-JIR, NY, 1977) was the editor-in-chief of the seven-volume *Kol Haneshamah* prayer book series. He is the Wiener Professor of Contemporary Jewish Civilization and director of the Center for Jewish Ethics at the Reconstructionist Rabbinical College, where he served as president for nearly a decade. He has written the first six volumes of *A Guide to Jewish Practice* as well as several other books and dozens of articles, including *Making a Difference: A Guide to Jewish Leadership and Not-for-Profit Management.* He earned his Ph.D. at the Wharton School.

Elaine Zecher (HUC-JIR, NY, 1988) is a rabbi of Temple Israel in Boston. She serves as the chair of the Worship and Practices Committee of the CCAR. She also worked on *Mishkan T'filah* as a member of the Editorial Committee and the Publishing Team. She is presently helping to edit *Mishkan T'filah for the House of Mourning*. At Temple Israel, she has actively engaged in creating creative and engaging worship. She was involved in Synagogue 2000 and is a member of the regional board of the ADL. She served as guest editor to the spring 2009 issue of the *CCAR Journal*, which focuses on the theological issues about the High Holy Day liturgy.

Rabbi Sheldon Zimmerman (HUC-JIR, NY, 1970) has served as rabbi of Central Synagogue, NYC, Temple Emanu-el, Dallas, and is now rabbi at The Jewish Center of the Hamptons. He served as president of Hebrew Union College–Jewish Institute of Religion and also as president of the Central Conference of American Rabbis, executive vice-president of birthrightisrael, North America, and vice president of Jewish Renaissance and Renewal, United Jewish Communities. He is married to Judith, a clinical social worker and family and play therapist. They are blessed with a precious family: Rabbi Brian and Mimi Zimmerman, Kira and Jeffrey Kerstine, David Zimmerman, and Micol and Rabbi Danny Burkeman, and five grandchildren.

Related Essays from CCAR Journal: The Reform Jewish Quarterly, Spring 2009

Introduction: Getting to the Heart of the Discussion of a New Machzor

Elaine Zecher

Each year, as the High Holy Days approach, we, as the spiritual leaders of our congregations, are sure of one fact. The community will show. Regardless of spending hours in sermon preparation, pondering the worship experience, or organizing the sanctuary spaces, members, their friends, neighbors, and family will present themselves in vast numbers. We take their presence seriously and want it to be meaningful and powerful. If, however, they show up merely for some annual roll call of community duty, we have not succeeded in creating a transformative prayerful environment.

We, as leaders, recognize our sacred responsibility to cultivate a connection with the Divine whether we define it through relationship, peoplehood, mystery and awe, or in some other way. It is incumbent upon us, therefore, to focus significant attention on the liturgical images and metaphors of God that fill the pages of our *machzor*. If our goal is to enable our people to be touched by the experience of High Holy Day worship, we must step back and reflect on whether and how these images of God resonate with the people sitting in the pews and what effect such a portrayal has on their experience.

In this issue of the *CCAR Journal*, the Worship and Practices Committee of the CCAR has attempted to explore how we, as a community of worshipers, understand the Divine in our *machzor*. Our committee has posed a question and a challenge. As all of us enter into our worship spaces during this momentous time of year, how do we understand the way God is conveyed in our liturgy of the High Holy Days? The challenge that confronts us is to understand

ELAINE ZECHER (NY88) is a rabbi at Temple Israel, Boston

and respond to the theological message as we struggle with that which is dissonant in the language of those images. By asking the question and making it a challenge, our committee hopes all of us will discover a deeper understanding and a profound appreciation of the magnificence of our liturgical experience.

As our committee discussed our approach, we wanted the conversation to be more than a theological exploration. It is not just the content of the words that challenges us, but the act of believing and interacting with the words that has the potential for resonance. Abraham Joshua Heschel called this kind of inquiry, depth theology. He said, "Theology has often suffered from a preoccupation with the dogma, the content of believing. The act of believing; the questions, What happens within the person to bring about faith? What does it mean to believe?—all this is the concern of a special type of inquiry which may be called 'depth theology.' The theme of theology is the content of believing; the theme of depth theology is the act of believing, its purpose being to explore the depth of faith."[1]

As people reflect on their own lives and their search for meaning, the experience of Rosh HaShanah and Yom Kippur afford them the opportunity to plunge the depths within their inner lives to reach out and avail themselves of the divine encounter. It is a moment that allows a personal inquiry into a belief system. The High Holy Day experience has great potential for such an exploration when those who join in our communal worship feel touched by the words and images they use in praying and feel moved to act upon those words.

The five gifted authors of the essays in this issue of the Journal have offered a myriad of ways to respond to our question and challenge. We started with the *Un'taneh Tokef.* Many rabbinic colleagues have struggled with the complicated divine image offered by it. Daniel Plotkin performs a meta-analysis of how rabbis, through their sermons, have contemplated how *Un'taneh Tokef* speaks of God. He has collected, contrasted, and compared how our colleagues have reconciled and approached an understanding of God in this prayer. Maggie Wenig takes the prayer to a new level and considers its paradoxical point of view. Instead of rejecting that which might make us uncomfortable, she posits an alternative to rejection and opens new possibilities not only of reconciling whatever might have initially felt dissonant but also of appreciating its

INTRODUCTION: GETTING TO THE HEART OF THE DISCUSSION

significant place in our liturgical experience. Yoel Kahn investigates the specific image of Kingship and regal metaphors prevalent in our High Holy Day worship. He shares the struggle with such metaphors, analyzes their placement, and then posits a number of helpful responses. Joel Mosbacher has used his dissertation work on understanding the way adolescents comprehend God to further our own development as adults to appreciate God-concepts in our prayer. His work challenges us to open pathways to create meaning in the worship experience. Nancy Flam takes us with her on her own journey of articulating a theology of God that not only incorporates the High Holy Day themes of *din* and *rachamim,* but one which also takes all of life's experiences and the eternal Presence of God into account to bring a full and whole understanding of God.

This issue has an added bonus. The poems included here have been selected specifically for their connection to the theme of this issue. We received over 150 submissions. These poetic expressions bring their unique artistry to complement the articles.

The genesis for this issue came about through three different sources. First, my colleague Jeremy Morrison posed the question to me in a conversation about the nascent development of a new *machzor* for the Reform movement. He asked how we could proceed if we have not yet had a comprehensive exploration of how God is presented and conveyed in our liturgy. Second, Peter Knobel suggested the Journal as a vehicle to begin the conversation about a new *machzor* for the Reform Movement. Third, those who attended the Worship and Practices Committee meeting at the 2007 CCAR Convention brainstormed an approach. Many who attended have offered their own response within these pages, and we are grateful for their contribution.

This issue is meant to spark the discussion of how we understand and encounter the Divine during this most significant time in the Jewish calendar year. As we recognize that the community will fill the sanctuary on these important holidays, we can explore the ideas presented here on many levels and in many venues throughout our movement and beyond.

Notes

1. Abraham Joshua Heschel, "Depth Theology," in *The Insecurity of Freedom* (Philadelphia: JPS, 1966), pp. 117–118.

Giving Meaning to Our Days: Reimagining *Un'taneh Tokef*— A Survey of Selected Sermons[1]

Daniel Plotkin

When we consider the prayers and *piyutim* that are unique to the *Yamim Noraim* services there are several that may come to mind. *Avinu Malkeinu, Kol Nidrei,* and the Shofar Service are among the highlights of these days for many worshipers. Although those prayers are important to both the experience of worship and the meaning of the days, none of them pierce to the heart of the meaning of the *Yamim Noraim* in the same way as *Un'taneh Tokef,* the medieval (or earlier) *piyut* commonly ascribed to Rabbi Amnon of Maynce from the end of the 11th century.[2]

While it is clear that the legend of Rabbi Amnon is just a legend,[3] the prayer still evokes powerful images of the matters of life and death that hang in the balance during the *Yamim Noraim.* The text of the prayer evokes the images of God taking into account each and every life and determining its fate for the next year. It lists a multitude of ways in which one might die and concludes by offering an apparent way to change God's mind and escape punishment for one's sins. That way is through repentance, prayer, and *tzedakah* (translated as "charity" in *Gates of Repentance*).

This *piyut* says, on the surface, that God will punish all the bad people; reward all the good people; and if we apologize, pray, and give enough we can save our lives. This interpretation is validated in *The Complete Artscroll Machzor,* a traditional *machzor* that includes extensive commentary on the prayers of the service. Referring to *Un'taneh Tokef,* it makes a very unequivocal case for a literal interpretation:

DANIEL PLOTKIN (C02) is rabbi of B'nai El Congregation, St. Louis, Missouri.

GIVING MEANING TO OUR DAYS

The list that follows [*B'Rosh HaShanah*] makes clear that whatever happens to a person is a result of the judgment rendered by God after evaluating the sum total of the quantity and quality of his deeds. That the cause of a death seems natural, accidental, or violent is only its external appearance; even that is determined by the judgment of Rosh HaShanah.[4]

The early Reform Jews were not entirely comfortable with this liturgy in terms of both its apparent fatalistic message and the references to angels in the traditional text. Despite these misgivings, they included it in the *Union Prayer Book* in a somewhat edited form that removed the angels but kept the essence of the theme.[5] Even in the modern day, when it is common to speak of God in very intimate terms, this prayer remains in our liturgy, even with its difficult theological message. Rabbi Rachel Gurevitz, recounts that in a discussion with her congregation in which her congregants were given both the traditional text and a reinterpretation of the text by Sidney Greenberg, they appreciated the reinterpretation but had no desire to replace the original text.[6]

As will be shown, there is a great desire on the part of liberal rabbis to reinterpret the text. The difficulty that so many face in reading this powerful, but disturbing *piyut* is illustrated best by a recollection from Rabbi Harry K. Danzinger: "I sometimes have told the story of my being asked to speak to a church group when I was about 17. It must have been right after the Holy Days, and I told the Book of Life tradition as fact. One teen said, 'You mean my grandmother died because she was bad?' I never let [*Un'taneh Tokef*] go uncommented upon after that."[7] Clearly if a non-Jewish teen hearing of the traditions surrounding *Un'taneh Tokef* for the first time was so disturbed by the apparent meaning of the text, this is also a text that Jews struggle with in hearing it year after year.

Rabbi Danzinger's story suggests that the *p'shat* of *Un'taneh Tokef* creates theological difficulties for the modern reciter of this liturgy. The events of the past decade, from the terrorist attacks of 9/11, to the tsunami in the Indian Ocean in 2004, and the devastating effects of Hurricane Katrina on the New Orleans area in 2005, in addition to many other tragedies of recent years, make it clear that death sometimes, or maybe almost always, comes randomly and at any time. Is it likely that all (or even most) of the three thousand or so who perished in planes, in the Twin Towers, or in the

DANIEL PLOTKIN

Pentagon on 9/11 were bad people who deserved to die "by fire"? Is it possible that all of the victims of the Indian Ocean tsunami and Hurricane Katrina were slated for "by water" the year before those events happened? Is it plausible that the 2007 bridge collapse in Minnesota didn't happen until only people who were slated for death the previous Rosh HaShanah were on the bridge?

While some, including the previously quoted *Complete Artscroll Machzor*, would say yes to the above questions, the very placement of the *Un'taneh Tokef* into only the Yom Kippur Afternoon Service in the *Union Prayer Book* suggests that the *p'shat* interpretation of the *piyut* was discomforting to many of our Reform predecessors. Yet *Un'taneh Tokef* is not only within *Gates of Repentance*, but it is placed in the morning services for both Rosh HaShanah and Yom Kippur.

Looking at sermons and other public comments from the past 10 years it is clear that there is not unanimous agreement about how *Un'taneh Tokef* should be approached among the respondents. Some rabbis are able to look at the *p'shat* of the text and see it as a challenge to their members to work to improve their lives. Others reject the premise of the prayer, even to the point that they will not lead the prayer. Most rabbis included in this survey, however, fall somewhere in the middle of those extremes; speaking to their congregations about *Un'taneh Tokef*, they feel a need to reinterpret the prayer and offer a new way of looking at it rather than the fatalistic determinism that a plain reading of the text would seem to offer.[8] It is often in the line that reads, "But repentance, prayer and charity temper judgment's severe decree"[9] in which modern day rabbis find a way to temper or even reverse the apparent fatalism of the prayer.

Some are willing to accept much of the plain meaning even while acknowledging the difficulties the text seems to create in the mind of the worshiper. Rabbi Mordecai Rotem, in speaking to his congregation in 2007, states initially, "This prayer does not hold any theological truths that we as modern Jews can embrace without challenging them." He continues later, however, "This is the basic truth of life: We are not in control of our destiny.... That although we are not in control, there is still a chance for us to influence our fate, to tilt the scale in our favor."[10] Rabbi Jennifer Clayman echoes some of these sentiments in her *iyun* to her congregation, "We never know after all / when it may be too late. / Unetaneh tokef

GIVING MEANING TO OUR DAYS

/ reminds us / that, even though / the decree may be severe, / we **can** change it; / we can change our**selves**."[11] In each of these discussions of *Un'taneh Tokef,* the rabbi accepts the fact that we have minimal control over our lives and promotes the idea that we should use the resources at our disposal to influence our destiny at least a little bit.

Others, however, take almost the opposite view. Instead of using *Un'taneh Tokef* as a reminder of God's power over us and our limited ability to affect God's decisions as we saw above, some rabbis reject the core meaning of the prayer, while in some cases seeing in the threefold prescription (repentance, prayer, and charity) a redemptive quality to the *piyut* that makes it acceptable to use in liturgy. Rabbi Jordan Parr, in summarizing his discussions of *Un'taneh Tokef* with his congregants, cannot even accept the presence of this *piyut* in modern liturgy, especially in light of Hurricane Katrina and the Shoah, writing:

> Who by water, who by fire? This is vicious! To think that the people of New Orleans deserved their fate because they didn't do enough repentance, prayer and charity is simply cruel. To think that the Shoah happened because of a lack of Tzedakah is equally vicious. Yet, we know of rabbis who claim that the Holocaust happened because Jews did not keep Shabbat. We rightfully deplore this statement but yet, it is in keeping with the tenor of this prayer.[12]

Parr's rejection of *Un'taneh Tokef* comes from his strong belief in human free will, and he does not include it in the liturgy that he leads on the *Yamim Noraim,* concluding that the plain meaning of the text is too much to interpret away. Ultimately for Parr, *Un'taneh Tokef* is "a relic of a time gone by, [it] should remain a sacred text of academicians, hidden away in libraries and never seen by the common public."[13]

Of all who responded to requests for material for this article, only Rabbi Parr was willing to throw the text of *Un'taneh Tokef* entirely out of the liturgy. Rabbi Yoel Kahn, returning in 2005 to preach at Sha'ar Zahav of San Francisco, a congregation that had been hit hard by the AIDS epidemic during Rabbi Kahn's tenure, wanted to reject *Un'taneh Tokef* completely, but could not. He stated, "When I sat down to work on this sermon, I was

DANIEL PLOTKIN

determined to say, 'let's throw these words out.'" But ultimately he concluded that he could not throw out this text despite his uncertainty.[14] Rabbi Barry Block, serving his congregation in San Antonio, Texas, in 2005 suddenly found his congregation and city springing into action immediately before the *Yamim Noraim* to assist the refugees of Hurricane Katrina. In response to some individuals who suggested Katrina was divine punishment on New Orleans, Rabbi Block affirmed that the words of *Un'taneh Tokef* seem to validate this idea. Rabbi Block then asked his congregation that Rosh HaShanah, "Do we affirm that Katrina's dead drowned at God's command?" Instead he suggests the opposite, that events like Katrina seem to suggest that God may not have power at all. In his conclusion, Rabbi Block says that the power suggested at the end of *Un'taneh Tokef* belongs to us, not to God, that repentance, prayer, and charity are a way of us taking control over our world.[15]

Most rabbis who responded to the request for sermons and other material for this article fell in between the two extremes that have already been presented, seeking neither acceptance of the words in any literal sense nor a rejection of the prayer in any way. In most of these cases, the focus of the sermon was on the final line, the threefold prescription for averting God's decree. These responses fell into three categories: those who focused on interpretations of the Hebrew word "*ma'avirin*" (temper, as translated in *Gates of Repentance*) in order to reinterpret the meaning of the text; those who understood that the last line of the text made it clear that the decree is not necessarily how we die, but how we live; and finally, those who saw in the text of the prayer a definitive call to social action.

First, in looking at one particular sermon that focuses on the word "*ma'avirin*," Rabbi Joseph P. Klein understands the root of the word (*avar*), as "to make pass." While initially explaining that the phrase can be interpreted to mean that difficult times will pass if one performs the prescribed actions, he takes it a step further:

> And when I looked at the means by which we may "make pass" the severity of the decree, namely repentance, prayer and charity, I saw for the first time a progression in, "repentance to prayer to charity." Repentance is something I can only do within myself— by me and for me. Prayer is something I can only fully do with my family-of-faith, in the sanctuary and in the company of my

GIVING MEANING TO OUR DAYS

congregation. And charity is something I can only do by extending myself out into the greater community.[16]

Rabbi Klein's words hint at the direction that many of the other sermons take in interpreting *Un'taneh Tokef.* Many of the examples submitted do reject the literal or simple meaning of the *piyut* but use the final line in order to reinterpret the prayer much in the same way as Rabbi Klein. Taken as a whole, these sermons understand *Un'taneh Tokef*'s message as: We ultimately do not have control of the length of our life, but we have full control of how we live those days and it is up to each person to make those days meaningful.

Rabbi David Locketz, in a sermon that responded in part to the Interstate 35 bridge collapse that affected the Minneapolis-St. Paul, Minnesota, region in late summer 2007, invoked the themes of *Un'taneh Tokef* in discussing the seeming randomness in which 13 individuals lost their lives but many more could have. In speaking particularly about the imagery that invokes each person writing their signature in the book of life he said, "We have a say in how we live. There is so much we cannot control...but we can choose how we live during each of the days we are given."[17] Rabbi Irwin Zeplowitz emphasizes this point in a 2005 sermon, "Earthquakes, hurricanes and viruses do not distinguish between the righteous and the wicked...not because God is plotting the action but because that is the way the world works." Despite this, Rabbi Zeplowitz affirms the good in life stating that the lesson of *Un'taneh Tokef* and the *Yamim Noraim* is, "Far from being fatalistic, then, Yom Kippur teaches that we can weather the storms life brings."[18]

The final line of *Un'taneh Tokef* is the completion of the *piyut* with the threefold prescription according to Rabbi Brett Kirchiver in a 2005 sermon saying, "But through our actions in this world, we may come to understand those deaths as a part of life, the severity of those decrees may lessen...it is only through prayer and tzedekah as well as repentance that our inner selves may come to know the peace of acceptance."[19] Others echo this theme including Rabbi Neil Kominsky speaking in the immediate aftermath of 9/11 on Yom Kippur: "We don't magically avert disaster, but our performance of these mitzvot [*t'shuvah, t'filah, tzedakah*] helps to mitigate even a terrible situation."[20]

DANIEL PLOTKIN

While the lessons of *Un'taneh Tokef* as a call toward inward reflection and the taking of small actions are important ways of reimagining the text, some go further. For some the call of repentance,
prayer, and charity is even stronger, equaling the call of the Shofar:
According to Rabbi Paul J. Kipnes, "The Unetaneh Tokef, like the
blowing of the shofar, is our wake up call, reminding us that life is
fragile. Simply put, 'Stuff happens.' Recognize it and live with it.
This is *ro-ah ha-gezayrah,* the harsh reality of life."[21] Rabbi Thomas
Alpert, responding strongly to the events of Hurricane Katrina in
2005 goes even further, focusing on *tzedakah* as the main action that
will reduce the severity of the decree:

> We can avert the evil of the decree by doing *tz'dakah* in its broad-
> est sense. We can act to ease the burdens of individuals. We can
> bring supplies here to fill a truck bound for Mississippi to help
> evacuees. Our supplies will join those contributed by other Re-
> form congregations around our country in the Jacobs Ladder
> project. We can help our own needy here in Massachusetts, as
> the Massachusetts Board of Rabbis so powerfully reminded Gov-
> ernor Romney a few weeks ago. Here at Ohabei Shalom, we can
> give to the Brookline Food Pantry, Family Table and the Preven-
> tive Food Pantry at Boston Medical Center, a program affiliated
> with the Grow Clinic. We can assist in the synagogue's commit-
> ment to help children in Boston's schools improve their reading
> as part of the Greater Boston Jewish Coalition for Literacy. We
> can help individuals, but we can, and we must, do more. We can
> speak out against governmental actions that ignore or exacerbate
> the problems of class, race, and poverty in our society. We can
> keep those problems on the agenda, so that no one will again be
> left behind, as they were in New Orleans.[22]

Un'taneh Tokef is, as so many rabbis admit, a prayer that is nearly
impossible for rabbis to take in any literal sense. It would have been
almost too easy, however, to remove it from Reform liturgy. While
for many decades it occupied an out-of-the-way place in the Yom
Kippur Afternoon services, it is now in a prominent place in the
Amidah of both Rosh HaShanah and Yom Kippur services and there
is no reason to expect that will change in the future. In light of recent events, *Un'taneh Tokef* is a part of the liturgy that cannot simply
be glossed over, but rather it must be addressed, and it has been addressed in creative and unique ways. Even in rejection of *Un'taneh
Tokef,* the questions that it raises are addressed. For some there is no

GIVING MEANING TO OUR DAYS

acceptable interpretation, for others its sole source of redemption is the final line with its threefold prescription, and for others the whole of the *piyut* has meaning especially in light of the final line.

Despite the particular interpretation placed upon it, *Un'taneh Tokef* carries a powerful message. The message is one of uplift, of giving each individual control over his or her own life. Even if one rejects placing *Un'taneh Tokef* in the liturgy, it is a rejection that affirms the individual's personal control. Rabbi Stephen Fuchs, in his 1999 *Kol Nidrei* sermon, speaks to the power of the prayer, and the power of the days on which it is traditionally recited: It is important that however one interprets (or even if one rejects) the words of *Un'taneh Tokef*, we still can enrich our lives by acting as if our fate were in the balance for the coming year, "If we can act as if we come under God's scrutiny on this holiest of days—we can choose life and blessing—for ourselves and for others—and that is the choice that really matters!"[23]

Notes

1. The sermons were selected by the author from among sermons, *iyunei t'filah*, and other public statements by rabbis who replied to the author's request for sermons in a variety of e-mail forums and word of mouth. Those who contributed sermons and other materials are: Thomas Alpert, Barry H. D. Block, Jennifer Clayman, Harry Danzinger, Morley T. Feinstein, Matt Friedman, Stephen Fuchs, Rachel Gurevitz, Mark Hurvitz, Yoel Kahn, Paul Kipnes, Brett Kirchiver, Joseph P. Klein, Neil E. Kominsky, Shelly Kover Becker, Lew Littman, David Locketz, Jordan Parr, Jason Rosenberg, Mordecai Rotem, Walter Rothschild, Steven Rubenstein, Marc Saperstein, Richard S. Sarason, Leonard B. Troupp, Irwin Zeplowitz.

2. Although the traditional *piyut* is longer, for the purposes of this article *Un'taneh Tokef* will refer to the following paragraphs as translated in *Gates of Repentance* (1978), pp. 107–109:

   Let us proclaim the sacred power of this day: it is awesome and full of dread. For on this day Your dominion is exalted, Your throne established in steadfast love; there in truth You reign. In truth You are Judge and Arbiter, Counsel and Witness. You write and You Seal, You record and recount. You remember deeds long forgotten. You open the book of our days, and what is written there proclaims itself, for it bears the signature of every human being.

   The great Shofar is sounded, the still, small voice is heard; the angels, gripped by fear and trembling, declare in awe: This is the

DANIEL PLOTKIN

day of Judgment! For even the hosts of heaven are judged, as all who dwell on earth stand arrayed before You.

As the shepherd seeks out his flock, and makes the sheep pass under his staff, so do You muster and number and consider every soul, setting the bounds of every creatures life, and decreeing its destiny.

On Rosh HaShanah it is written, on Yom Kippur it is sealed: How many shall pass on, how many shall come to be; who shall live and who shall die; who shall see ripe age and who shall not; who shall perish by fire and who by water; who by sword and who by beast; who by hunger and who by thirst; who by earthquake and who by plague; who by strangling and who by stoning; who shall be secure and who shall be driven; who shall be tranquil and who shall be troubled; who shall be poor and who shall be rich; who shall be humbled and who exalted.

But REPENTANCE, PRAYER and CHARITY temper judgment's severe decree.

3. Lawrence A. Hoffman, *Gates of Understanding 2* (New York: CCAR Press, 1983), pp. 75ff.

4. Nasson Scherman and Meir Zlotowitz, eds., *The Complete Artscroll Machzor: Rosh Hashanah* (Brooklyn, NY: Mesorah Publications, 1985), pp. 482–483. This explanation of *Un'taneh Tokef* is repeated in the Yom Kippur Edition as well.

5. Hoffman, p 75. In all editions of *The Union Prayer Book II, Un'taneh Tokef* is found only in the Yom Kippur Afternoon Service.

6. E-mail to author from Rabbi Rachel Gurevitz, December 20, 2007.

7. E-mail to author from Rabbi Harry K. Danziger, December 20, 2007.

8. This survey of sermons cannot take into account the opinions of those rabbis who have chosen not to address *Un'taneh Tokef* with their congregations.

9. As translated in *Gates of Repentance*, p. 109.

10. Rabbi Mordecai Rotem, sermon (Temple Rodef Sholom, Waco, TX, Rosh HaShanah Morning, 2007).

11. Rabbi Jennifer Clayman, *iyun*, alternative service for Rosh HaShanah and Yom Kippur (Temple Emanu-El, Westfield, NJ, 2007). Emphasis is Rabbi Clayman's.

12. E-mail to author from Rabbi Jordan Parr, January 9, 2008.

13. Ibid.

14. Rabbi Yoel Kahn, sermon (Congregation Sha'ar Zahav, San Francisco, CA, Yom Kippur Morning, 2005).

15. Rabbi Barry Block, sermon (Beth El, San Antonio, TX, Rosh HaShanah Evening, 2005).

GIVING MEANING TO OUR DAYS

16. Rabbi Joseph P. Klein, sermon (Temple Emanu-El, Oak Park, MI, Rosh HaShanah, 2005).

17. Rabbi David Locketz, sermon (Bet Shalom Congregation, Minneapolis, MN, Rosh HaShanah Evening, 2007).

18. Rabbi Irwin A. Zeplowitz, sermon (The Community Synagogue, Port Washington, NY, Yom Kippur, 2005).

19. Rabbi Brett Krichiver, sermon (Stephen S. Wise Temple, Los Angeles, CA, High Holy Days, 2005).

20. Rabbi Neil Kominsky, sermon (Temple Emanuel of the Merrimack Valley, Lowell, MA, Yom Kippur Evening, 2001).

21. Rabbi Paul J. Kipnes, "Who Shall Live and Who Shall Die? Why God is Not Making These Decisions...or Stuff Happens: Figuring Out How to Live with the Book of Life," High Holidays, 2002.

22. Rabbi Thomas M. Alpert, sermon (Temple Ohabei Shalom, Brookline, MA, Second Day Rosh HaShanah, 2005).

23. Rabbi Stephen Fuchs, sermon (Congregation Beth Israel, West Hartford, CT, Yom Kippur Evening, 1999).

The Angels Proclaim It, But Can We? "The Whole Earth Is Full of God's Presence"

Nancy Flam

We enter the season of the *Yamim Noraim* with complex emotions: excitement for the possibilities of a new year ahead; regret over our past failings; some mixture of doubt and hope (if we are honest with ourselves) about our ability to change; joy in celebrating the holidays with family, friends, and community; and fear about what decree lies in wait for us regarding the coming year: Will we rest or will we wander, will we live or will we die? We engage with the words of the *machzor* and strive to relate to the awesome, complex, and inscrutable God it depicts. And at some point in these long days of liturgy and prayer, perhaps often, we wonder how to think best about God.

My own *Yamim Noraim* theology emerged most clearly for me from the dialogues I have had with ill Jews, but perhaps most of all in relation to one woman whom I will call Rebekah.

The Search for Meaning

When Rebekah was diagnosed with breast cancer, she felt ambivalent. On the one hand, she had all the "expected" responses: fear, anger, sadness. On the other hand, she began to feel relief, as if an enormous burden was being lifted from her. Having entered "crisis mode," Rebekah was no longer able to "do" her regular life: working as a high-powered psychiatrist, taking charge of household

RABBI NANCY FLAM (NY89) is co-director of Programs at the Institute for Jewish Spirituality, New York, NY

Another version of this essay appeared previously in *Sh'ma* 24, no. 475, May 27, 1994.

THE ANGELS PROCLAIM IT, BUT CAN WE?

management, her family's financial planning, and so on. All of those concerns receded as she began to manage the one great task before her: how to seek treatment and recover health.

The shock of serious diagnosis propelled Rebekah to examine her life, determine what was of real value, and restructure the way she was spending her time and energy. Without question, she would have preferred to have been spared life-threatening illness and grown to reorder her life in a gentler fashion. Yet, somehow, she was experiencing her illness as a blessing at the same time as she believed it to be a curse.

Rebekah sought a theological framework with which to understand her illness. She refused to believe that God actually sent her this disease with the intent of helping her reorder her life; she didn't believe that God worked that way. Her illness seemed to her a random event in the universe: unearned, without moral cause. And yet, she was able to find some good; in fact, she was creating some good out of the painful circumstances.

Meaning Beyond Morality

It was important to Rebekah to resist the urge to attribute divine intent to her illness: either as punishment or as a "blessing in disguise." Such formulations, though emotionally compelling, seemed facile. Searching her deeds, she reckoned that there was nothing she did or failed to do that was commensurate with this affliction. Some part of her wished there *were* a correlation between "sin" and "punishment," because she might then be able to affect her situation positively through *t'shuvah*. But she did not believe that God intervened this way in individual human lives, meting out rewards and punishments.

Likewise, she could not accept her illness as a divinely intended "blessing" sent by God to help her change her ways, what rabbinic theology calls *yisurin shel ahavah* (chastisements of love), afflictions sent by God as prods to do *t'shuvah*. Although some good emerged from her suffering, she did not believe that this was the reason for her affliction.

Victor Frankel asserts that humanity's essential drive is to make meaning. Rebekah struggled to find the meaning of her illness. But her experience suggests to me that disease may be devoid of moral meaning; perhaps disease has nothing to do with merit

NANCY FLAM

or demerit and is simply a necessary though sometimes agonizingly painful feature of this physical creation. When Elisha ben Abuya watched the obedient young boy climb the ladder to send the mother bird away before collecting its eggs, falling on the way down to a horrifying and untimely death, Elisha ben Abuya denounced God as the arbiter of justice. There was no justice in the boy's death. The boy had simply slipped from a ladder that did not support him; his death expressed the laws of gravity and physics, not a moral law.

Din is the Divine Imposition of Limits

To Elisha ben Abuya's mind, there was no *din* and no *dayan* (judge) in this picture. But I think the element of *din* is here. By this I do not mean "judgment" or "justice" in the way the Rabbis usually mean it, the way we usually think about "judgment" during the *Yamim Noraim.* I mean a morally neutral *din: din* as the imposition of limits, the correct determination of things, the *din* Cordovera talks about as inherent in all the things insofar as all things need to remain what they are, to stay within their boundaries.[1]

Midat hadin (the divine attribute of *din*), then, carries within it the necessity of limits and finitude. Disease and death are expressions of *midat hadin.* Physical bodies are limited; they are created with a finite capacity for life and health. They are vulnerable to disease, injury, and decay. We are created and, without exception, pass away. This is part of God's holy design. It is with this understanding that I am able to accept the instruction to recite *Tzidkuk HaDin* upon hearing bad news, specifically upon hearing of a death. The core of the prayer blesses God as *Dayan ha-emet* (the judge of truth). On the level of *p'shat, Dayan ha-emet* implies moral judgment, of course, where God knows in God's wisdom who should die, when and for what reasons.

But the tradition hints of a morally neutral *din* as well. Consider the new year of *Tu BiSh'vat,* what is sometimes referred to as the *yom din* for trees. Certainly it is not the righteous trees that will bear fruit in the new year, but rather those whose structures are fitting, those that can conduct water efficiently from root to branch. So perhaps *Dayan ha-emet* makes better sense on the level of *d'rash.* Perhaps *Dayan ha-emet* refers to God who sets down the hard and fast laws of physical creation.

THE ANGELS PROCLAIM IT, BUT CAN WE?

To say *Dayan ha-emet* would affirm that *din* and God's truth are expressed when there is illness or death: not moral law, but natural law, the God-given truth of limits and finitude. Blessed is *Adonai* our God, Ruler of the universe, who sets limits and ordains the physical laws of creation. Contemplating such a view of God's *din* on *Yom HaDin* might enrich our sense of connection with the Divine.

Rachamim Is the Expression of Healing

Whereas illness expresses *midat hadin*, healing expresses *midat harachamim* (the divine attribute of mercy). *Rachamim* is classically envisioned as the force that mitigates the severity of the *din*; in cases where *midat hadin* would exact strict punishment, *midat harachimim* comes to commute the sentence, to soften the decree. *Rachamim* makes it possible for us to live within the reality of *din*. Though originally, according to one midrash, God thought to create the world with the attribute of *din* alone, God found that the world would not endure without *rachamim*. The two principles had to work together in the formation and daily re-creation of the world.

To my mind, this is indeed how the world works. Our human acts of mercy, compassion, and empathy make it possible for us to endure, to suffer the sometimes excruciatingly painful limits and losses of creation.

And it seems to me that the Jewish impulse is to add to the principle of *rachamim* so that it might outweigh, indeed ideally, messianically, overcome the power of *din*. It doesn't seem to be our task to add to the power of *din*. Consider the instruction that we should imitate God's ways. God's ways are various, but the examples given in our sources about "following in God's ways" are all instances of *rachamim:* to clothe the naked, visit the sick, comfort the mourner, bury the dead. We are not told to imitate God in strictness and severity. Perhaps the very nature of *din* as setting the principles of creation precludes human imitation, whereas the nature of *rachamim* invites it. As Abraham Joshua Heschel wrote in *The Prophets*: "Justice is a standard, mercy an attitude; justice is detachment, mercy attachment; justice is objective, mercy personal."[2]

Softening the Edges of *Din* with *Rachamim*

When it comes to illness, our acts of *rachamim* can affect our experience of *din*. We may not be able to make disease disappear, but we

NANCY FLAM

can profoundly affect how we cope with illness, thereby "softening the decree," if you will. In the Talmud, *N'darim* 39b, we learn that a visitor can take away part of a sick person's pain, can affect the experience of illness. Enough love, Rav Huna asserts, might entirely eradicate the pain, the *tza'ar*, the subjective burden.

I would go further. Acts of *rachamim* may not only make the limits more bearable, but may actually affect the limits themselves. The growing field of mind-body medicine suggests this possibility. For instance, Dr. David Spiegel of Stanford University conducted a classic study where he found that women with metastatic breast cancer who provided emotional support and care for one another lived twice as long as those who did not receive such care. While all the women eventually died of cancer, the realm of *din*, of limits and infinitude, was moved.

Our classic Jewish sources speak of the power of *rachamim* to affect the realm of *din*. Consider Rabbi Akiva's visit to his sick disciple: upon the cleaning of the sick man's room and tidying up, the man revived. A simple act of care and dignity cured the patient of his ills.[3] Or consider the various people Rabbi Yohanan ben Zakkai would visit: upon honest conversation and a show of care, Yohanan ben Zakkai would reach out his hand and the fellow would be cured, not just comforted. As if our very human love, compassion, and empathy, as well as our research and treatment, could move nature to overcome previously known limits. As if our love, our attention, our presence, our bestowal of dignity could heal both spiritually and physically.

This is the messianic vision toward which we strive: to overcome the limits of *din* with the power of *rachamim*. I do not suggest that *din* ought to be or could be eliminated entirely. The same midrash that says that the world cannot be ruled by pure *din* also states that it would not stand if guided only by *rachamim*. But our desire, our vision, is to move the world toward holding a greater share of *rachamim* than of *din*. Even God is imagined to exclaim in *B'rachot* 7a, "O that I might forever let my mercy prevail over my justice."

Recognizing *Dayan Ha-emet*

At moments of blessing, release, relief, healing, beauty, or communion of spirits, it is not hard for us to affirm God's presence. It is decidedly more challenging to affirm God's presence in the midst of loss or limitation. But, as Jews, this is what we are called upon to do. In the Book of Isaiah, God says: "I the Lord do all these things."[4]

Sometimes we recognize God only in what is positive, in blessing, as *Hatov v'HaMetiv,* "the One who is good and who brings goodness." But such a view mistakes a part for the whole and leaves open the possibility of a dualistic theology. If God is the One who inspires us with strength to cope with difficult circumstances such as illness, who or what is responsible for the fact of illness itself, the limitations of creation that bring us so much suffering? This is God too, *Dayan ha-emet,* the Maker of limits and finitude.

At the time of the *Yamim Noraim,* contemplating the reality of God's *din* as well as *rachamim,* we are invited into the possibility of constructing a theology that affirms the truth of our experience as well as the truth that the *Zohar (Tikkunei Zohar 122b)* teaches: "There is no place where God is not."

While this theology of *din* and *rachamim* emerged out of my intensive work with the ill, it has deepened and broadened through my work over the past decade, not specifically with those who are ill, but through my experience with a wide variety of Jewish professionals and laypeople seeking spiritual vitality and truth at all points in their lives. Influenced by Chasidism, mindfulness practice, feminism, and my own life as a mother and friend, it is this last line from the *Zohar* that I now see as so central to the theology we might live during these High Holy Days: "There is no place where God is not."

The Whole Earth is Filled with God's Presence

One of the central refrains of the early Chasidic movement was "*M'lo kol ha-aretz k'vodo;* The whole earth is full of God's Presence" *All* of creation—human, animal, vegetable, and mineral—is made of divine substance, *all* of its variety in form but God's donning "the coat of many colors," God's infinitely creative way of refracting the One into the many. A great portion of my own spiritual curriculum has been geared to training my consciousness to see the One behind the many. Only then can I affirm experientially, "There is no place where God is not."

We long to leave nothing out, to find a way to banish none of our life's experience as "other." One of the brilliant teachings of

NANCY FLAM

the Baal Shem Tov concerned how to work with "alien thoughts" (*machshavot zarot*) in prayer: intrusive, distracting, compelling thoughts that would captivate one's attention and interrupt one's prayer. Rather than struggling to conquer them, forcefully applying one's will to banish the thought from consciousness, the Baal Shem Tov taught another way. Since all of creation and all of experience is an expression of the Divine, and nothing at all could possibly exist without the animating divine spark in it, why not investigate the distracting thought to identify its Godly energy? A lusty thought, for instance, must come from the root of *chesed* (love). So instead of wrestling the thought or image to the ground and turning one's back on it, we might turn to face it head-on and "take it to its (divine) root," release its energy into the animating, Godly energy of *chesed*. In this way, the thought and its animating energy is not so much rejected as it is transformed.

This ability to embrace and skillfully work with all of one's experience is a central goal of mindfulness practice. Originally taught by Southeast Asian Buddhists, mindfulness meditation was brought to America and has been steadily gaining popularity as a secular practice with which to study and work with the mind and body. It teaches the art of being present, of living consciously in the body, mind, and heart in each moment, and not fleeing one's experience. No matter how painful, frightening, or otherwise unpleasant and uncomfortable one's particular experience in any moment, mindfulness practice teaches one how to stay present to what is happening in the body and mind, applying the ultimately comforting strategy of what Pema Chodron calls, "the wisdom of no escape." When we learn how to resist escaping from our experience, from fleeing from what is unpleasant (sometimes excruciatingly so), we are ultimately rewarded by a sense of nonseparation. Constriction of awareness (through any kind of pain, tightening, clutching, etc.) tends to lead to a sense of separation from God. With mindfulness practice, we draw a larger circle around our experience to include all of it as an expression of God's reality: limitation as well as expansion, pain as well as pleasure, *din* as well as *rachamim*. What happens, happens. The most important spiritual task that confronts us at each moment is to be spaciously present to what is happening in the phenomenal field of our awareness. In so doing, our pleasures become richer and our pain more tolerable.

THE ANGELS PROCLAIM IT, BUT CAN WE?

The key to this ability lies in the cultivation of *daat*, or awareness. Through meditation practice, we learn to develop a witnessing awareness that can (ideally) be present to all experience, of whatever emotional valence. Instead of "becoming" any particular thought, emotion, or physical sensation, instead of our awareness becoming completely absorbed into its gravitational pull, we rest in a greater awareness of thought, emotion, or sensation itself simply "happening." We do not identify with our experience as who we are. Rather, we rest in a spacious awareness of what presents itself to consciousness, moment after moment. We cultivate a compassionate, witnessing awareness that in Jewish theology we might call *"HaMakom"* (the Place/Space): the expansive, steady place of consciousness itself. Perhaps this interpretation of *"Ha-Makom"* provides another way of understanding the words we say to a mourner upon the death of a loved one: *"HaMakom yinachem etchem...."* May the Place/Space that is greater than your suffering, greater than this moment of excruciating loss, provide you comfort. May you be comforted by spacious awareness.

We strive to become beings who can hold it all, "the full catastrophe," as Jon Kabat-Zinn titled his book on mindfulness practice (quoting Nikos Kazantzakis): experiences of God's *din*—painful moments of constriction and limitation—as well as of *rachamim*—glorious moments of ease and well-being. We long to create a strategy of consciousness and of living, and an accompanying theology, which can help us be present to the entire gamut of our experience, throwing nothing out. Feminist thought has taught us that the body, for instance, is not to be "transcended." Physical experience is not to be "overcome." Such dualistic thinking itself becomes a source of suffering. Physical sensations, emotions, and thoughts are all to be witnessed and held, as a parent strives to embrace and be present to all the experiences, both painful and joyful, of his or her child.

For too many of us, too often, what we experience as painful we judge as "bad." But if we take the analogy of awareness or *daat* to be like a loving parent, and painful moments of consciousness to be like the appearance of the child who has skinned her knee, we understand better that a more skillful application of consciousness would be to learn to sit lovingly with our own painful experiences, rather than to judge them or ourselves as bad. Or when we cannot do that for ourselves (for even with extensive mindfulness training we are, nonetheless, limited and not always able to manifest such

NANCY FLAM

awareness), we do that for each other. We help each other resist the temptation to interpret our experience as abandonment by God, or as rejection.

This is not to say that we do not work to change painful circumstances. As I explained earlier, we certainly seek to move the limits of *din* toward the side of *rachamim.* We strive to ameliorate pain, injustice, and all other kinds of suffering through our love, care, therapies, medicine, and just actions, for instance. As Jews, we dedicate ourselves to lessening suffering in all its forms. We apply our best efforts, all the while aware that we are not in control of outcomes. As we imitate God's *rachamim* and with great dedication try to increase it, we learn how to be with what is in the moment without banishing it as "other," and we learn how to be with whatever does or does not result from our efforts. God—life, reality, creation—will be what it will be. *Ehyeh asher Ehyeh.*

The classic, dualist rabbinic theology of God "out there" and we humans "over here," especially prominent as we engage with our liturgy during the High Holy Days, is itself a source of pain for many of us, and can make it challenging to actually experience all of life as taking place within the field of God's loving regard. Without a spiritual practice that teaches us how to inhabit God's spacious *Makom,* moment by moment, we are left vulnerable to feeling alienated from our own pain, discomfort, or suffering; it becomes something *other* than "who we really are," and *other* from God who is classically envisioned as "all good." When God is envisioned as "out there" instead of as "in here" (deep within our capacity for steady, compassionate awareness), most of us moderns lose our capacity to experience the whole of our lives as manifesting an aspect of God's being. For this reason, the Chasidic call that "the whole world is filled with God's Presence," and the *Zohar's* declaration that "there is no place where God is not," become invitations to us for developing awareness. My own experiences suggest to me that one aspect of our current Jewish communal project becomes one less of traditional theology, of thinking thoughts about God, than one of spiritual practice, of manifesting God-awareness in every moment. In a post-modern world where classic Jewish theology has largely broken down, working with the truth of our own experience becomes, as it is to both the religious existentialist and the phenomenologist, the most compelling arena for theological exploration and creativity.

THE ANGELS PROCLAIM IT, BUT CAN WE?

During these High Holy Days, we need to allow the truth of our own experience to inform our theologies so that we might live into them, or, when we must, die into them, with integrity.

Notes

1. Pardes Rimonim, ch. 8.

2. Abraham Joshua Heschel, *The Prophets* (New York: Harper & Row; Philadelphia: Jewish Publication Society of America, 1962), p. 220.

3. Talmud, B'rachot 39b.

4. Isaiah 45:7.

Wrestling with God's Image in the High Holy Day Liturgy

Yoel H. Kahn

אֲדֹנָי, שְׂפָתַי תִּפְתָּח, וּפִי יַגִּיד תְּהִלָּתֶךָ.

Adonai, open up my lips, that my mouth may declare Your praise.

— Psalm 51:17

Preparing to pray is in itself a prayer.
Or so I say. I will begin tomorrow.
Having fled here, though none pursue. Fled where.
Within, far, to the desert place, the sorrow
place. For what I have done. For surely the matter is known.
But see, turn aside, look, the thorn tree, the heart
is not consumed; burning, it does not burn
to ash. It has a voice: Friend, pilgrim, start
now on your way. You can't save your prayer for the world
to come, vagrant one, it is your call, the knowing
to turn and answer, *Wilderness of God,*
hard mountain, I am here. A pilgrim going
to the farthest place is praying, or too can pray
if the place be near, since going is the way.[1]

—Dan Bellm, "The voice in the fire" (*Parshat Sh'mot*),
from *Practice: A Book of Midrash*

In *Pirkei Avot*, we learn, "Ten things were created on the eve of the first Shabbat at twilight. These are they: the mouth of Miriam's well; Balaam's ass; the manna; Moses' staff; the hole in the earth which swallows Korach...."[2] Other versions of the story propose variations in this list, but all share the same idea: at the very last moments of twilight before the first Shabbat, a few exceptional things were created. These are phenomena described in the Torah that violate the laws of nature, and to which the Rabbis declared a one-time exception to the principle *olam ke-minhago noheg* ("The world goes according to its natural course").

YOEL H. KAHN (NY85) is Rabbi of Congregation Beth El, Berkeley, California.

WRESTLING WITH GOD'S IMAGE IN THE HIGH HOLY DAY LITURGY

This midrash is a story about the indigestible. What do we do with the stuff offered by our tradition that we simply cannot swallow? For our ancestors, the solution in this case was to create a special exception for a small group of occurrences, and then to declare, *Dayeinu,* enough already—leaving them, as it were, integrated but quarantined. Much as we love the Jewish religious tradition, it contains plenty of aspects—in teaching, text, and practice—that we can't swallow. Earlier generations of Reform Jews were confident that they could distinguish between what was intrinsic and essential to Judaism, and what could be jettisoned because it was not. We, on the other hand, may be less confident of our own discernment in these matters, but at the same time we may be more open to the possibilities of significance and meaning that the tradition can offer. And yet, there are many aspects of historical Jewish teaching and practice, from *nidah* to *tahanun,* that have no place in Reform Judaism.[3]

I love the High Holy Days. I love the music and the gathering of the people, and despite my seasonal grumbling, I find deep fulfillment in my role as organizer, officiant, and preacher. Sometimes I am overwhelmed by my connection to the extended community, linked across time and space to the generations of our people. Adrienne Rich writes of the faith of those who

have kept beyond violence the knowledge
arranged in patterns like kente-cloth

unexpected as in batik
recurrent as bitter herbs and unleavened bread

of being a connective link
in a long, continuous way....[4]

At other times, to be honest, I am so much on "automatic pilot" that the words and music wash over me without penetrating. But when I do what we ask our people to do—to be fully present, to pay close attention to the liturgy, and to reflect on its message—I find myself torn between my devotion to the words (words polished smooth by generations of our people, words that resonate deeply with historical Jewish teaching and my own religious language) and my discomfort with language and imagery that are

YOEL H. KAHN

so incongruent with my life experience and my faith. While most of the time I am caught up in the poetry, history, melodies, and multivocality of the liturgy, I am sometimes like the congregant who suddenly stopped reading aloud from the Yom Kippur *machzor* one year, turned to his companions, loudly exclaimed, "This is such bull!" and walked out. I wanted to run after him, shouting, "Just wait for the haftarah! The prophet Isaiah felt the same way!" Then I wondered, why am I always in need of the corrective and the counter-text?

At the center of the historical liturgy of the High Holy Days is the celebration of God's enthronement and majesty.[5] From the substitutions in the *chatimot*, in which "the King" replaces "God," to the shofar service, the liturgy of the High Holy Days calls our attention to the centrality of this core rabbinic idea. For myself and for many others, the theological assertion of God's absolute power and of our human smallness and powerlessness is deeply untrue and unsatisfying. While the rabbinic tradition offers other images of both God and humanity, the High Holy Day liturgy lifts up the language and imagery of divine sovereignty.

My discomfort begins with the gendered language of sovereignty, but it certainly does not end there. What do we gain by substituting or alternating *Imeinu Malkateinu* for *Avinu Malkeinu*? For most liberal Jews, I believe, the result is not the least bit satisfactory; it appears to be a gratuitous substitution that does not significantly alter the force of the prayer or the imagery.[6] God as the powerful King is the overarching image of rabbinic theology, and it's the central motif throughout the daily, Shabbat, and High Holy Day liturgy. The recitation of the *Sh'ma* is an act of "accepting the yoke of the Kingdom of Heaven," the *G'ulah* blessing recites how our ancestors at the shore of the sea "witnessed His power...[and] freely acclaimed Him King,"[7] and the normative explanation for the custom of taking three steps forward before beginning the *Amidah* is that one is "entering the presence of the Sovereign."

All the same, it is possible to pray faithfully in a synagogue and to fully engage in the worship experience without noticing or engaging these ideas or this imagery. For the most part, while they are the background against which our practice has been shaped, the historical complex of naming and declaring God's sovereignty need not be an explicit part of the liturgy we experience. We do not introduce the *Sh'ma* as "accepting the yoke of the Kingdom

WRESTLING WITH GOD'S IMAGE IN THE HIGH HOLY DAY LITURGY

of Heaven," we sing *Mi Chamochah* and skip over the body of the *G'ulah* prayer that precedes it, and any Reform rabbi can readily offer a Buberian, dialogical interpretation of taking three steps forward to signify entering into an intimate conversation.

At the High Holy Days, however, it is much harder to overlook such imagery. The central themes of the season are the enthronement of, and judgment by, the Holy One, Blessed Be. The special liturgy of the day begins with the proclamation, "THE KING sits on an exalted and elevated throne." The shofar service begins with the *Malchuyot* readings and verses—and here, too, I must acknowledge my simultaneous discomfort with and deep devotion to historical practice and liturgy. Even without medieval *piyutim,* the fundamental shape of the High Holy Days' liturgical message is a vertical axis, with the Living and Eternal God-King (*Melech El chai v'kayim*) above, and humanity ("whose origin is dust and whose end is dust") below. We hasten to quote the last line of *Un'taneh Tokef*—"for the hand of every person is signed there"—but this is small compensation for the tradition's overwhelming emphasis on petition for God's mercy and kindness, and our need for unmerited grace, *ki ein banu maasim.*

My discomfort is not due simply to an outdated metaphor; we have no trouble freely invoking and understanding the rich agrarian imagery that permeates the Bible and our sacred literature, even though the vast majority of us left the long-since-mechanized farm a couple of generations ago. What does not work for so many today is the continual emphasis on God's absolute power and our own frailty—an imagery of imbalance that is fundamentally dissonant with how we experience ourselves in the world and with our core Reform Jewish teachings about human responsibility and engagement. Peter Knobel and others have called this rebalancing of the divine-human relationship the "theology of human adequacy."[8] I seek a theological language and liturgical imagery that recognize and honor both human adequacy and human frailty.

Within our diverse movement, the theology of human adequacy—which might be called more adequately a "theology of partnership"—is perhaps the most characteristic contemporary Reform Jewish theological and liturgical language. It is the emphasis on human agency as the vehicle for realizing God's powers and the divine-human partnership that distinguishes this teaching from secular humanism on the one hand and a traditional religious

YOEL H. KAHN

language of dependence on the other. Beginning with the midrash about Nahshon at the parting of the sea, liberal Jews, and especially their rabbis, seek out and lift up all those places in which "Your might, O God, is everlasting" can be re-read as "Help us to use our strength for good and not for evil."[9]

For the Rabbis, nothing described in the Torah could be dismissed, no matter how uncomfortable it may have made them. In *People of the Book*, Moshe Halbertal calls the effort to frame or understand a received text in the best possible light, or in a way consistent with the reader's values and world view, "the charitable reading" of the text. In this way, the midrash about the phenomena created at twilight on the first Shabbat is a complex effort to create a "charitable reading" of a group of problematic stories in the Torah.[10] Our inclination, of course, is to read the Torah and the entirety of the Jewish tradition as charitably as possible. Yet what sets us apart from other Jews today, and from prior generations of Jews, is our readiness to acknowledge that not every text or teaching is amenable to a charitable reading. Consistent with our own theology of human adequacy in our own day, we do not "accept the decree," but instead turn away from such texts and teachings.

I hasten to point out that many of us, clergy and congregants alike, are untroubled by the imagery of the historical liturgy. We can and do find deep meaning, comfort, and truth. History, language, and message all resonate. Others can even bring charitable readings of the very texts that distress me the most, as Margaret Wenig does with *Un'taneh Tokef* elsewhere in this issue. For such individuals, the attempt to erase the distance, to level the disparity between God above and the human (individual and collective) below, disrupts the very imagery that so resonates for them and that is at the core of their experience of the High Holy Days. In an essay about the language of contemporary liberal Jewish prayer, Lois Dubin writes,

> I do not want to pray to myself or to ourselves as humans. I do not want to pray only to a human community or to the forces immanent in nature. When I pray, I want to maintain a sense of transcendence, of Otherness beyond. I want to imagine something Other, something beyond us; something that conveys a sense of the forces beyond ourselves and our control, a sense of the mystery and tragedy we often face, and the truth of our finite limits.

WRESTLING WITH GOD'S IMAGE IN THE HIGH HOLY DAY LITURGY

I want to address that dimension of Otherness, for without it, I cannot express honestly my deepest longings and fears.[11]

This passage is a corrective to my own position; it is a firm reminder that although many share my alienation from the imagery and language of the received liturgy, there are many others who do not. Accordingly, if our task is to create a liturgical experience that addresses contemporary liberal Jewish sensibilities, it must be nuanced and inclusive rather than dogmatic and exclusive.[12] If my personal discomfort with the core metaphor of the High Holy Day season colors my reading and hearing of every aspect of the liturgy, surely the comfort and resonance that the metaphor brings others only increases their receptivity and relationship to the very same texts.

With this sensibility in mind, let us turn to five techniques that Reform Jews use to create a meaningful liturgical experience when faced with potentially dissonant texts.

1. Including the Historical Text in Hebrew, and Omitting the Translation

Gates of Prayer's Shabbat Evening Service VI, the "religious naturalism" service, includes the *Bar'chu* but does not have a translation. In the compiler's mind, there was clearly no appropriate, alternative, nontheistic language to offer, but respect for the historical liturgy in Hebrew was required. Although we often offer alternative English settings for traditional texts, the wholesale recitation of Hebrew passages without a vernacular translation is unacceptable to our Reform community today. The message sent by presenting and reciting passages in Hebrew without providing access to a translation is that the historical liturgy is a symbolic or magic ritual whose manifest content is of no interest or importance. Purely as a practical matter, the increasing proportion of well-educated Jews and native Hebrew speakers makes the Hebrew text more accessible than it was for earlier Reform communities.

2. Radical Reformulation of the Language

In her *Book of Blessings*, Marcia Falk not only argues for a reformulation of the language of blessing, but encourages us to move completely beyond dualistic language in favor of an evolving, inclusive vocabulary of immanence.[13] Powerful as Falk's poetry and language are, for most Reform Jews her nontheistic imagery strays too far from the historical liturgy to fulfill their goals of familiarity, historical integrity, and theological authenticity. While many Reform Jews are uncomfortable with the balance between human agency and divine decision and action as portrayed in the received liturgy, most do not want the distinction between them to be erased. They seek to name and honor both human power and frailty, *Adonai Tz'vaot* and *Shechinah.* The intermediate step of recasting the blessing formula without substantive change to the body of the text itself does not resolve objections to the pervasiveness of the metaphors.[14]

3. Framing *Kavanot*

By the time Lurianic Kabbalah began to spread its influence in the century after Luria's death in 1572, the extant liturgy was well established and codified. Liturgical innovations that reflected the kabbalistic sensibility did not, by and large, penetrate the language of the prayers. Instead, innovation was channeled into the creation of entirely new prayer structures, such as midnight *tikkunim* and framing *kavanot* that preceded the recitation of the authorized prayers. These introductory settings did not alter the language or performance of the received prayer; rather, they were intended to inform and direct the *kavanah* of the worshiper so that the next action would be performed in conformity with the halachah yet understood in an original theological fashion.[15]

The introduction to the candle lighting in *Gates of Repentance*, Rosh HaShanah Evening Service II, is an example of a Reform Jewish *kavanah,* invoking the language of human agency and abstract divinity: "May the light of the divine shine forth to lead us, to show us the good we must do, the harmony we must create. Let the fire we kindle be for us a warming flame, whose brightness shows us the path of life."[16] As with the kabbalistic formulae printed in other *siddurim,* the goal of this passage is to explain the true significance and intent of the prayer and ritual that follow.[17]

No section of the High Holy Day liturgy is more powerful and more challenging than *Un'taneh Tokef.* In this medieval *piyut,* invoking an ancient, mythic image, God sits on the throne of judgment and decides the fate of each living creature, declaring, depending on their merits, "who shall live and who shall die." A litany follows,

WRESTLING WITH GOD'S IMAGE IN THE HIGH HOLY DAY LITURGY

listing the many ways in which death can arrive. At the end, we learn that our own actions have the power to alter the force of, but not lift, the decree. In *Gates of Repentance, Un'taneh Tokef* is presented in full and faithfully translated.[18] It is preceded, however, by a page-length reading that changes the focus from God as the Judge to a humanistic reflection about how we manage our own challenges. Decisions are not recorded or sealed in the Book of Life, but rather:

On Rosh HaShanah we reflect,
On Yom Kippur we consider:
Who shall live for the sake of others,
Who, dying, shall leave a heritage of life.[19]

4. Creative Translation/Interpretation

Offering a framing *kavanah*, followed by a faithful presentation of the historical liturgy, is often combined with interpretative English readings that are offered in place of the faithful English translation.[20] Perhaps the most venerable, specifically Reform solution is to offer a nonliteral translation—yet surely a charitable translation from the perspective of the translator. Reflecting an evolving sensibility, the editor of *Gates of Prayer* went through the manuscript and made all references to people inclusive but left all the references to the Holy One in the masculine; in *Mishkan T'filah*, humanity and divinity are gender-neutral. Most Reform rabbis probably hold that this is a nonliteral but extant rendering of the original. Such insertions range from relatively small changes that are made throughout a service or liturgy to entire passages that bear only the slightest resemblance to the original source. The relationship of these carefully crafted English liturgical readings to the historical text to which they are anchored is parallel to the relationship of midrash to biblical verse. Some midrashic readings have become so familiar over time that they are part of the normative Jewish understanding of the text. We consider others to be overly determined by the agenda and historical circumstances of the authors and compilers, and we do not find them illuminating of the underlying text or compelling.

5. Complementary readings

The fifth response to challenges presented by the historical liturgy is to bring complementary English texts that do not necessarily

YOEL H. KAHN

speak directly to the language or imagery of the Hebrew prayer. A few poems are used in this way on the left hand pages of *Mishkan T'fila*—for example, the juxtaposition of Judy Brown's "What Makes a Fire Burn" opposite *Chatzi Kaddish* on page 224. Strong, even fierce English texts, whether in poetry or prose, can be effective precisely because they are not directly trying to redeem or rework the Hebrew prayer. Such texts unapologetically invite the worshiper to explore a completely new set of metaphors and images that are not derived from or dependent upon the historical liturgy. Consider Ellen Bass's poem, "Change":

> This is where I yank the old roots from my chest
> like the tomatoes
> we let grow until December, stalks
> thick as saplings.
>
> This is the moment when the ancient fears
> race like thoroughbreds, asking for more
> and more rein. And I, the driver,
> for some reason they know nothing of
> strain to hold them back.
>
> Terror grips me like a virus
> and I sweat, fevered,
> trying to burn it out.
>
> This feat is so invisible. All you can see
> is a woman going about her ordinary day,
> drinking tea, taking herself to the movies,
> reading in bed. If victorious
> I will look exactly the same.
>
> Yet I am hoisting a car from mud ruts
> half a century deep. I am hacking
> a clearing through the fallen slash
> of my heart. Without laser precision,
> with only the primitive knife of need, I cut
> and splice the circuitry of my brain.
> I change.[21]

This poem could be used as a *kavanah*, framing the High Holy Day *Amidah*. I would propose, however, using this poem as a

WRESTLING WITH GOD'S IMAGE IN THE HIGH HOLY DAY LITURGY

complement or response to *Un'taneh Tokef.* Bass's plainspoken, humanistic poem does not invoke religious imagery or vocabulary; for me, it is a more fulfilling and spiritually engaging passage than the widely used, toned-down, humanistic rewriting of the received text that appears in *Gates of Repentance.* The evocation of awe and trepidation is as rich as in the medieval *piyut,* but the setting has moved from the heavenly court to the kitchen table. Strong, spiritually engaged texts by contemporary writers, which do not try to paraphrase or compete with the language and imagery of our historical texts, can open up meaning, resonance, and connection for many who would not otherwise respond to the language of the liturgy, while reinvigorating the liturgical landscape for all.[22]

A well-known Talmudic passage speaks about the multivocality of the biblical text. First, Rabbi Abbaye interprets Psalm 62:12— "God has spoken once, twice have I heard this…"—to mean that any particular verse can be used in support of multiple teachings. The school of Rabbi Ishmael goes further, imagining the multiplicity of possible meanings and interpretations found in any particular text, citing Jeremiah 23:29: "'Is not My word like fire?' declares Adonai, 'And like a hammer which shatters a rock?'"[23] Our theology of human agency and capacity can and should extend the tradition's insistence on the multivocalic possibility in every verse of the *Tanach* to the siddur as well, even if we recognize the prayer book as an entirely human creation. If the Torah speaks *b'lashon b'nei adam* (in human idiom), is it too far to imagine that over the last two thousand years, our human prayer language has also come to speak, as it were, *b'lashon shamayim* (heavenly idiom)?

While I was once quite ready to overhaul the entire historical liturgy, I am no longer willing to do so. While there are still metaphors, themes, and texts that I cannot digest, my capacity to hold and honor them so that others may explore them has grown over the years; I am trying to practice aesthetic and theological *tzimtzum.* While it is necessary and valuable to continue to emend, reimagine, and revise the historical liturgy, I have redefined my own task, trying less to "fix" or make palatable the historical texts than to seek to bring ever richer and deeper counter texts—the Yom Kippur morning haftarah reading being the example par excellence— that can inform and open up the liturgy.

Avivah Gottlieb Zornberg teaches that true prayer always means opening ourselves to encounter: it is confronting the unexpected,

YOEL H. KAHN

seeking to step outside of the ordinary. The language of prayer, whether an ancient text or a contemporary source, seeks to put into words the internal experience we have or that we seek to evoke. Many of us are yearning for a prayer life that is authentic and honest, a prayer language whose metaphors and images are both comfortable and provocative, a prayer experience that reaches deep within and deep beyond the self. The particular privilege of Reform Jews is the freedom to hold more than one set of metaphors, to speak in more than one language.

Notes

1. Dan Bellm, *Practice: A Book of Midrash* (San Francisco: Sixteen Rivers, 2008). Used by permission.

2. *Pirkei Avot* 5:8. Compare similar ideas in *Genesis Rabbah* 5:9 and *Exodus Rabbah* 21:6.

3. *Nidah* is the complex of laws regulating menstrual purity; *Tahunun* is the name of the short section of supplicatory prayers in the daily service; it has never been part of Reform liturgy.

4. Adrienne Rich, "Sources," section XV, in *Your Native Land, Your Life* (New York: W. W. Norton, 1996), p. 17.

5. I believe that "historical liturgy"—rather than the more common "traditional liturgy"—is a more accurate and neutral term to refer to pre-modern Jewish practice and its preservation and interpretation across the varieties of contemporary Judaism. After more than 150 years, Reform liturgical texts and customs are now surely worthy themselves of being considered "traditional."

6. *Gates of Repentance* (revised, 1996), p. 549, has a litany "Shechina, M'kor Chayenu," with creative, original Hebrew, and *Shechinah* translated nine different ways in English. This was clearly an effort to address just such concerns.

7. *Gates of Prayer*, p. 132.

8. Elyse Frishman and Peter Knobel use it in the Introduction to *Mishkan T'filah*, p ix. Rabbi Edwin Goldberg sums up the "theology of human adequacy" in a comment about the opening reading for Shabbat Service I on page 3:

> The new reading reflects a perspective of strength rather than humility. Instead of beseeching God out of a place of relative worthlessness, we recognize that we have the potential to perform many mitzvot and thereby improve the world. We ask for God's help in efforts already begun. We are far from helpless supplicants. In these words, we are more like able partners of God. ("Ten Minutes of Torah," 6/12/2008, http://urj.org/torah/ten/.)

WRESTLING WITH GOD'S IMAGE IN THE HIGH HOLY DAY LITURGY

9. *Gates of Repentance*, p. 310.

10. Moshe Halbertal, *People of the Book: Canon, Meaning, and Authority* (Harvard University Press, 1997). The classic description of Halbertal's "charitable reading" is Maimonides' assertion in the *Guide to the Perplexed* (II, 25) that he could as easily defend the claim that the world is eternal as the one he does that the world was created in time; see Halbertal's discussion, p. 29. The example from *Pirkei Avot* is my own.

11. Lois C. Dubin, "Who's Blessing Whom?: Transcendence, Agency, and Gender in Jewish Prayer," *Cross Currents* 52, no. 2 (Summer 2002). http://www.crosscurrents.org/dubin.htm.

12. The historical liturgy was sometimes phrased with the specific goal of making some people so uncomfortable that they would not want to participate; see Lawrence Hoffman, "Censoring In, Censoring Out: A Function of Liturgical Language," in *Ancient Synagogues: The State of Research*, ed. Joseph Guttman (Chico, CA.: Scholars Press, 1981) 19–37.

13. Marcia Falk, *The Book of Blessings* (San Francisco: HarperSan Francisco, 1996), pp. 420–421.

14. For a summary of the halachic standards for licit blessings, see Ruth Langer, *To Worship God Properly: Tensions between Liturgical Custom and Halakhah In Judaism* (Cincinnati: Hebrew Union College Press, 1998), pp. 19–40; compare the discussion by Falk, *Book of Blessings*, pp. xvi–xvii.

15. Kabbalat Shabbat is a singular example; it is an entire liturgical unit, but it is appended to the front end of the Shabbat evening service. Before its widespread adoption, the Shabbat evening service began with Psalm 92, the Psalm for Shabbat. A hint of this history is the custom of greeting the mourners immediately before Psalm 92, the prior beginning of the Shabbat evening liturgy, and after *L'chah Dodi*, the last element of the "new" Kabbalat Shabbat service.

16. *Gates of Repentance*, p. 49.

17. In *Covenant of Blood: Circumcision and Gender in Rabbinic Judaism* (Chicago: University of Chicago, 1996), pp. 19–21, Lawrence Hoffman describes how women who grew up on the Union Prayer Book explain that the meaning of lighting candles is that "Light is a symbol of the Divine." The candle-lighting sensibility of these women was formed by the kavanah in the Union Prayer Book, which included this phrase.

18. The introductory kavanah is given the rubric *Un'taneh Tokef* in Hebrew but is not given an English translation. This is the book's style for the major modules of the service; e.g., *Sh'ma Uvirchoteha* and *T'filah*.

19. *Gates of Repentance*, p. 311.

YOEL H. KAHN

20. For example, the many asterisked passages in *Gates of Prayer*.
21. © Ellen Bass. Used by permission. For more of her work, see www. ellenbass.com.
22. The complementary readings may, of course, generate new dissonances.
23. TB *Sanhedrin* 34a.

Searching for God in the 7th Grade

Joel Mosbacher

It is clear from my learning in the Doctorate of Ministry program that people's ideas and beliefs about the power of God can evolve, just as our ideas about our parents do. Older children and adolescents don't feel they were lied to because when they were small their parents allowed them to believe that mother or father kept them from all harm. Nor do older children lose all faith in their mother or father when they finally realize that their parents are fallible. And so I believe that Jews can sustain a loving relationship with God even when they find that God is not the figure they imagined in childhood.

Through worship, our synagogues have the capacity to foster greater theological and psychological maturity, but I fear we often miss that opportunity. I know that in my congregation historically, while we prayed to God often, we rarely spoke frankly about our personal beliefs about God. I have examined this phenomenon most closely in teenagers, but I would suggest that we can use the experience of our young people's theological development (or lack thereof), as a window into how we might best create a *machzor* for Jews of any age.

This is a pastoral issue insomuch as the failure to continue to develop their spiritual life impedes young people's ability to rely on their Jewish identities for comfort, consolation, and strength at one of the most confusing times of their lives, namely adolescence. So, too, such stunted growth will leave them at a loss pastorally as adults, as they face all of the complexities of life.

This is a theological issue because our synagogue, and perhaps many others, is failing to give our kids adequate permission

JOEL MOSBACHER, D.Min. (C98) is Rabbi at Beth Haverim Shir Shalom, Mahwah, New Jersey and language to speak to God from their own unique hearts and perspectives.

On a micro level, the issues that I am herein attempting to address are relevant to people of all ages—not simply 13- and 14-year-olds. When a person's spiritual growth is stunted in some way, his or her spiritual life in general will be impeded, and that hindrance will last a lifetime unless he or she addresses the "blockage" in some way.

On a macro level, to my knowledge, many Jewish congregations struggle with these issues. Many congregations struggle to connect their young people in a spiritual way, so that their religious education is as much about substance as it is about form. If what I suggest here has validity, it may be useful as we strive to create liturgies of all sorts for adolescents and beyond.

As we know, the Jewish tradition is rich with a wide variety of types of prayer expression. From the fixed prayer language and timing of the rabbinic tradition to the meditation and contemplation of the mystical tradition, from the traditionally masculine God language of much of Jewish history to an increasing diversity of God language, Jews in search of a spiritual home and a familiar prayer language can find it in the tapestry of their own highly variegated sacred tradition.

So, too, though, over much of the past two thousand years, Jewish prayer has become increasingly codified and formulaic, perhaps out of necessity; since the Jews were exiled all over the world after the destruction of Jerusalem in the year 70 C.E., Jews have relied in part on common prayer as a tie that binds the highly diverse Jewish communities of the world. Through prayer, it is possible for people to view that diverse history as their heritage to inherit and to encourage them to embrace that which brings them closest to their spiritual source.

What, after all, is prayer for? I am particularly drawn to the reflections on prayer of thinkers such as the medieval philosopher Bahya Ibn Pakuda and modern-day teacher Rabbi David Wolpe who provide compelling answers to this ultimate religious question. I feel that these thinkers will motivate meaningful reflection on the power and potential that prayer can have on one's life.

Bahya describes prayer as having parts. "The words of prayers," he says, "are like the husk covering the grain, and reflection on their meaning is like the kernel. Prayer itself is like the body, and

SEARCHING FOR GOD IN THE 7TH GRADE

reflecting in its meaning is like the spirit. If we merely utter the words of prayers while thinking about matters other than prayer, it is like a body without a spirit, a husk without a kernel, the body is present but the heart is absent."[1]

And Wolpe reminds us that the Rabbis call prayer the service of the heart. "The sacrificial metaphor is suggestive. Jewish prayer is built upon the idea that an offering is being made to God. Something is being given—the fervor and fullness of our souls. 'One's prayer is not heeded,' says the Talmud, 'unless God is approached with one's heart in one's hands (Tannit 8a).'"[2]

These theological concepts of prayer—that the words of prayer without the intentionality of the heart is empty and that prayer is a genuine offering to God—are among the consequential ideas that can bring new significance to prayer for our people.

Aryeh ben David writes that "serious prayer needs to be an authentically personal experience."[3] Prayer at its best reaches the depths of our hearts, and the Jewish *machzor* is designed to be the jumping off point for the plumbing of these depths. At times, though, the words of the *machzor* take over and dominate the meditations of our hearts. We can go through the pages of the *machzor* without ever truly personalizing them, without making them our own, without being transformed in any way. In this kind of prayer experience, our hearts are rarely touched, and so it should come as no surprise that we feel no spiritual connection to God.

Rabbi Larry Kushner says that prayer is like the hokey-pokey, and that what it's all about is putting our whole selves in.[4] The challenge in our lives is to find ways to put our whole selves into prayer experiences, whether that is as a part of ritualized communal prayer or daily as we go about our lives. Even the ancient rabbis of our tradition, who had no shortage of words to prompt us within the prayer book, recognized the need to leave space for silent and personal prayer at the end of the *Amidah,* the petitionary section of the Jewish worship service. The challenge for us is to find that space throughout the worship service, and, at best, throughout our lives.

When it comes to developing a High Holy Day liturgy—any liturgy, truth be told, the most important thing I can suggest is that we not underestimate the depth of our congregants' ability to reflect deeply and theologically. At the moment in the year when they are perhaps most open to thinking and struggling with what

JOEL MOSBACHER

they believe, we have a rare opportunity to give them permission to explore their inherited traditions regarding faith and God. We can either slam the door closed intentionally or inadvertently, or we can open new doors of spiritual formation for them.

I think that it is not an overstatement to suggest that what we do with this slim opportunity can make or break the theological growth of our congregants. If they feel that the *machzor*, the *siddur*, the religious school, the Jewish professionals, or the service in their synagogue is a place where prayer happens formulaically and without discussion or reflection, we are leaving their theological development to chance. If, however, their synagogue is a place where Jews actually talk about God, share their faith, their doubts, and their spiritual journeys, I think it far more likely that they, too, will continue to explore a variety of expressions of faith. It will be far more likely that they will find old/new language to talk about what they do and do not believe, rather than tossing faith aside as irrelevant or antiquated.

In this paper, I speak admittedly from my own experience alone, working in a congregational setting. So, too, I completed the Doctorate of Ministry program through HUC-JIR in 2007 and wrote a Demonstration Project entitled "Searching for God in the 7th Grade: A Curriculum for Developing Images of the Divine." It is out of this work and this experience that I have come to the conclusions herein.

The goals of our synagogue's Hebrew school program are, like most supplementary Jewish schools, I suspect, primarily to give them some basic Jewish literacy and competence, and to prepare them with the technical Hebrew reading skills to become *b'nei mitzvah*. In my view, our congregational school does a fairly good job with these goals. I conduct an interview with the students as they approach their *b'nei mitzvah*, and among other information I gather in that interview, I have for seven years explored with them their feelings of Jewish competence regarding prayer and the prayer experience.

The kids by and large succeed nicely with the technical tasks of leading the service as they become *b'nei mitzvah* and generally seem to enjoy their religious education. The pastoral issue I see here is that many students come to the day of their *b'nei mitzvah* frequently expressing a high level of uncertainty about the role of prayer and spiritual connection in their lives. They know that they

SEARCHING FOR GOD IN THE 7TH GRADE

have learned specific words and prayers for the purpose of "suc-
ceeding" on the day they become bar or bat mitzvah, but when I
ask them about regular, meaningful prayer or spiritual experiences
they've had, they seem almost universally to *not even understand
the question*. They often seem disillusioned by the experience overall; they have learned the *keva* of Jewish prayer, but very little *kavanah*; they have learned the traditional words, but not how to put
their intentionality, their feelings and emotions, into the process of
prayer. If this is true of the Shabbat morning service, with which
they are most familiar, how much the more so it is with High Holy
Day liturgy.

The result as I see it is another cadre each year of *b'nei mitzvah*
who have learned through our program a number of prayers, but,
for the most part, who have not learned how to pray. Jewish tradition asserts religiously that becoming bar or bat mitzvah means
that a person has achieved a degree of maturity in the Jewish community, and yet their faith development remains stunted in para-
lyzing ways. A critical analysis of the process might reveal a severe
lack of enduring understandings that might inform their Jewish
lives in the decades that follow.

Since the summer of 1995 when I was first training as a chaplain
intern in the Clinical Pastoral Education program at Jewish Hospital in Cincinnati, Ohio, I have been continually amazed by the disparity between the level of comfort with personal prayer and personal relationship to God expressed by Jews and non-Jews. Jewish
Hospital was Jewish largely in name alone—the daily census was
80 to 85 percent non-Jewish—and so most of my encounters with
patients were of an interfaith sort. The non-Jews I would visit in the
hospital tended to be much more comfortable if and when I would
suggest that we pray together. To this day, even when I visit my
own congregants in the hospital—even people who I know fairly
well—I get quite a range of responses to an invitation to prayer.
There are those who welcome the invitation and who launch right
into their own composed prayer. There are those who are familiar
with the traditional *Mi Shebeirach* and ask me if I would recite it on
their behalf. But my completely anecdotal experience in this regard
is that the vast majority of my congregants I pastor to—in the hospital, in my office, or in their homes—are unfamiliar or uncomfortable with the idea of personal prayer, of personal connection with
the Holy One of Blessing.

JOEL MOSBACHER

There are times when I offer to pray with my congregants that I get a truly puzzled look. When I delve with those folks into the reason for their puzzlement, I get a variety of responses. At times, they feel inadequate and unprepared to speak to God in an informal way. Their puzzlement is of this sort: "Pray? What do you mean pray? What do you mean speak to God? It's not Shabbat. It's not High Holy Days. We don't have a minyan here. We don't have a prayer book. What do you mean pray?" This confusion and inadequacy grows, I think, from some sense that the only times when Jews can pray is when they are in a formal, structured, communal prayer setting.

At other times I think, the perplexity grows from a misunderstanding of what prayer is limited to. It takes this form: "Pray? What do you mean pray? If the rabbi wants to pray with me or for me, does that mean he thinks I am going to die?" This confusion, too, grows from a lack of understanding about the ways and settings that Jews have historically reached out to God. Many Jews are familiar with the idea that there is a kind of "deathbed confessional"—the *vidui*. As many Jews seem to be married to the idea that Jewish prayer only emerges in a formal, fixed setting, they must assume that the only alternative to praying in a formal synagogue service is praying only in the direst of circumstances. Hence the apparent conclusion: "If it's not Yom Kippur and the rabbi wants to pray, I must be near death."

I was raised in a very committed Reform Jewish household, and my entire extended family was and remains very Jewishly involved. I attended religious school three days a week, and I attended a very Jewish summer camp every year for 15 summers as a camper and on staff. I felt that becoming bar mitzvah was for me a very fulfilling experience. Obviously, I felt so positively inclined toward the role of Judaism in my life that I decided to become a rabbi. And yet I have to say that through it all, and with the benefit of hindsight, I cannot say that I was particularly well-equipped by my Jewish "village" to develop my spiritual, theological side to maturity.

Of course, all of us will pass through moments of deep pain and loneliness in our lives. For many, sustaining an image of a loving God may help pass through the valley of shadows. In my experience as a rabbi, many who turn to God in these moments come to feel a greater sense of autonomy, realizing that their parents are not the only source of judgment or power, and they themselves hold vast storehouses of spiritual strength to cope with the curves that life has thrown them.

Nonetheless, many parents who truly want their children to develop into strong adults have trouble speaking to them about God. They have no difficulty telling their kids stories that they know not to be literally true, but which nevertheless contain deep truths. These same parents encourage their kids to participate in secular expressions of belief in magic; from tooth fairies to birthday wishes made on a candle, these ideas seem safe to parents who somehow may dismiss their child's belief in the power of prayer or God in their lives. Rabbi Edythe Mencher, of the Union for Reform Judaism's Department of Jewish Family Concerns, tells the following story from a father.[5]

> Eventually the kids will find out that we are the tooth fairy. I don't mind if my kids believe in magic that we can eventually show them came from the loving devotion of relatives—but what happens when they find out, as they will, that believing in God doesn't mean that everything they want will come true—there will still be wars and hunger. Won't we have kind of lied to them? Won't they be disillusioned—in God and in us?

Somehow, many adults are comfortable helping children in their evolving feelings about magic. But when it comes to their faith, they are stymied as to how to respond.

Time and again when I speak to congregants and we discuss their beliefs in God, I hear versions of this response: "I wish other rabbis had spoken about God this way." Why is it that many parents, and even more ironically, many religious leaders, have such a difficult time speaking to young people about God? Could it be that they themselves have not considered what they believe? That their faith, itself, is stunted, underdeveloped? If that is the case, it should come as no surprise that a parent or a clergyperson might have difficulty opening up God conversations with young people.

Erich Fromm traces the evolution of the God-idea in his text *The Art of Loving*, following the ways in which ideas about God seem to change even within the Torah itself. He calls it "the maturing idea of monotheism,"[6] which begins with matriarchal phases of religion that eventually lead to a patriarchal one, at least in many cultures.

JOEL MOSBACHER

Once the patriarchal phase develops, here, too, an evolution takes place, from "a despotic, jealous God who considers man, whom he created, his property, and is entitled to do with him whatever he pleases,"[7] into a loving father "who himself is bound to principles which he has postulated; it goes in the direction of transforming God from the figure of a father into a symbol of his principles, those of justice, truth, and love."[8] Ultimately, the most striking development in this evolution involves God's revelation to Moses. Moses tells God that the Hebrews will not believe that he has been sent by God unless God tells them his name; Moses understands that he faces a largely idol-worshiping people who are accustomed to having names attached to their deities. God's response is to tell Moses *"Ehyeh-Asher-Ehyeh,"* which Fromm suggests we might most accurately translate as "my name is nameless."

Fromm suggests that the consequences of this maturity "can only lead to one conclusion: not to mention God's name at all, not to speak *about* God." In that way, Fromm continues, "God becomes what he potentially is in monotheistic theology, the nameless One, an inexpressible stammer, referring to the unity underlying the phenomenal universe, the ground of all existence." Perhaps this is one reason why Jews struggle so much to discuss God; we are inheritors of a tradition that urges us not to name or depict God at all.

Clinical Principles

There are many psychological theories of children's concepts of prayer. If we divide child development into four stages, we see this division of theories. Goldman suggests that children from ages 5–9 go through a "magical phase," where prayer is the sole cause of events, and God acts immediately; they then progress from ages 9–12 to a focus on "semi-magical" prayer which is still causative, but other forces are shaping the reality at play; finally to a stage from age 12+ where "nonmagical" prayer is about relationship, not causation, and kids at this age doubt the efficacy of prayer altogether.[10] At this exact moment of development, we in the Jewish community ask them to prepare sacred texts, affirm for the first time publicly their faith, and bestow the title bar or bat mitzvah upon them. It seems an ironic twist, but perhaps an appropriate

SEARCHING FOR GOD IN THE 7TH GRADE

one, and should inform how we develop liturgies for them, and for all Jews who shared a similar experience.

I am further compelled by the writing of Ann and Barry Ulanov in their *Prayer as Primary Speech,* in which they discuss primary process, projection, and fantasy. In one sense, they suggest, prayer is not something we do; it is a part of who we are—at some deeper level, we are all engaged in inner conversations, not just in words, but images, feelings, and values. On another level, prayer is something we do when we begin to address the one who speaks and gradually bring into consciousness the interaction we have with the One who is addressed. The Ulanovs suggest that prayer is a process of listening carefully to that primary speech, of carefully entering the totality of our innermost being. When through prayer we acknowledge and examine images, feelings, impulses, and fantasies, we are able to let go of inadequate images and move to deeper understandings.[11] It is precisely those deeper understandings that we might hope to help our congregants reach for. Rather than settling for the increasingly inadequate God-images of childhood, perhaps we can, if nothing else, give our people permission to examine their past images and perhaps move toward deeper understandings.

Anna Maria Rizzuto discovered that a person's evolving views of God parallel an increasingly nuanced view of other important figures in his or her life. The small child may conceive of a God similar to her own parents—possessing great power and authority to punish or reward, as well as being a source of nurturing care. The school-age young person may view God as a source of rules and structure. The adolescent may view God as an authority figure against whom to rebel. On this view, then, gradually into adulthood God may come to be viewed less as an omnipotent external force and more as a wellspring of meaning, values, and comfort.[12]

Rizzuto describes the God-idea as a transitional object that never goes away but evolves based on where we are in our lives. She argues that God may lose meaning due to rejection, being ignored, suppressed, or being found temporarily unnecessary. But we never fully repress God, Rizzuto suggests, just as we never fully repress any other object. God remains as a transitional object, always available "for further acceptance or further rejection."[13]

So, too, the psychic process of creating and finding God never ends in the course of human life. Rizzuto states that the process

JOEL MOSBACHER

of re-imaging God follows closely the developmental stages, the psychic defenses and adaptations of human experience, as well as a need for meaningful relationships with oneself, others, and the world at large.

Fromm suggests, too, that as God-ideas evolved from anthropomorphic to pure monotheistic ones, it made all the difference in how we relate to God. "The God of Abraham can be loved, or feared, as a father, sometimes his forgiveness, sometimes his anger being the dominant aspect."[14] If this is so, Fromm argues, "inasmuch as God is the father, I am the child. I have not emerged fully from the autistic wish for omniscience and omnipotence." He continues further that in this way, "I still claim, like a child, that there must be a father who rescues me, who watches me, who punishes me, a father who likes me when I am obedient, who is flattered by my praise and angry because of my disobedience." Fromm concludes that "quite obviously, the majority of people have, in their personal development, not overcome this infantile stage, and hence the belief in God to most people is the belief in a helping father," which Fromm calls "a childish illusion."[15] As I read these words, the refrain of *Avinu Malkeinu* echoed in my head. I began to wonder what additional language for God we might add to this ancient and evocative prayer.

If we get stuck at this stage, Fromm suggests, we never attain a more nuanced belief system. Ideally, I think, we would develop God-ideas that mature from "the beginning of the love for God as the helpless attachment to a mother Goddess, through the obedient attachment to a fatherly God, to a mature stage."[16] What that mature stage will yield can only be revealed, I think, once we are able to see past the earlier stages.

As significantly, Rizzuto argues that the God-images we develop will, reflecting what we have done, affect our sense of ourselves. As we are all unique individuals, so, too, are our God-ideas. We may imagine God as great, as hidden behind some illusory but real door, an enemy, or a frightening mystery. At times, we go through our daily lives for extended periods of time without reaching out to God to either keep us company or to intervene in our lives.

Like jugglers we sometimes call in our God and toss him around; sometimes we discard him because he is either too colorless for

SEARCHING FOR GOD IN THE 7TH GRADE

our needs or too hot for us to handle. Some of us never get him out of the magician's box where we placed him in our childhood; others never stop throwing him around, either for pleasure or because they cannot stop touching him in spite of their ability to keep him in their hands for long (perhaps he is too slippery or too dangerous); others are content simply to know that he is there if needed; others find him so fascinating that they want nothing else.[17]

If, as Rizzuto argues, our God as transitional object never is fully suppressed, then it is a particularly important challenge to continue to examine that object, to test where it sits in our psyche and to nurture its evolution. All religions create official or more private rituals to facilitate and mark the resolution of critical moments. Generally, these rites dramatize the breaking of old bonds and the formation of new ones between people. By bringing God in as an active participant in the process, ritual provides a new opportunity for the reshaping of God-images and the individual's relationship to it. This certainly should be true for Jews in their formal prayer experiences.

I believe that through a thoughtful *machzor*, we can help our congregants not abandon God as they abandon their younger years, but instead to examine their foundational beliefs, struggle with them, and begin to refashion them in ways that will allow them to take God with them on their journeys. I hope that we can help our members explore this connection, in all its complexity, and perhaps to imagine coming out the other end with faith made stronger for their adult lives.

When given the opportunity to reflect meaningfully as I worked with teens through my D-Min project, I was heartened to find meaningful conversation and, I believe, impact over the course of the sessions. I deeply enjoyed the conversations we engaged in, and I felt highly engaged and connected to the students. I feel that as I look back at each student, they each grew in their self-understanding, which was a big part of their ability to grow theologically in an expansive way during that time. The students were deeply respectful of each other in our time together—so much so that it was surprising to me. I feel that this was due, in part, to both the relevance of the material to their own lives and the safe atmosphere we were able to create together.

I observed real gains in the students' ability to reflect more deeply than they previously had about their spiritual beliefs and how they might inform their everyday lives. The discussions clearly challenged their belief systems and even challenged misconceptions that some students had about "proper" ways to believe. My experience confirmed in many ways what I had anticipated—that they were unaccustomed to discussing the specifics of their own faith in this religious school setting, if at all. Where some of them may have been inclined initially to be dogmatic about their belief or nonbelief, the conversations seemed to give them permission not only to explore alternative ideas about God, but on an even more fundamental level, permission to question and challenge altogether in ways they seemed at the beginning not to feel authorized to do. What became abundantly clear to me is that the need they felt to pray was really just below the surface; once they were willing to give voice to their feelings, the prayers nearly leaped out of their souls in ways that moved all of us. I learned from this experience, and extrapolate from it, that people are eager to talk about and explore what they believe, if given the chance. This should, I think, inform the ways in which we contemplate the composition of a *machzor* liturgy. I believe that the development of a new *machzor* gives us the opportunity to give Jews of all ages the opportunity to pray what is in their hearts. Let us give them wings to let their souls fly.

Bibliography

Ben David, Aryeh. *The Godfile.* Unpublished paper used with permission of the author.

Fromm, Erich. (1956) *The Art of Loving.* New York: Harper and Row.

Green, Arthur and Holtz, Barry W. (eds.) (1993) *Your Word is Fire.* Woodstock, VT: Jewish Lights.

Hood, R. W., (ed.). (1995). *Handbook of Religious Experience.* Birmingham, AL: Religious Education Press.

Kushner, Lawrence. (1998) *Invisible Lines of Connection: Sacred Stories of the Ordinary.* Woodstock, VT: Jewish Lights.

Ochs, Carol. (2001). *Jewish Spiritual Guidance.* Melbourne, FL: Krieger Publishing.

Ochs, Carol. (2001). *Our Lives as Torah: Finding God in Our Own Stories.* San Francisco: Jossey-Bass.

SEARCHING FOR GOD IN THE 7TH GRADE

Ochs, Carol. (2004). *Reaching Godward: Voices from Jewish Spiritual Guidance*. New York: URJ Press.

Rizzuto, A. M. (1979). *The Birth of the Living God: A Psychoanalytic Study*. Chicago: University of Chicago Press.

Wolpe, David J. (2004). *Floating Takes Faith: Ancient Wisdom for a Modern World*. Springfield, NJ: Behrman House.

Winnicott, D. W. (1953). "Transitional objects in traditional phenomena." *International Journal of Psychoanalysis,* 34 (2). 89-97.

Ulanov, A., & Ulanov, B. (1982). *Primary Speech: A Psychology of Prayer*. Atlanta: John Knox Press.

Notes

1. Arthur Green and Barry W. Holtz, eds., *Your Word is Fire* (Woodstock, VT: Jewish Lights, 1993), p. 94.

2. David J. Wolpe, *Floating Takes Faith: Ancient Wisdom for a Modern World* (Springfield, NJ: Behrman House, 2004), p. 180.

3. Aryeh Ben David, *The Godfile* (unpublished paper used with permission of the author), p. 7.

4. Lawrence Kushner, *Invisible Lines of Connection: Sacred Stories of the Ordinary* (Woodstock, VT: Jewish Lights, 1998), p. 75.

5. Edythe Mencher, "Our Children Need God," *Reform Judaism* (Summer 2006), p. 67.

6. Erich Fromm, *The Art of Loving* (New York: Harper and Row, 1956), p. 65.

7. Ibid., p. 63.

8. Ibid., p. 64.

9. Ibid., p. 67.

10. R. W. Hood, ed., *Handbook of Religious Experience* (Birmingham, AL: Religious Education Press, 1995), p. 155.

11. A. Ulanov and B. Ulanov, *Primary Speech: A Psychology of Prayer* (Atlanta: John Knox Press, 1982), p. 226.

12. Anna Maria Rizzuto, *The Birth of the Living God: A Psychoanalytic Study* (Chicago: University of Chicago Press, 1979), p. 177.

13. Ibid., p. 179.

14. Erich Fromm, *The Art of Loving*, p. 62.

15. Ibid., p. 65.

16. Ibid., p. 75.

17. Anna Maria Rizzuto, *The Birth of the Living God*, p. 180.

The Poetry and the Power of Paradox[1]

Margaret Moers Wenig

When I was a child, my parents and teachers told me about a man who was very strong. They told me he could destroy the whole world. They told me he could lift mountains. They told me he could part the sea. It was important to keep the man happy. When we obeyed what the man had commanded, the man liked us. But when we didn't obey what he had commanded, he didn't like us. He hated us. Some days he hated us so much, he killed us; other days, he let other people kill us....

So begins the memoir of the contemporary Jewish writer, Shalom Auslander. It continues:

The people of Monsey were terrified of God, and they taught me to be terrified of Him, too....they taught me...about a man named Moses, who escaped from Egypt, and who roamed through the desert for forty years in search of a Promised Land, and whom God killed just before he reached it—face-plant on the one-yard line—because Moses had sinned, once, forty years earlier. His crime? Hitting a rock. And so, in early autumn, when the leaves choked, turned colors, and fell to their deaths, the people of Monsey gathered together in synagogues across the town and wondered aloud and in unison, how God was going to kill them: —Who will live and who will die, they prayed—who at his predestined time and who before his time, who by water and who by fire, who by sword, who by beast, who by famine, who by thirst, who by storm, who by plague, who by strangulation and who by stoning.

I can't imagine raising children this way. We have learned that positive reinforcement is a much healthier way to train children

MARGARET MOERS WENIG (NY84) is Instructor in Liturgy and Homiletics at HUC-JIR, NY and Rabbi Emerita of Beth Am, The People's Temple, NY

The liturgical selections, *Unetanah Tokef* and *Ein Kitzvah*, referred to throughout the essay, can be found at the end of this piece.

THE POETRY AND THE POWER OF PARADOX

and even dogs. Corporal punishment of students is a thing of the past in most states, and we know that even our penal system is as likely to produce recidivists as it is to reform criminals. These days, punishment and inspiring fear of punishment is unpopular in our class and culture, abhorrent in fact.

So was the notion of punishment anathema to Albert Einstein: "I cannot imagine a god who rewards and punishes the objects of his creation."[3]

For that very reason, most liberal siddurim removed Deuteronomy 11:13–21[4] as the second paragraph of the *Sh'ma.* And Isaac Mayer Wise omitted the first three stanzas of *Un'taneh Tokef* including the litany of punishments Auslander begins to cite above.[5]

From his version of *Un'taneh Tokef,* Wise omitted more than the list of ways in which we might die, suffer, or flourish. He also omitted the verse of the poem that in many *machzorim* is highlighted with a special type face: *U't'shuvah, u't'filah, u'tzedakah ma'avirin et ro'ah ha-g'zeirah* ("Repentance, prayer, and righteousness..."). Of course Wise had to omit this statement since it is the second half of the earlier articulated notion that "On Rosh HaShanah it is written and on Yom Kippur it is sealed...," which he excised. But he might have omitted it for other reasons as well because that statement too is considered abhorrent by some. Marc Saperstein worried in the pages of this journal that *"u't'shuvah, u't'filah, u'tzedakah..."* might communicate to the 11-year-old girl sitting before him one Rosh HaShanah morning that it was within her power or the power of her mother who was then dying of cancer

> to arrest the cancer through penitence, prayer and charity. Would the mother's untimely death after an agonizing struggle prove that she and the members of her family had not engaged sufficiently in penitence, prayer and charity and that they were therefore responsible for the consequences?[6]

No, he concluded. That cruel message is not contained in these words. For the *paytan* does not claim that *t'shuvah, t'filah,* and *tzedakah* will **annul, cancel, or rend** the decree, but merely that they will ease the passage of the worst of the decree. The poet eschewed the expressions *m'vatlim et ha-g'zeirah* (as in *B'reishit Rabbah* 44:12) or *m'karin g'zar dino shel adam* (as in *Bavli, Rosh HaShanah*

MARGARET MOERS WENIG

16b) and substituted *ma'avirin et ro'ah ha-g'zeirah,* a much more modest promise.

Yet, even Rabbi Saperstein's understanding of these words would be unlikely to satisfy some who experience as abhorrent the notion of punishment in *Un'taneh Tokef* as well as the notion that human effort could mitigate such punishment. Dr. Lawrence Hoffman is an articulate spokesman for people who feel this way:

> I deliberately omit the God of *Un'tane tokef,* the God who seals our fate with death by fire, water, and strangulation, not because the Jewishly elite among us could not divert, invert or even subvert it to give it meaning—rabbis like to save what we have studied and fallen in love with, rather than admitting (as the classical reformers properly did) that **it causes unnecessary pain and is therefore wrong.** We can willingly believe what we know is not true; **we cannot happily abide what we know is hurtful. Evangelical Christians have abandoned the God of punishment, and so should we.**[7] (Emphasis added.)

I do not experience *Un'taneh Tokef* as hurtful. On the contrary. But I will take a lesson here from one as naturally argumentative as I am, Grace Paley, *aleha hashalom,* who said: "I never argue with those with whom I truly disagree."[8]

One of the major disagreements surely to arise in discussions of a new Reform *machzor* will be over the inclusion or exclusion of *Un'taneh Tokef.* The purpose of this article, however, is not to argue with Dr. Hoffman in an attempt to change his mind or the minds of those for whom he speaks. For once someone has testified that *Un'taneh Tokef* is "hurtful," how can we justify imposing it on those it has hurt? I would not presume to argue with those who have been hurt by this poem that they should not feel what they do in fact feel. Nor would I dare to say to them that they should endure this pain for the sake of some greater good. Reciting *Un'taneh Tokef* or hearing it recited is not akin to receiving a painful inoculation against a highly infectious disease for the sake of protecting the wider population from the spread of it. Reciting *Un'taneh Tokef* or hearing it recited is not akin to paying painfully high taxes for the sake of universal health care and generous unemployment insurance as many citizens of the EU must do. It does not benefit anyone else if one hurt by *Un'taneh Tokef* endures its pain. Moreover, as a feminist and a gay person, I have myself argued for the elimination or alteration

THE POETRY AND THE POWER OF PARADOX

of Jewish laws, customs, and liturgical components on the grounds that they hurt some people. So the argument: *"Un'taneh Tokef* hurts" wins hands down. Thus my purpose here is not to argue or convince but merely to testify to my own experience of *Un'taneh Tokef* and to the experience of others who feel as I do:

> "To me this is the center of the service." "It is one of the more beautiful and memorable parts of the service." "I am swooning with the emotions of it. To leave this out would be like amputating a limb." "How can you remove the *Un'taneh Tokef!*...it is so central to the Days of Awe! I never saw it as a negative blame-the-victim poem, to me it was actually comforting."[9]

How the editors of a new Reform *machzor* will navigate their way through the irreconcilable experiences of those Dr. Hoffman represents who experience *Un'taneh Tokef* as hurtful and those like me who don't and who in fact experience it as crucial and even comforting, remains to be seen.[10]

Three factors affect my experience of *Un'taneh Tokef:*

1. My understanding of the figurative language of the poem
2. My longing for concrete and powerful imagery in liturgy
3. My view that the poem is constructed as a series of tensions, contrasts, contradictions, and paradoxes that build to a dramatic climax in the very stanza of the poem that our current *machzor,* the *Gates of Repentance,* unfortunately left out.

An Understanding of the Figurative Language of the Poem

Many a *darshan* or *baal t'filah* has given a sermon, *iyyun t'filah,* or *kavanah* interpreting the figurative language of this poem.[11] I offer several in the endnotes to this article. The one I cite here cuts to the core issue: How do we understand the notion of divine punishment, which is considered anathema to many modern minds? In her commentary on the second paragraph of the *Sh'ma,* Dr. Judith Plaskow writes:

> It is not necessary to read this paragraph of the *Sh'ma* as a literal statement about divine reward and punishment. In a world whose survival depends partly on the human capacity to value creation and care for it wisely, it is possible to interpret the passage more

naturalistically. If we are able to develop an ecological consciousness, if we treat the earth with respect, if we are aware that we
are embedded in a great web of life of which God is the ultimate
source and sustainer, then the earth will bear fruit for us and the
rain will come in its season. But if we believe we can trample on
or transcend the constraints of nature, if we forget the sacredness
of all things and make idols of our own wealth and power, 'the
earth will not grant its produce,' and both we and our world may
perish.[12]

It will come as no *chidush* to you that many understand the references to judgment and punishment in *Un'taneh Tokef* as figurative
language, the literal meaning of which is simply that our deeds
have consequences. If you don't wear a seat belt, if you speed, and
if you drive while drunk, you increase the risk of hurting yourself
and others. I don't need to multiply the analogies, since readers of
this article can supply long lists of their own. While some lucky
folks do seem to escape painful consequences of dangerous behavior, many find it useful to believe that our actions are likely to have
consequences, even if we do not learn for years or ever what those
consequences may be.

The inverse, however, is not a given: if people suffer in an au-
tomobile accident, or from a disease, I and many others do not
conclude that their suffering is a function of any fault of their own.
There are some who do believe that "everything happens for a reason" or that God "never sends us more than we can handle" or
that "suffering is a gift to purify our soul," but many of us do not
believe we know the will or the ways of God sufficiently to be able
to make any such claims. Even the unknown author of *Un'taneh
Tokef* may have understood his references to God figuratively, since
many of those references he borrowed from biblical verses where
the subject of the verses was not God at all but human kings instead. Many of us have never taken the words of this poem literally, but we value them for the moral challenge they pose and for
their vividness and power.

A Longing for Concrete and Powerful Imagery in Liturgy

Catherine Madsen is among those who crave concrete and powerful liturgical language. Her craving largely unsatisfied, she has
leveled harsh criticism against many contemporary liturgies. If
you overlook the judgments in her words and understand instead

THE POETRY AND THE POWER OF PARADOX

the pain of her unfulfilled yearnings, you will appreciate why the graphic language in *Un'taneh Tokef* might appeal to her as it does to me and to others.

> Across the board, [contemporary liturgical language, Jewish and Christian is]…all flat, unconvincing contemporary English without the least idea of ardor or terror or splendor. You can be as intellectually daring as you want in modern Judaism, but [in the language used by modern Jewish thinkers or liturgists] you're not going to get that live coal…
>
> How can you maintain a religious allegiance by reciting dispirited platitudes? Why should you bother? How can people who write the platitudes imagine that they're doing their religion a favor, or even keep their minds on the job? We are the only species on the planet with language; why aren't we using it better?
>
> The face of your beloved doesn't have to smile at you all the time….
>
> Modern prayer books deal heavily in abstraction…They underestimate our energy and our intelligence by making their dominant mood light reverie rather than moral imperative. They are embarrassed by metaphor and they flee powerful emotion. They depersonalize God…. They avert their eyes from our own terrifying powers of destruction and exploitation, our endless capacity for self-deception…. All this has the effect of depersonalizing us, removing us from the world of decisions and consequences into a world of bloodless intellectual counters….
>
> …liturgy is never only one voice; it is an assembly of voices gathered from holy texts and earlier liturgies, each speaking in the voice of intimate address…. What [good] liturgy never is [is] a homogenized voice, without alarms or surprises; never a safe inoffensive voice that requires no response.[14]

The first three stanzas of *Un'taneh Tokef* include images that evoke in me ardor and terror, emotions that ring true. I know that we are judged, that our deeds have consequences, that some of our fate appears to be in our hands and much of it does not, that some mistakes we can fix and others we simply have to live with. If, like Isaac M. Wise, we removed these portions of *Un'taneh Tokef*, we would lighten its message to be sure. But, in the hearts of many of us, we would, at the same time, diminish its credibility and tame its power. Moreover, if we omitted the first three stanzas of this poem we would destroy what I believe to be its logical structure and eliminate the mounting tension to the dramatic climax of the poem.

MARGARET MOERS WENIG

A Series of Tensions, Contrasts, Contradictions, and Paradoxes and Their Dramatic Climax

Un'taneh Tokef is in its logical structure similar to the oft-quoted instruction of the Sages: "Every person should carry in a pocket two pieces of paper. On one should be written: 'From dust you came and to dust you shall return.' And on the other: 'For your sake was the world created.'"

Neither of these statements is literally true. We did not come from dust, nor was the world created for our sake. Yet we consider each statement to convey meaning even though the meanings of the two statements express opposite views of our place in the world (one humble the other exalted). Yet we are instructed to "believe" both of them. We claim that each statement is "true" (i.e., meaningful) on its own. But neither statement, on its own, conveys the entire truth. And so we are instructed to keep both pieces of paper in our pockets.

Un'taneh Tokef strikes me as an honest expression of some of the fundamental contradictions or paradoxes of life. Some theologies or world views, myths, or liturgies endeavor to eliminate contradictions. Some endeavor to preserve them. Some would attribute greater intellectual or even moral value to the latter than to the former, as perhaps the following authors would:

"The test of a first-rate intelligence is the ability to hold two opposed ideas in the mind at the same time and still retain the ability to function." (F. Scott Fitzgerald)

"It is best that you grasp the one without letting go of the other." (Mordecai Kaplan, quoting Eccl. 7:18)

"Jewish thinking and living can only be adequately understood in terms of a dialectic pattern, containing opposite or contrasted properties. As in a magnet, the ends of which have opposite magnetic qualities,...[some key religious] terms are opposite to one another and exemplify a polarity which lies at the very heart of Judaism." (Abraham Joshua Heschel, God in Search of Man)

"Survivors' endurance, persistence, resiliency in new and complex situations is primarily derived from having integrated major mental and emotional paradoxes into their ways of functioning." ("Characteristics of The Survivor Personality," by Al Siebert, Ph.D. quoted on NPR's *The Infinite Mind*)

THE POETRY AND THE POWER OF PARADOX

I am in no position to prove or disprove F. Scott Fitzgerald's claim. I see no need to claim more than that a preference for contradictions, tensions, and paradoxes in liturgy is merely a matter of taste as the architect quoted below expressed his preference for contradiction in his métier:

"I like complexity and contradiction in architecture. I do not like the incoherence or arbitrariness of incompetent architecture nor the precious intricacies of picturesqueness or expressionism. Instead, I speak of a complex and contradictory architecture based on the richness and ambiguity of modern experience, including that experience which is inherent in art." (Ronni Venturi, *Complexity and Contradiction in Architecture,* 1962)

Un'taneh Tokef is full of contrasts, tensions, contradictions, ambiguities, and paradoxes. It has rhyming and rhythmic structure to be sure. But one might say that its logical structure consists of a series of paired contrasts, contradictions, and paradoxes: I list them here in the figurative language of the poet. (My own understandings I reserve for the end notes.)

God has the power to inscribe and record	but it is we who have inscribed our our names (and deeds) in the Book[15]
God communicates through the sound of a Great Shofar	and through a still small voice[16]
God's throne will be established in CHESED (mercy, loving kindness, covenant love)	God will sit on it in EMET (pure truth, unaffected by emotion)
God is DAYAN[17]	and RO'EH[18, 19]
God is Judge and forgets nothing	yet God is slow to anger and easy to appease[20]
God fixes the limits of every living creature and inscribes the decree of their Judgment....who shall live and who shall die	yet God doesn't want anyone to die[21]

MARGARET MOERS WENIG

On RH it is written, on YK sealed	yet *t'shuvah, t'filah, and tzedakah ma'avirin et ro'ah ha-g'zeirah*
Even though God doesn't desire the death [of the sinner]	all human beings [sinner and righteous alike] will die
Even though some things can temper the severity of the decree	nonetheless, to dust we shall all return
Humans are mortal	God is eternal[22]
God sets the limits of human life	God's years have no limit

If we carry the "two pieces of paper in our pockets" presumably we are to read the humbling message when we are feeling excessive pride and the other message, hyperbolically reminding us of our worth, when we are feeling worthless. During the Ten Days of Repentance, when we are already acutely aware of our failings and their damaging consequences, which of the opposing messages in *Un'taneh Tokef* are we to hear with greater emphasis? Is the *piyut* meant to further frighten us or to reassure us? Is it meant to condemn us or to comfort us?

There is no question which sides of the opposing messages Wise thought ought to be most heavily emphasized. Lest any rabbi, cantor, or choir, erroneously emphasize the first stanza ("*Un'taneh Tokef*..."), the second stanza ("*U'v'shofar gadol*..."), or the third ("*B'rosh HaShanah yikateivun*..."), Rabbi Isaac M. Wise omitted them altogether. Wise began his *Un'taneh Tokef* with *Ki k'shimcha*:

This is Your glory. You are slow to anger, ready to forgive. It is not the death of sinners You seek, but that they should turn from their ways and live. Until the last day You wait for them, welcoming them as soon as they return to You. You have created us and You know what we are; we are but flesh and blood.... (*GOR's* translation)

THE POETRY AND THE POWER OF PARADOX

Equally important, Wise did not conclude the *piyut* as *GOR* does or *UPB II* did with *"V'atah hu melech el chai v'kayam,"* the often musically dramatized affirmation of God's sovereignty and eternality (in stark contrast to our own humble lives and ultimate demise). Instead, Wise concluded *Un'taneh Tokef* with *"Ein Kitzvah"* the crucial stanza that follows *"v'atah hu melech el chai v'kayam"* and which climaxes on a very different note:

> Your years have no limit. Your life no end. None can know your glory, nor explain your essence. Your name is worthy of You, and You are worthy of Your name, *u'sh'meinu karata bishmecha,* **and our name You have linked with Yours.**[23]

U'sh'meinu karata bishmecha is the only sentence in this entire *piyut* in which the verbs are in the perfect tense. For this reason alone, these words stand out. They have a definiteness, a certainty to them. The time frame of the rest of the *piyut* is ambiguous for all the rest of the verbs are either gerunds (e.g., *U't'shuvah, u't'filah, u'tzedakah ma'avirin et ro'ah ha-g'zeirah*) or in the "imperfect" tense. I believe that *"u'sh'meinu karata bishmecha,"* is meant to be the climax of *Un'taneh Tokef* not *"U't'shuvah u't'filah, u'tzedakah ..."* nor *"V'atah hu melech...."* It is these words that deserve to be highlighted by typeface and musical setting, pauses and inflection. "Our name You have linked with Yours": Something of us can endure. We are part of an ongoing chain of humanity, of Jewish tradition. We are but one link but the chain endures. Our lives are fleeting but we may write books or compose music that will be remembered generations after we have died. We may teach students, who will teach students, who will teach students, for generations to come. One single deed of loving-kindness we perform may send ripples far into the future. Despite our failings and despite our inescapable mortality, at our core resides something enduring and worthwhile. Perhaps it is "the faith of those despised and endangered that they are not merely the sum of damages done to them... [but] a connective link in a long, continuous way of ordering hunger, weather, death, desire and the nearness of chaos," as Adrienne Rich put it.[24] Or perhaps it is the faith that

> Though our deeds are stained with blood, this we know: You have set in the inmost sanctuary of our being Your law of justice, love

MARGARET MOERS WENIG

and peace. The flame which burns upon that altar may flicker, but it can never be quenched. For that flame is Your eternal spirit, burning within us. (in *GOR's* "From Creation to Redemption," p. 417)

If you read or hear the entire *piyut* in light of this dramatic claim; if you read or hear the entire *piyut* as if it is building up to this climax, as members of one congregation do, then you can understand why they would say:

...as a child [*Un'taneh Tokef*] was frightening to me...it does... have a punitive feel and...it was quite damaging to me as a child. I think it of it as part of why I had a difficult time with some aspects of Judaism for a time. However, the version of the prayer that we use...[(i.e., the entire *piyut* unabridged, including *Ein Kitzvah*)] does not have that same punitive feel...and should definitely be included.[25]

No matter what terrible things happen, [no matter what] personal demons plague us, [no matter how] ephemeral life may be, God is eternal...it is the God waiting till the very last second...that I cling to with an almost childlike fervor. And for those 10 days in particular we ARE very much God's children. *Avinu Malkeinu.*

To me this is the center of the service, a prayer/poem that never fails to bring me to tears. It is a great mistake...to take literally every instance of poetry in prayer and delete it...in so doing the whole community is hurt. We have a right to be moved to contemplate what we have done and what we have failed to do through the past year, we have a right to appeal to G-d for a recognition of human frailty, which the Creator created us with, we have a right to believe we and G-d are linked in a mystical way. To think of God waiting for us to return is the center of a spiritual life I try to keep all year. When each member of the [volunteer] choir sings his or her line:

Our origin is dust and dust is our end.
Each of us is a shattered urn
grass that must whither
a flower that will fade
a shadow moving on
a cloud passing by
a particle of dust floating on the wind
a dream soon forgotten

THE POETRY AND THE POWER OF PARADOX

I am more profoundly moved by the quavering tiny voices [of the volunteers] than by the powerful trained ones. It is human frailty that moves me and makes me feel there is something so admirable about a human being who can sing that way before G-d and the congregation, to let her human and flawed nature be known.

It also seems to me that a belief in the power of repentance, prayer and charity is at the core of our religion. I don't take this prayer to be a literal bargaining but a profession of faith—that my life, which is like a particle of dust, matters; that my acts make a difference. It's not that they buy me time or health but that they give me life for the time I have.... if we take the poetry out of our services we will have nothing left but predigested, politically correct pap.[27]

The melody that ... [we sing] for

Your years have no limit, Your life no end,
None can know Your glory, nor explain your essence,
Your name is worthy of You, and You are worthy of Your name,
Your name is worthy of You, and You are worthy of Your name,
and our name, our name,
You have linked with Yours,[28]

is to me the most beautiful/tender/heart-rending/spiritual/moving/...[of the High Holiday liturgy]. That moment is the highlight of the service and perhaps of my year.[29]

These congregants aren't alone in sensing, through the inclusion of *Ein Kitzvah*, the uplifting climax of *Un'taneh Tokef*. A Modzitzer setting of *Ein Kitzvah*, that is light, playful, almost circus like, makes it clear that by the time these worshipers arrive at the end of the *piyut* they too are happy.[30]

Alas, it is this very stanza, this very climax that the *UPB II* and *GOR* omitted.[31] I, for one, want to recite *Un'taneh Tokef* or hear it recited unabridged and accurately translated[32] because it speaks "truth" to me, ultimately comforts me, and contains some of the most powerful and evocative language in our *machzor*.

One doesn't even have to believe in God to find meaning in this poem. Many secular Israelis have found even the terrifying first three paragraphs of *Un'taneh Tokef* evocative. They have listened over and over again on the radio to a setting composed by Ya'ir Rosenblum and sung by Hanoch Albalack. The song was recorded

MARGARET MOERS WENIG

for the film *Unetane Tokef* documenting the affect on Kibbutz Beit Hashita of the death of 11 of its sons during the Yom Kippur War. In this setting the most comforting portions of the poem (i.e., *Ki k'shimcha* and *Ein kitzvah*) are omitted. It is the awareness of mortality so palpably brought home by the litanies: *mi yichyeh, u'mi yamut* and *adam y'sodo m'afar v'sofo v'afar . . .* that rang true for the composers and consumers of this song. Did they believe that the deaths of soldiers in the Yom Kippur War was a punishment for the sins of those very soldiers? I doubt it. At least not in any simple quid quo pro sort of way.

Why do I, for one, want to hear all of *Un'taneh Tokef,* not only the comforting parts? An answer comes from the octogenarian violinist Olga Blum, founder of Barge Music in Brooklyn. Olga was once asked by Mayor Ed Koch: "Olga, why don't you put the barge on pilings so that when a large boat passes and causes a wake, the barge won't rock any more and the piano won't ever roll across the stage during a performance (as it once did)." Olga replied: "I will never put the barge up on pilings because all beauty, all art is in some way a wrestling with impermanence and death." *Un'taneh Tokef* is an artistic wrestling with impermanence and death, with deeds and their consequences, with power and powerlessness, with fear and reassurance, with mistakes and second chances. Perhaps the ultimate paradox is that life hurts but is still worth living.

Un'taneh Tokef **from** *Gates of Repentance*

וּנְתַנֶּה תְּקֶף קְדֻשַּׁת הַיּוֹם כִּי הוּא נוֹרָא וְאָים. וּבוֹ
תְּנַשֵּׂא מַלְכוּתֶךָ וְיִכּוֹן בְּחֶסֶד כִּסְאֶךָ וְתֵשֵׁב עָלָיו
בֶּאֱמֶת. אֱמֶת כִּי אַתָּה הוּא דַיָּן וּמוֹכִיחַ וְיוֹדֵעַ וָעֵד,
וְכוֹתֵב וְחוֹתֵם וְסוֹפֵר וּמוֹנֶה, וְתִזְכֹּר כָּל־הַנִּשְׁכָּחוֹת,
וְתִפְתַּח אֶת־סֵפֶר הַזִּכְרוֹנוֹת, וּמֵאֵלָיו יִקָּרֵא וְחוֹתַם
יַד כָּל־אָדָם בּוֹ.

Let us proclaim the sacred power of this day:
it is awesome and full of dread.
For on this day Your dominion is exalted,
Your throne established in steadfast love;
there in truth You reign.
In truth You are
Judge and Arbiter, Counsel and Witness.

THE POETRY AND THE POWER OF PARADOX

You write and You seal, You record and recount.
You remember deeds long forgotten.
You open the book of our days,
and what is written there proclaims itself,
for it bears the signature
of every human being.

וּבְשׁוֹפָר גָּדוֹל יִתָּקַע וְקוֹל דְּמָמָה דַקָּה יִשָּׁמַע.
וּמַלְאָכִים יֵחָפֵזוּן וְחִיל וּרְעָדָה יֹאחֵזוּן וְיֹאמְרוּ: הִנֵּה
יוֹם הַדִּין. לִפְקֹד עַל צְבָא מָרוֹם בַּדִּין, כִּי לֹא יִזְכּוּ
בְעֵינֶיךָ בַּדִּין. וְכָל־בָּאֵי עוֹלָם יַעַבְרוּן לְפָנֶיךָ כִּבְנֵי
מָרוֹן. כְּבַקָּרַת רוֹעֶה עֶדְרוֹ, מַעֲבִיר צֹאנוֹ תַּחַת
שִׁבְטוֹ, כֵּן תַּעֲבִיר וְתִסְפֹּר וְתִמְנֶה וְתִפְקֹד נֶפֶשׁ כָּל־
חָי, וְתַחְתֹּךְ קִצְבָה לְכָל־בְּרִיָּה וְתִכְתֹּב אֶת־גְּזַר דִּינָם.

The great Shofar is sounded,
the still, small voice is heard;
the angels,
gripped by fear and trembling,
declare in awe:

This is the Day of Judgment!
For even the hosts of heaven are judged,
as all who dwell on earth
stand arrayed before You.

As the shepherd seeks out his flock,
and makes the sheep pass under his staff,
so do You muster and number and consider
every soul,
setting the bounds of every creature's life,
and decreeing its destiny.

בְּרֹאשׁ הַשָּׁנָה יִכָּתֵבוּן וּבְיוֹם צוֹם כִּפּוּר יֵחָתֵמוּן.
כַּמָּה יַעַבְרוּן וְכַמָּה יִבָּרֵאוּן, מִי יִחְיֶה וּמִי יָמוּת, מִי
בְקִצּוֹ וּמִי לֹא בְקִצּוֹ, מִי בָאֵשׁ וּמִי בַמַּיִם, מִי בַחֶרֶב
וּמִי בַחַיָּה, מִי בָרָעָב וּמִי בַצָּמָא, מִי בָרַעַשׁ וּמִי
בַמַּגֵּפָה, מִי בַחֲנִיקָה וּמִי בַסְּקִילָה. מִי יָנוּחַ וּמִי יָנוּעַ,
מִי יַשְׁקִיט וּמִי יִטָּרֵף, מִי יִשָּׁלֵו וּמִי יִתְיַסָּר, מִי יֵעָנִי
וּמִי יַעֲשִׁיר, מִי יִשָּׁפֵל וּמִי יָרוּם.

MARGARET MOERS WENIG

On Rosh HaShanah it is written,
on Yom Kipur it is sealed:
How many shall pass on, how many shall come to be;
who shall live and who shall die;
who shall see ripe age and who shall not;
who shall perish by fire and who by water;
who by sword and who by beast;
who by hunger and who by thirst;
who by earthquake and who by plague;
who by strangling and who by stoning;
who shall be secure and who shall be driven;
who shall be tranquit and who shall be troubled;
who shall be poor and who shall be rich;
who shall be humbled and who exalted.

וּתְשׁוּבָה וּתְפִלָּה וּצְדָקָה
מַעֲבִירִין אֶת־רֹעַ הַגְּזֵרָה.

But REPENTANCE, PRAYER, and CHARITY
temper judgment's severe decree.

כִּי כְּשִׁמְךָ כֵּן תְּהִלָּתֶךָ, קָשֶׁה לִכְעֹס וְנִוֹחַ לִרְצוֹת. כִּי
לֹא תַחְפֹּץ בְּמוֹת הַמֵּת כִּי אִם בְּשׁוּבוֹ מִדַּרְכּוֹ וְחָיָה.
וְעַד יוֹם מוֹתוֹ תְּחַכֶּה־לּוֹ, אִם יָשׁוּב מִיַּד תְּקַבְּלוֹ.
אֱמֶת כִּי אַתָּה הוּא יוֹצְרָם וְיוֹדֵעַ יִצְרָם כִּי הֵם בָּשָׂר
וָדָם.

This is Your glory; You are
slow to anger, ready to forgive.
Lord, it is not the death of sinners You seek,
but that they should turn from their ways
and live.
Until the last day You wait for them,
welcoming them
as soon as they turn to You.

You have created us and know what we are;
we are but flesh and blood.

אָדָם יְסוֹדוֹ מֵעָפָר וְסוֹפוֹ לֶעָפָר. בְּנַפְשׁוֹ יָבִיא לַחְמוֹ.
מָשׁוּל כַּחֶרֶס הַנִּשְׁבָּר, כְּחָצִיר יָבֵשׁ וּכְצִיץ נוֹבֵל, כְּצֵל
עוֹבֵר וּכְעָנָן כָּלָה, וּכְרוּחַ נוֹשָׁבֶת, וּכְאָבָק פּוֹרֵחַ,
וְכַחֲלוֹם יָעוּף.

וְאַתָּה הוּא מֶלֶךְ אֵל חַי וְקַיָּם!

THE POETRY AND THE POWER OF PARADOX

[Our] origin is dust,
and dust is [our] end.
Each of us is a shattered urn,
grass that must wither,
a flower that will fade,
a shadow moving on,
a cloud passing by,
a particle of dust floating on the wind,
a dream soon forgotten.

*But You are the King,
the everlasting God!*

Ein Kitzvah

Your years have no limit
Your length of days no end
None can imagine Your glory
Nor explain Your name
Your name is worthy of You
And You are worthy of Your name
And our name You have linked with Yours.

אֵין קִצְבָה לִשְׁנוֹתֶךָ, וְאֵין קֵץ לְאֹרֶךְ יָמֶיךָ:
וְאֵין לְשַׁעֵר מַרְכְּבוֹת כְּבוֹדֶךָ, וְאֵין לְפָרֵשׁ עֵלוּם שְׁמֶךָ:
שִׁמְךָ נָאֶה לְךָ וְאַתָּה נָאֶה לִשְׁמֶךָ,
וּשְׁמֵנוּ קָרָאתָ בִּשְׁמֶךָ.

Notes

1. My thanks to those who read and commented on an earlier draft of this article: Drs. David Blumenthal, Lawrence Hoffman, Richard Sarason, Rabbi Sharon Kleinbaum, and Steven Rosenberg.
2. Shalom Auslander, *Foreskin's Lament: A Memoir* (New York: Riverhead Books, 2007), pp. 1–3.
3. Quoted by Corey Powell in *God in the Equation: How Einstein Transformed Religion* (New York: Simon and Schuster, 2003), p. 252
4. "If you will carefully obey my commands...I will give rain for your land...Beware lest your heart be deceived, and you turn and serve other gods and worship them; for then the Lord's anger will blaze against you, and he will shut up the skies so that there will be no rain..."

MARGARET MOERS WENIG

5. *Tefilot B'nai Yeshurun l'Yom Kakippurim, k'fi Minhag America* (Cincinnati: Block and Co., 1866).

6. Marc Saperstein, "Inscribed for Life or Death," CCAR Journal (Summer 1981), pp. 18–26.

7. Lawrence Hoffman, "Principle, Story and Myth in the Liturgical Search for Identity" (unpublished ms)

8. Quoted in one of the tributes to Grace Paley at a memorial service in her honor held in the Great Hall of Cooper Union College, New York, November 6, 2007.

9. From members of Beth Am, The People's Temple, New York, in e-mail messages to the author in winter 2008.

10. Responding to Dr. Hoffman's claim leaves us no choice but, minimally, to find a way to make it possible and easy, acceptable and comfortable for those who cannot abide *Un'taneh Tokef* to absent themselves from the sanctuary during its recitation. Just as some Jews leave the sanctuary while *Yizkor* is recited (albeit for very different reasons), and mourners, during shivah, absent themselves from *Kabbalat Shabbat* and enter the sanctuary only after *L'chah Dodi*, so too those pained by *Un'taneh Tokef* could leave during its recitation and be ushered back upon its conclusion. There should be no stigma attached to those who cannot abide *Un'taneh Tokef*. They should not be excluded, as women and gay people used to be, from any honor or role in the synagogue. They should not be forced to explain or justify their feelings or be burdened with the task of convincing a rabbi, cantor, or ritual committee of the legitimacy of those feelings. Their feelings should be honored. Period. End of story. Alternately, the hurtful parts of *Un'taneh Tokef* could be sung *b'lachash* (*soto voce*) as it is the custom to chant the curses in *Parshat Ki Tavo* in an undertone and as some *baalei korei* now chant Lev. 18:22 and 20:13 (prescribing death for a "man who lies with a man as one lies with a woman,") in an undertone. And, following the example of *Mishkan T'filah*, different but parallel prayers or teachings could appear on the opposite page for the benefit of worshipers who wish to ignore the chanting of *Un'taneh Tokef*. Of course, some congregations may choose to omit *Un'taneh Tokef* altogether as most Sephardi *machzorim* do (since they are disinclined to interrupt the *Amidah* with *piyutim*). Some Sephardi *machzorim* print *Un'taneh Tokef* in the back of the book with a superscription saying "It is the custom in some congregations to recite *Un'taneh Tokef* before the Torah scrolls are placed into the ark." See, e.g., *Machzor Kol Yehudah, The Orot Sephardi Rosh Hashanah Machzor*, ed. Rabbi Eliezer Toledano (Lakewood, NJ: Orot, 2002), p. 522.

11. While the second stanza of this poem concludes with the words, *"v'tachtoch kitzvah l'chol b'riah, v'tichtov et g'zar dinam"* of which God is most definitely the subject, many have noticed and considered

THE POETRY AND THE POWER OF PARADOX

significant the fact that **God is not the subject** of "B'Rosh HaSha-nah yikateivun u'v'Yom Tzom Kippur yeichateimun" where the verbs are in the passive voice. As Dr. Joel Hoffman said in a post-Katrina *d'rash,* "In *Un'tane tokef* the reason it says, 'it is written' and not 'God writes' is that we do the writing. We write down who shall live by water and who by fire, etc. This past year we all witnessed Katrina, but let us not believe that it was a natural disaster. It was a natural phenomenon and a governmental and political disaster. This year, we have to decide who we are going to write in the book of life (by supporting them with *tzedakah*), and who in the book of death (by not supporting them). Let us be clear if, as the richest nation in the world, we let children die in Africa we have written them in the book of death, not God." Summarized by him in an e-mail to me, October 21, 2005.

Others notice and consider significant the fact that the litany begins not with "who shall live and who shall die" but rather with "**how many** shall pass on…," which Rami Shapiro compares to

> the fatality statistics made public prior to any major American holiday. We know from experience that a certain number of people will be killed on our highways, but we do not know in advance who the victims will be. Does this mean we are in the hands of a fate over which we have no influence? Not at all. While we cannot know who will die, we can take every precaution to see that we are not among the victims. We can stay home. We can use seat belts. We can drive with extreme caution. Or we can drive drunk, recklessly, heedlessly, and increase our chances of being a victim. That there will be victims is not in our hands. Whether we will be among them, is—at least to a certain extent.

> The second section is more personal: who will live and who will die, and how. What does it mean to die "at one's predestined time or before?" If the date of my death is predestined, how can I die before it? The prayer is not talking about duration of time, but about fullness of time. We all know people who lived short but full lives and people who live long but empty lives. The point isn't the length but what we do with the time we have.

> The rest of the second section deals with ways of living that are detrimental to living life fully. Who by water, drowning in self-pity? Who by fire, consumed with the fires of rage? Who by the sword, brought down by our own violence? And the beast, never using the gifts of reason, compassion and love that make us human? Who by famine, starving for love? Who by thirst, all dried up without friends or interests outside our own aches and pains? Who by storm, in constant emotional turmoil? Who by plague, by disease, a loss of balance, a loss of self? …If we choose to live in these ways, we will die by these ways. (Rami Shapiro, "Random Thoughts on the *Un'tane Tokef,*"*Raayonot: A*

MARGARET MOERS WENIG

Journal from the Reconstructionist Rabbinical Association, Vol. 8, No. 2 Fall 5752, 1991], pp. 7, 8.)

12. From Lawrence A. Hoffman, ed., *My People's Prayer Book: Traditional Prayers, Modern Commentaries, Volume I, The Sh'ma and Its Blessings* (Woodstock, VT: Jewish Lights, 1997), p. 110.

13. *"Tinase malchuto"* in Nu. 24:7 which refers to Israel's king becomes *"tinase malchutecha"* in *Un'taneh Tokef. "V'huchan b'chesed kiseh v'yeshev alav b'emet"* from Isaiah 16:5 where it is a reference to the throne of the king of Judah becomes *"v'yachon b'chesed kishecha; v'teshev alav b'emet"* in the poem. *"Markevot k'vodecha"* in Isaiah 22:18 where it is a reference to the chariots of human foes of God is unaltered but in the context of the poem refers to God's chariots. *"Ayom v'nora hu"* in Habbakuk 1:7 describing the Kasdim, becomes *"ki hu nora vayom,"* God's day of Judgment in *Un'taneh Tokef.*

14. Catherine Madsen, "Spiritual Sobriety and the Iconic Voice: How We Recognize Language We Can Trust," *CCAR Journal* (Winter 2003), p. 5, 6, 7-8, 9.

15. "God writes and records" / "But when God opens the Book, God reads what we have written."

    Our deeds matter. As insignificant as they may seem at the time, our deeds have lasting impact. Every action, every choice has an impact on the future course of events. The impact may be reversible, but not always. People may notice and remember what we have done, they may even remember deeds we have long forgotten.

    We create ourselves. We write the stories of our own lives. We may be given certain genes. We may be born into a poor or a wealthy family, in a time of peace or in a time of war, we may have had nurturing parents or neglectful parents or even abusive parents but how we respond to the circumstances in which we find ourselves, how we play the hand we have been dealt is up to us. God only reads what we ourselves have written.

16. "Shofar"/"Still Small Voice"

    Revelation comes in the form of Beethoven's Ode to Joy and in the Rocky Mountains, in a volcano and at Mt. Rainier. It comes when Maria Callas sings Tosca and when Moshe Ganchoff davens. It comes in Louis Armstrong's trumpet. It comes when seeing the Guggenheim Museum at Bilbao or Central Synagogue. It comes in the brilliant insight of a great teacher or preacher. But revelation also comes in the slow movement of Beethoven's Fifth Piano Concerto, in the dwarfed trees above the arctic circle, in the call of a bird, and the chirping of crickets or in a child's voice or through a realization that grows slowly over time or in the silence of a corpse.

THE POETRY AND THE POWER OF PARADOX

17. "God is judge"

We are judged. Our children judge us. Our congregants judge us. Our parents and our partners judge us. Our students and our teachers judge us. Outside of us are standards to which we are held. Sometimes we live up to them. Sometimes we don't. We don't always know what the standards are until we violate them. Sometimes we don't learn we've violated them until years later when a child refers to a hurt we unknowingly inflicted or when a friend refers to an unintended betrayal or when a business decision that impacted the lives of many turned out, with the benefit of hindsight, to be a poor one. We are judged. God judges us. The universe judges us. Our actions have consequences.

18. "God is shepherd"

A judge and a shepherd play very different roles. When he reaches the words *"k'vakarat ro'eh edro,"* one of the world's greatest scholars of medieval piyutim, Professor Raymond Scheindlin, who also serves as *baal musaf* on Rosh HaShanah at Congregation Baith Israel Anshei Emes in Brooklyn, segues seamlessly into Ben Zion Shenker's melody (the one "everyone" knows) for Psalm 23. I will never forget the first time I heard it. He sang these words of *Un'taneh Tokef* to the melody we all know for *"Adonai roi lo echsar"* for only a phrase or two. But that was all it took. Suddenly this stanza of *Un'taneh Tokef* that had always inspired terror in me hinted at comfort. The Shepherd who makes me lie down in green pastures, who restores my soul, whose presence quells my fears, is the same Shepherd who "seeks out his flock and makes us pass under his staff." Suddenly I noticed that in this stanza of the poem God is not only *dayan* but also *ro'eh*, not only Judge but Shepherd ,and the Shepherd's job is to protect his sheep and not allow them to fall prey to predators or accidents, thirst or starvation, or to wander off and become lost.

19. "God is Judge"/"God is Shepherd"

People judge us and impose their expectations upon us but some also give love and care for us. A teacher takes notice of us and encourages us. A board member runs interference for us in a synagogue battle. A donor gives us money to use as we please. Parents fed us, carried us when we cried. An angel took us under his wing, a mentor taught us the ropes. A supervisor stopped us from doing something dangerous, steered us back on course and never told a soul. Food satisfies us. Sleep refreshes us.

20. "God judges"/"God is easy to appease"

There is no statue of limitations on *t'shuvah*. Asking for forgiveness, even years after the fact, may go a long way towards mollifying a person we have deeply hurt. Showing a sincere willingness to change may soften the hardened heart of those who

MARGARET MOERS WENIG

loved us once. And if they are not mollified, they should be, for that is how God would react to a penitent soul: Slow to anger and quick to forgive. That is the way we should react as well. Yes, we judge. Yes, we bear grudges. Yes, we recall hurts, we may even horde them. We may be completely justified. But if those who have hurt us genuinely do *t'shuvah*, no matter how long it takes them, it is our job to let go of the anger we long harbored against them.

21. "God decrees the limit(s)" / "God does not want us to die"

    We are mortal. No one lives forever. Some things are simply not in our hands. (We may have a genetic predisposition for breast cancer or manic-depressive illness or heart disease.) But God gives human beings minds to study diseases and sometimes find treatments and cures.

22. "We are dust" / "God is Eternal"

    In 100 years no one may remember that we ever existed. People killed in the Shoah, entire families, entire towns were wiped out without tombstones or yahrzeits. Even without the devastation of near-genocide, immigration and the passage of time alone can erase the past. I knew my grandparents but not their parents. No one is alive anymore who knew that generation of my family. Congregants in another generation will not know that it was we who _____ (fill in any of the accomplishments of which you are most proud). No matter how healthy or careful or cautious or righteous we may be, we all die eventually. The person who dies at 100 is no less mortal than she who dies at 30. We are all mortal.

    But there are elements of the universe that preceded us and that will outlast us: energy, light, change, atoms, force, mass. If kayam means not eternal but essential or enduring then we can include elements of culture and society: love, hate, fear, gratitude, hunger, procreation, longing, and satisfaction as well as ideas such as freedom, responsibility, goodness, evil, justice, truth, and falsehood. When we are long gone civilization will continue without us.

23. I am not claiming that *Un'taneh Tokef* ends with the words "*U'sh'meinu karata bishmecha,*" merely that it climaxes there. In Goldschmidt's edition and in orthodox machzorim (Ashkenazi) "*U'sh'meinu karata bishmecha*" is followed by "*Ashe l'maan...,*" which segues into the K'dushah.

24. From "Sources XV" in *Adrienne Rich's Poetry and Prose A Norton Critical Edition*, selected and edited by Barbara Charlesworth Gelpi and Albert Gelpi, (NY: WW Norton & Co.,1993) p. 108.

25. Hannah Hahn, member of Beth Am, New York, in an e-mail to the author, March 8, 2008.

THE POETRY AND THE POWER OF PARADOX

26. Janet McDowell, member of Beth Am, New York, in an e-mail to the author, March 7, 2008.

27. Marcia Golub, member of Beth Am, New York, in an e-mail to the author, March 7, 2008.

28. At my request, our (former) Music Director, David Feinberg, composed a musical setting to an English translation of *Ein Kitzvah* (as well as to English translations of *Ki k'shimcha* and *Adam y'sodo*).

29. Dan McCracken, member of Beth Am, New York, in an e-mail to the author, March 8, 2008.

30. *Ein Kitzvah* composed in the early 1930s by Reb Koifman-Yidel Idelson recorded on *Chagim uzmanim: Modzitz Classics, Eighteen Songs, Volume One, Sung by Ben Zion Shenker*, Mosdos Modzitz, 1992.

31. *Ein Kitzvah*, was also omitted from *Kavanat ha Lev (Hatenua l'yahadut mitkademet b'Yisrael*, Jerusalem 5749/1988), from the *New Machzor*, edited by Sidney Greenberg and Jonathan Levine (Bridgeport, CT: The Prayer Book Press of Media Judaica, Inc., 1977) but it IS included in *On Wings of Awe*, edited and translated by Richard Levy (Washington DC: B'nai Brith Hillel Foundations, 1985); in the *Mahzor for Rosh Hashanah and Yom Kippur: A Prayer Book for the Days of Awe*, edited by Rabbi Jules Harlow (NY: Rabbinical Assembly, 1972) in *Seder Hatefilot, Forms of Prayer for Jewish Worship Edited by the Assembly of Rabbis of the Reform Synagogues of Great Britain, III Prayers for the High Holidays, 5745-1985*, edited by Jonathan Magonet and Rabbi Lionel Blue (see Musaf for Rosh HaShanah and Yom Kippur, (Finchley, London: The Reform Synagogues of Great Britain) pp. 224ff and 4456ff) and in *Machzor Kol Haneshamah* (Elkins Park, PA: The Reconstructionist Press, 1999).

32. Since the imperfect in Hebrew can be translated either as certain future or, as is often the case in liturgical Hebrew, as the optative (expressing wish or desire) or precative (expressing entreaty, e.g., "*Yivarechecha*... May God bless you and keep you") we have some latitude in understanding the meaning of the plethora of imperfect verbs in this poem.

Many have noticed the strong similarities between the first two stanzas of *Un'taneh Tokef* and *Dies Irae*, from the Requiem Mass of the Roman Catholic liturgy (attributed to Friar Thomas of Celano of the 13th Century). (Eric Werner found an 8th Century Byzantine hymn which may have been the Ur text of both *Dies Irae* and *Un'taneh Tokef.*) What's clear in *Dies Irae*, however, is that the events described therein (e.g., "...the trumpet will assemble all before the throne...the book will be brought forth...the judge will be seated...") are expected to take place not annually but at the end of time on the final Day of Judgment. In contrast, *Un'taneh Tokef's* parallel images: "*uvo tinase malchutecha, v'yachon b'chesed*

MARGARET MOERS WENIG

kishecha; v'teshev alav b'emet … v'tizkor kol hanishkachot, v'tiftach et sefer hazichronot" are all imperfect verbs that are usually translated not as future tense verbs but as present tense verbs, as though these events are taking place as we speak.

What would *Un'taneh Tokef* feel like if we read the imperfect verbs, especially in the first half of the poem not as certain future tense verbs or as present tense verbs (as they are often translated to be) but as optative or precative verbs? It would sound something like this:

> …on this day **may** Your dominion be exalted. **May** Your throne be established in mercy…. **May** You open the book of memories…. As a shepherd seeks out his flock…so may You muster and number…. May You set the bounds of every life and inscribe the decree of their judgment. Please God, on Rosh HaShanah may it be written and on Yom Kippur may it be sealed.

In other words:

> May our fate be determined by You, God, through justice and mercy rather than by human evil or human error or by accident or by arbitrary forces. We look all around us God and some of the wicked prosper and some of the righteous suffer. If only our fate were determined by You, rather than by negligent doctors or drunk drivers or genetic rolls of the dice or parental neglect or human hatred or simply being in the wrong place at the wrong time.

> Please God, may You (not anyone else) set the bounds of every life, may pure truth tempered by loyal love determine our fate. Under those circumstances, repentance, prayer, and righteousness would temper judgment's severe decree. You, who are slow to anger and easy to appease, You would not want anyone to die because of his sins. You, who know our weaknesses, our frailties, our limitations of character and circumstance, You will wait patiently for us to return. And You, who know that ultimately we are but dust, have none the less, linked our name, our essence with Yours.

Related Essays from
CCAR Journal and
Journal of Reform Judaism

Back Issues

II. *Rosh Hashanah Morning*

The voice, imperious, spoke,
And Abraham recalled a long-off day when first
        the voice had called
And said: "Leave now and go!
I am your God, trust Me, have faith!"
And he had left;
Left the ancient nest of home and land,
Trusting in the unseen voice.
And now again the voice, imperious,
Stabbing through to where the very self lay moored.
"Take now your son, your only son, your son so loved.
Take Isaac, wood and knife."
He understood.
Again, again the call to trust
"Trust Me. Have faith."

EPHRAIM M. ROSENZWEIG is Rabbi of Judea Reform Congregation, Durham, North Carolina.

FOR THE DAYS OF AWE

What did he think, that ancient man?
What was his faith?
That God who pledged tomorrows would not cut off today?
Without belief was not his life a stone upon his heart?
Without belief and faith would he not move in endless circling path,
Where with that faith he would move on to destiny?
What did he think, that ancient man?
Standing aloft the mountain reared by time,
Looking down and back into that far-off day,
Do we mock his act of faith?
Do we look with shocked regard upon the knife
Uplifted in the father's hand —
Then do we send our eyes and thoughts in swift survey
      across time past,
And wonder at the lives which lived by faith?

The floods of time . . .
Have they leached out all faith from this our earth, our soul?
Have the rivered rains of time washed out the salt which savored
      for the soul its meat and drink?
Do we in truth believe in nothing but what eyes perceive,
Or mind's extension of our eyes supports
In formula and theorem?
Does truth reside alone in what man can probe and prove?
What then is faith to us?
What is faith when mind is all,
And he who does not see with reasoned proof is blind?

The sun will rise. In this there's faith,
And in the tides,
And in the seasons' greens and browns and reds,
And in the circling stars.
In this there's faith:
That yesterday is wedded to today,
Which in its own turn carries all tomorrows in its womb.
Is this our faith?
Then what is life itself, that we continue on,
Enduring agonies and ills,
Fearing tomorrow, even as we harvest riches from today?
Or what is love if there's no faith
Save in the calculated proof?

Summer, 1973   69

EPHRAIM M. ROSENZWEIG

How simple is that man who thinks
He does not live by faith!
Were there not faith, we could not lie abed at night
For fear of waking in the cradling arms of death
Or to disastered life.
Of if we did awake to anguished life,
We would not press our way with dream and hope
Into another night.
Were there not faith,
Would man and woman take each other's hand,
And binding each to each
Say Amen to life?
—And seed another life
And watch our children grow from strength to strength.
Against all spectral deaths, we live by faith
That there will be another day
And still another, still another day,
And that as we grew from infancy
In far too fast a sweep of time,
So too our children, and so too their own.
What an act of faith is this,
That we commit our lives and theirs to unknown days
Whose nights can fall in terror,
And yet whose sun can rise and set and rise again
With hope.

Who lives without that abject faith?
We do not hear the voice imperious which sends us on our way,
But still it speaks.
And we have faith that life will nourish us with good and strength,
That good will flower if we care for it,
And evil wither from its own self-poisoning.
We live by faith or not at all.

Do not wonder, then, at Abram's faith,
Or at the faith that shored up countless lives.
Their faith was faith in God,
That if for good He touched their lives,
Then give Him thanks!
And if for ill, this too might be for good,
For it is upon a stone the knife is honed.
And who can know what ebb and flow or life

FOR THE DAYS OF AWE

Is cast upon the sands?
Or what today will take, or what
Tomorrow may return.
Standing atop the mountain built by time,
Do we mock the act of faith?
We do not know what moves the heart and soul,
But this we know:
That born into this breed of man,
We rise to life, close the door of day with hopeful sleep,
Seek for each other in friendship and in love,
Bring life to birth, watch over it,
Move hesitantly along the trembling years,
Knowing only that we must have faith
In what we do
And are. And in
A hand that moves our own.
How painful to be man. And yet
What glory crowns our head,
With faith's small candle lighting up the way.

Somewhere is God.
Need He watch over us, as over Abraham?
Or did some fragile spark of His vast light
Ignite the wick of that small candle in the dark,
Which is the faith by which we live?
I do not know,
No more than any man.
It is enough that faith warms life, and lights the way to love,
And though blown to halting flicker by the howling winds of life,
Spring up anew
To light the night
Until the dawn proclaims another day.

Ephraim M. Rosenzweig

The Torah And Haftarah Readings For The High Holy Days

Bernard M. Zlotowitz

The Torah and Haftarah readings of Rosh Ha-Shanah and Yom Kippur are enigmatic. The reason for the selection of the particular Scriptural lessons by the rabbis is intriguing. The Torah readings do not seem truly to represent the meaning of the *Yomam Noraim,* or to convey the awesomeness of the Holy Days and the scriptural significance and edification that one would expect for these special occasions. The question we shall try to answer in this paper is what truly impelled the rabbis to make the selections they did.

I. *High Holy Day Readings*

A. Traditional Readings for Rosh Ha-Shanah

The Scripture reading for the New Year, as laid down by the Mishnah (*Meg.* 3:5), is Lev. 23:23-41. However, by the time of the Gemara, Rosh Ha-Shanah was observed for two days (instead of one as in Mishnaic times). The Talmud, therefore, declared that, "On New Year we read *On the seventh month* (Num. 29:1), and for *haftarah, Is Ephraim a darling son unto me?* (Jer. 31:20). According to others, we read, *And the Lord remembered Sarah* (Gen. 21), and for *haftarah* the story of Hannah (1 Sam. 1). Nowadays that we keep two days, on the first day we follow the ruling of the other authority, and on the next day we say, *And God tried Abraham* (Gen. 22) with *Is Ephraim a darling son to me?* for *haftarah.*"[1]

The basis for the selections by the Mishnah of Lev. 23:23-41 and by the Gemara of Num. 29:1 is obvious: these passages deal with the injunction to observe Rosh Ha-Shanah.[2]

The sounding of the ram's horn is connected with the "binding of Isaac, (Gen. 22)" as reward for Abraham's unquestioning faith; Isaac is spared and a ram is sacrificed in his stead. According to the

BERNARD M. ZLOTOWITZ is rabbi of Temple Sinai of Bergen County, Tenafly, New Jersey.

BERNARD M. ZLOTOWITZ

Midrash, God promises: "Sound before Me a ram's horn so that I may remember on your behalf the binding of Isaac the son of Abraham, and account it to you as if you had bound yourselves before Me."[3]

Gen. 21 is read because God remembered Sarah on the New Year, i.e., she conceived Isaac (*R.H.* 10b). The childless Rachel[4] and Hannah were also remembered on the New Year (*R.H.* 10b) which accounts for these Scriptural readings.

The Talmud applies the hermeneutic principle of *gezerah shava* to justify the readings of Rosh Ha-Shanah: "'On New Year Sarah, Rachel and Hannah were visited.' Whence do we know of this? R. Eliezer said: We learn it from the two occurrences of the word *visiting,* and the two occurrences of the word *remembering.* It is written concerning Rachel, *And God remembered Rachel* (Gen. 30:22), and there is an analogous mention *remembering* in connection with New Year, as it is written, *a solemn rest, a remembering of the blast of the trumpet* (Lev. 23:24). The double mention of visiting [is as follows]: It is written concerning Hannah, *For the Lord had visited Hannah* (Is. 2:21), and it is written concerning Sarah, *And the Lord visited Sarah* (Gen. 21:1)."[5]

The Scriptural lessons for the Day of Atonement are *After the death* (Lev. 16),[6] and for the *haftarah, For thus saith the high and lofty one* (Isa. 57:14-58:14). For the Afternoon Service the reading is Lev. 18 which deals with forbidden marriages, and the *haftarah* is the Book of Jonah.[7]

According to A. Z. Idelsohn, Lev. 16 is read because it gives "an account of the service of the High Priest on that day."[8] The *haftarah* speaks of fast and repentance, which is a logical reading for Yom Kippur. The laws treating of forbidden marriages are read at the *Minhah* service because, according to Rashi (*Meg.* 31a), the temptation to sexual offense is very strong. Jonah serves as a reminder that "there is no escape from God's judgment which . . . may be influenced by repentance."[9]

B. Reform Readings

According to Jakob Petuchowski, "Reform Judaism made its first appearance on the stage of Jewish history as a movement for liturgical reform."[10] The dynamics of reforming the prayer book and arriving at a theology consistent with the contemporary spiritual needs of the Jewish people are reflected in the Scriptural readings selected by different Reform Jewish communities.

THE TORAH AND HAFTARAH READINGS FOR THE HIGH HOLY DAYS

1. Rosh Ha-Shanah
   a. 1858 - Einhorn, David, *Olath Tamid*
      (1) Torah: Gen. 21:1-34
      (2) Haftarah: I Sam. 1,2:1-10
   b. 1866 - Wise, Isaac M., ed., *Minhag America*
      (1) Torah: Gen. 22; Nu. 29:1-6
      (2) Haftarah: Jer. 31:2-21; Ps. 98
   c. 1873 - Szold, B. and Jastrow, M., *Avodath Israel*
      (1) Torah
         (a) First day: Gen. 21:1-31   ) Hebrew
         (b) Second day: Gen. 22:1-24) only:
                                              not translated
      (2) Haftarah: Jer. 31:15-20 (only English)
   d. 1904 - Hamburg Prayer Book
      (1) Torah
         (a) First day: Gen. 21:1-34
         (b) Second day: Gen. 22:1-24
         (c) Both days: Nu. 29:1-6
      (2) Haftarah - none
   e. 1908 - *Seder Tefillah: Israelitische Gebetordnung*, Stuttgart
      (1) Torah
         (a) First day: Gen. 21
         (b) Second day: Gen. 22
         (c) Both days: Nu. 29:1-6
      (2) Haftarah
         (a) First day: I Sam. 1:1-2:10
         (b) Second day: Jer. 31:1-19
   f. 1922 - *Gebetbuch fuer die neue Synagogue*, Berlin
      (1) Torah
         (a) First day: Gen. 21
         (b) Second day: Gen. 22:1-19
      (2) Haftarah
         (a) First day: I Sam. 2:1-10
         (b) Second day: Jer. 31:2-20
   g. 1922 - Union Prayerbook (revised; original 1894)
      (1) Torah: Gen. 22
      (2) Haftarah: Isa. 55 (1922 ed.) but I Sam. 2:1-11 or Neh.
                    8 (1894 ed.).
   h. 1923 - Liberal Jewish Prayer Book, London
      (1) Torah: Dt. 10:12-21a
      (2) Haftarah: Isa. 55:6-13

BERNARD M. ZLOTOWITZ

    i. 1929 - West London Synagogue: *Forms of Prayer,*
          (originally pub. 1840's)
     (1) Torah: Gen. 22:1-19; Nu. 29:1-6
     (2) Haftarah: I Sam. 1:1-2:10
         (read in *Minhah* Service)
    j. 1945 - Union Prayerbook
     (1) Torah: Gen. 22
     (2) Haftarah: I Sam. 2:1-11 or Neh. 8
  2. Yom Kippur
    a. 1858 - Einhorn, David, *Olath Tamid*
     (1) Morning:
       (a) Torah: Lev. 16
       (b) Haftarah: Isa. 57:14-21 and 58
     (2) Afternoon:
       (a) Torah: Lev. 19:1-37
       (b) Haftarah: Book of Jonah
    b. 1866 - Wise, Isaac M., ed., *Minhag America*
     (1) Morning:
       (a) Torah: Lev. 16; Nu. 29:7-11
       (b) Haftarah: Is. 57:14-58:14
     (2) Afternoon:
       (a) Torah: Ex. 32:11-14; 34:1-10
         (Hebrew only)
       (b) Haftarah: Book of Jonah;
         Micah 7:18-20
    c. 1873 - Szold, B. and Jastrow, M., *Avodath Israel*
     (1) Morning:
       (a) Torah: Lev. 16 (Hebrew only)
       (b) Haftarah: Is. 57:14-58:14 (English only)
     (2) Afternoon:
       (a) Torah: Lev. 19:1-18 (Hebrew only)
       (b) Haftarah: Jonah 2:3-10 (English only)
    d. 1904 - Hamburg Prayer Book
     (1) Morning:
       (a) Torah: Lev. 16; Nu. 29:7-11
       (b) Haftarah: none
     (2) Afternoon:
       (a) Torah: Lev. 18 (ed. 1841)
             Lev. 19:1-18 (ed. 1904)
    e. 1908 - Seder Tefillah: *Israelitische Gebetordnung,*
          Stuttgart

THE TORAH AND HAFTARAH READINGS FOR THE HIGH HOLY DAYS

    (1) Morning:
        (a) Torah: says Lev. 18 in error, but gives
                 text from Lev. 16; Nu. 29:7-11
        (b) Haftarah: Isa. 57:14-21; 58:1-14
    (2) Afternoon:
        (a) Torah: Lev. 18
        (b) Haftarah: Jonah 1:1-4:11; Micah 7:18-20
  f. 1922 - *Gebetuch fuer die neue Synagogue,* Berlin
    (1) Morning:
        (a) Torah: Lev. 18
        (b) Haftarah: Isa. 57:14-58:14
    (2) Afternoon:
        (a) Torah: Lev. 19:1-18
        (b) Haftarah: 3:1-4:11
  g. 1922 - Union Prayerbook (revised; original 1894)
    (1) Morning
        (a) Torah: Dt. 29:10-30:6
        (b) Haftarah: Isa. 57:14-58:14
    (2) Afternoon:
        (a) Torah: Ex. 33:12-34:10 (1945 ed. Lev. 19:1-3,
                 9-18, 33-37)
        (b) Haftarah: Jonah 3:1-4:11
  h. 1923 - Liberal Jewish Prayer Book, London
    (1) Morning:
        (a) Torah: Dt. 29:10-15, 29; 30:11-20
        (b) Haftarah: Isa. 57:14-58:14
    (2) Afternoon:
        (a) Torah: Lev. 19:1-4, 9-18
        (b) Haftarah: Jonah 1:1-4:11
  i. 1929 - West London Synagogue: *Forms of Prayer*
         (originally pub. 1840's)
    (1) Morning
        (a) Torah: Lev. 16; Nu. 29:7-11
        (b) Haftarah: Isa. 57:14-58:14
    (2) Afternoon:
        (a) Torah: Dt. 30:1-20
        (b) Haftarah: Jonah 1:1-4:1; Micah 7:18-20
  j. 1945 - Union Prayerbook
    (1) Morning:
        (a) Torah: Dt. 29:9-14; 30:11-20
        (b) Haftarah: Isa. 57:14-58:14

BERNARD M. ZLOTOWITZ

(2) Afternoon:
  (a) Torah: Lev. 19:1-4, 9-18, 33-37
  (b) Haftarah: Jonah 3-4

II. Discussion and Analysis

Why did the rabbis make the particular selections that they did? If we accept their reasons at face value, certain other questions arise: e.g., if the basis of their choice for Rosh Ha-Shanah was that God "remembered," they might have used the rationale equally well that God created the world on Rosh Ha-Shanah (*R.H.* 10b); thus they might have selected the creation story for the Torah reading to commemorate the birthday of the Universe. Why *Adonai pakad* in preference to *Bereshit?* The argument advanced by Ely Pilchik is very cogent: The *Akedah-*story has less immediate relevance to our day than the Creation story.[11] Would not Pilchik's thesis have been equally valid at the time when the readings were canonized during the first centuries of this era? Why then did our sages choose God *remembers* Sarah, Hannah, etc.? The rabbis were certainly not arbitrary in that selection. Unquestionably there was a definite reason and purpose for their selections. Stanley Dreyfus suggests that the Torah and *haftarah* readings for the *Yamim Noraim* have an overall unifying theme: a polemic against Christianity.

Christianity teaches that Jesus was born of a virgin, was crucified as a vicarious atonement for men, was buried and resurrected on the third day. The early Christians were predominantly Jews. Even ben Zoma "converted to Christianity and became a professing Christian."[12] To combat the danger of apostasy, certain rabbis adopted a doctrine similar to that of Christianity, i.e., Judaism also has a Christ-figure, born in a supernatural fashion, who was sacrificed and then rose from the dead. Did not the founders of Reform in the early part of the nineteenth century face a similar situation when thousands of young people were converting to Christianity? They introduced changes in the liturgy influenced perhaps by the Lutheran ritual but kept within the bounds of the Jewish faith. Similarly, the rabbis in the first centuries of this era adopted Torah readings which might effectively combat the fundamental teachings of Christianity and thereby save untold numbers of Jews for Judaism.

To have designated *Bereshit* as the Torah reading for Rosh Ha-Shanah would have played into the hands of the early Jewish-Christians and might have been disastrous for the future of the Jewish community. *Bereshit* describes the creation of the world and the first

THE TORAH AND HAFTARAH READINGS FOR THE HIGH HOLY DAYS

man, Adam. Jesus is considered the second Adam in the New Testament, "the son of Enos, the son of Seth, the son of Adam, the son of God" (Lk. 3:38). " 'The first man Adam became a living being; the last Adam became a life-giving spirit (1 Cor. 15:45)." Thus a reading of the Creation story to commemorate the day of Creation—which would have been logical—was deliberately avoided. Under the circumstances the Rabbis chose a far more relevant passage: the *Akedah*. This passage has all the elements of sacrifice, vicarious atonement, and the necessary mythology to stem the tide of conversion to Christianity. The *Akedah* is an anti-Christian polemic.

> . . .all scholars who have dealt with the *Akedah*-tradition have said, and some have sought to locate the explanation in the collision between Christianity and Judaism . . . the tradition that something was done to Isaac when he lay bound on the altar—certain scholars suggested— —must have originated in times when the supreme sacrifice of the Christian messiah was invoked as demonstration that the complete, the perfect act had been enacted only on Golgotha, that the act on Moriah was only a preamble, a partial adumbration of the greater and full one later. And since those who rejected the Gospels refused to be outdone in manifestations of loving God with all heart and soul and being, they appropriated ideas—said these scholars—that were in actuality anathema to the God of the patriarchs and their descendents.[13]

The Jews, too, have a vicarious atonement in the person of Isaac: He is sacrificed, his blood serves as the redemption of Israel, and he is resurrected: "Now the moment the knife touched Isaac's throat his soul took flight . . . Forthwith the Holy One said to Michael: 'Do not let the father slaughter him.' (And the angel) said to Abraham: 'Lay not thy hand upon the lad.' Whereupon Abraham unbound the lad and his soul returned to him: and he stood upon his feet and recited the resurrection-of-the-dead benediction."[14] Thus Isaac is sacrificed and resurrected. Also his blood serves as a vicarious atonement: "Isaac said to him: Father, have no fears. May it be His will that one quarter of my blood serve as an atonement for all Israel."[15]

Jewish tradition goes one better than Christianity. Unlike Jesus who cried, *Eli, Eli, lama sabachthani?* (Matthew 27:46), Isaac insists that the binding be secure to avoid trembling, so that the sacrifice be a perfect one without blemish.[16]

Isaac, like Jesus, carries his own cross. The Midrash commenting on "And Abraham took the wood for the burnt offering, and put it on his son Isaac" (Gen. 22:6), states that it was "like one bearing his own cross."[17] The parallelism is inescapable.

BERNARD M. ZLOTOWITZ

Though Isaac is the Christ-figure, Judaism could not countenance an immaculate conception. But the rabbis developed something akin to it. "The Lord remembers Sarah." Sarah who is far beyond the age of child-bearing is visited by God and at the age of ninety (Gen. 17:17) conceives and gives birth to Isaac—a miraculous event, indeed. The same concept is continued in the *haftarah*. The childless Hannah miraculously conceives and bears a child. Rachel, too, has a similar experience, but with one major difference. The children of Israel idealize her as the mother-figure par excellence of the Jewish people and invoke her aid, as do Christians with Mary. In a word, Rachel becomes a Jewish surrogate—or Mary-figure. "Rachel weeps for her children" (Jer. 31:15, cf. Matthew 2:18) and "refuses to be comforted." The implication is clear. She is a unique personage, and God must heed the anguish of her soul. The Midrash unveils the mystery of Rachel's privileged access to God:

> Then, with the suddenness of a flash, Rachel our mother stood before the Holy One, blessed be He: "Lord of the world," she said, "Thou knowest how overwhelming was Jacob's love for me, and when I observed that my father thought to put Leah in my place, I gave Jacob secret signs, that the plan of my father be set at naught. But then I repented me of what I had done, and to spare my sister mortification I disclosed the signs to her. More than this: I myself was in the bridal chamber, and when Jacob spake with Leah, I made reply, lest her voice betray her. I, a woman, a creature of flesh and blood, of dust and ashes, was not jealous of my rival. Thou, O God, everlasting King, Thou eternal and merciful Father, why wast Thou jealous of the idols, empty vanities? Why hast Thou driven out my children, slain them with the sword, left them at the mercy of the enemies?" Then the compassion of the supreme God was awakened, and He said: "For thy sake, O Rachel, I will lead the children of Israel back to their land."[18]

Witness the crowds who, to this day, pray at Rachel's tomb, asking her to intercede on their behalf with God. Is this not similar to Roman Catholics who turn to Mary, "Mother of God," to intercede on their behalf?

"From earliest times Mary's intercession was believed to be especially efficacious on behalf of men and the church, and she is called upon to meet every kind of need."[19] Thus the theological refutation of the Christian notion of Christ and Mary is that we Jews, too, have such concepts, but ours are better.

The *payyetanim* (who arose either in the fourth or fifth centuries C.E.), understood the anti-Christological meaning of the Scripture lessons and fought vigorously to suppress the idea of Isaac as a Christ-figure with all the implications thereof. To them the selection

THE TORAH AND HAFTARAH READINGS FOR THE HIGH HOLY DAYS

of the reading of the *Akedah* represented an attempt to account for the blowing of the *shofar*, and/or to remind God that just as Abraham was ready to heed His command to sacrifice his son, *be-zechut zeh* God should similarly heed the petitions of Abraham's descendants and temper Judgment with Compassion (*rahamim*).

Two examples will suffice to highlight the view of the *payyetanim:*

(1) *Tamim paale'cha . . . ke-ma'achelet ha-ma'achila me-az ne'erechet: yahad av u-ven, be-lechtam le-har ha-mor. Tevah le-hachen mi-pekadecha li-shemor. Hinnucham netzor rahamim li-chemor.*[20]

(2) *Asher mi ya'aseh . . . ve-tizkor lamo akedat Yitzhak, ki-shevu'atecha. Ve-tahafoch middat ha-din le-rahamim, ki chen middatecha.*[21]

The link between the blowing of the *shofar* on the High Holy Days and the *Akedah* is very weak. Originally it served as a means of calling the people to war or to drive away evil spirits.[22] Later the *shofar* became associated with the *Akedah:* "All the more does the *shofar* remind God to be kind to His people, because it is made of the horn of a ram. It thus recalls the binding of Isaac and his redemption by a ram. Therefore God recalls that, as He saved Isaac, He is to save His people. He is to save them not only from His harsher judgment, but also from the trials, persecutions they are the victims of, and from their subjection to the nations."[23]

To eradicate any remote resemblance of the Scripture lesson to Isaac as a Christ-like-figure, the *payyetanim* understood *pakod* in the *Musaf* of Rosh Ha-Shanah as "judgment" and not "visited" e.g. in the *U-Netaneh Tokef,* the words *Ve-yomeru, hinneh yom ha-din, li-fekod al tzeva marom ba-din.* The very fact that the *payyetanim* tried to redirect the thrust and meaning of the Rosh Ha-Shanah Scripture lesson is indicative that they understood the original intent of the rabbis: to create a Christ-like-figure in Isaac and thus combat Christianity. The *payyetanim* objected to the portrayal of Isaac as a Christ-figure and successfully discredited this notion. The proof of their success is that later generations did not even relate the *Akedah* passage to anti-Christian polemic but rather to the *shofar*.

A similar rationale—anti-Christian polemic—was used for the selection of the Yom Kippur scriptural lessons. The Torah reading for the morning service is the ritual of the scapegoat, which is merely another form of vicarious atonement. Though this rite was discontinued with the destruction of the Temple in Jerusalem, its concept was so deeply imbedded in the Jewish psyche that a substitute had to

BERNARD M. ZLOTOWITZ

be introduced; namely, the *Kapparot*-ceremony on the morning of
the eve of Yom Kippur. Thus, unlike the Christians, the Jews could
claim two means of vicarious atonement: Isaac the Christ-figure, and
the scapegoat of Lev. 16.

The Haftarah for Rosh Ha-Shanah morning *Ha-ven yakir li
Efrayim* is a further refutation of Christianity's contention that Israel
has been rejected. The Church's claim that it is the true Israel and that
Israel (the Jewish people) has been rejected for denying Jesus is
answered with a resounding "no" in this Haftarah:

> Is Ephraim my dear son?
> Is He my darling child?
> For as often as I speak against him,
>   I do remember him still
> Therefore my heart yearns for him:
>   I will surely have mercy on him,
>   says the Lord.[24]

Though God speaks against Israel, Israel is nevertheless His child on
whom He has mercy.

Jonah (the Yom Kippur Afternoon *haftarah*), too, is the Christ-
figure: As Jonah was in the belly of the fish for three days and then
emerged alive, so Jesus was in the belly of the earth three days and
then emerged (Matthew 12:40). Jonah is an answer to the particularism of Christianity. Christianity taught that salvation is possible only through belief in Jesus. Jonah stands as a refutation of this.
The people of Nineveh repent and God saves them. Belief in God
alone is the path to salvation.

Thus far we have satisfactorily explained the reason for all but
one of the Scriptural selections for the High Holy Days. We have yet
to indicate how the Torah reading for Yom Kippur afternoon fits into
our theory.

Idelsohn attributes to Abudraham the reason for selecting
'arayot (Lev. 18:1-30): "to remind the people of these ethical principles in sexual life."[25] At first glance, this is the most obvious
explanation. The Day of Judgment is the most opportune time to
remind the people of their obligation to observe proper moral conduct. But there is yet another dimension to be considered which is not
readily apparent: the rabbis included *'arayot* primarily as an attack
against Christianity. Paul had taught that once Jesus came, the Law
was no longer obligatory.[26] Such rituals as circumcision, dietary
laws, and Sabbath need no longer be observed. But certain early
Christians, in their zeal to overthrow the Torah, rejected the moral as
well as the ceremonial law. They adopted a libertarianism which the

THE TORAH AND HAFTARAH READINGS FOR THE HIGH HOLY DAYS

leaders of the New Testament times tried to curb. Paul's strong denunciation reflects widespread immoral practices among the new Christians: "It is actually reported that there is immorality among you, and of a kind that is not found even among pagans; for a man is living with his father's wife" (1 Cor. 5:1).

Under the circumstances, what would be more natural as a Scripture lesson for Yom Kippur than 'arayot as an anti-Christian polemic. Proper sexual behavior was the very foundation of Jewish family survival. The message the rabbis preached was that the Christians had lost all sense of moral values; if their faith were embraced, not only would family life be endangered, but the moral level would sink lower than that of the heathen. The heathen certainly would not permit a son to marry his father's wife, yet the Christian, according to Paul, was committing this heinous sin. Even a convert to Judaism is not permitted to violate this basic moral teaching, though he is accounted as a new born child—*Ger she-nitgayer ke-katan she-nolad domeh (Orah Hayyim: 268)*—, on the premise that the Jew could not have a lesser degree of morality than the heathen.

What better Scriptural passage could serve the interests of the Jewish community in their feud with Christianity than that of 'arayot? What would be more natural than to read the laws of forbidden marriages with its emphasis on morality on the holiest day of the year, in contradistinction to the immoral practices of certain early Christians? In the context of the times, this passage was certainly another natural refutation of Christianity.

Harry M. Orlinsky, in another connection, adds strength to our theory when he points out that the term *Mosheh Rabbenu* came into vogue also as an anti-Christian polemic. ". . .it is worth noting that in post-biblical times, Moses came to be called *Mosheh Rabbenu*, 'Moses our Teacher/Master.' I wonder whether the biblical term '*ebed Adonai* for Moses gave way in time to *Rabbenu* because 'Servant of the Lord' had come in Christian circles to designate Jesus; but the matter requires very careful study."[27]

III. The Reform Attitude toward the High Holy Day Scripture Lessons:

The Reform Movement dispensed with the reading of the sacrifices on Yom Kippur and substituted *Attem Nitzavim* (Dt. 29:9-14; 30:11-20). Reform found sacrifices objectionable and thus removed any reference to them from the liturgy. "You stand this day" was a logical substitute, for it encompasses the theme of Yom Kippur, in

BERNARD M. ZLOTOWITZ

that all mankind stands before God in judgment on that day.

Because of the influence of the Victorian ethic, *'arayot* was deleted in favor of the message of justice and brotherly love (Lev. 19). The Reformers could make this change without any qualms because the significance of the original Scripture lessons had lost all meaning for them. The Christ-figure motif had long since been forgotten.

IV. Conclusions

A common thread runs throughout the Torah and *haftarah* readings for the High Holy Days: a polemic against Christianity. The Scriptural readings are interwoven by the same thematic lesson:

1. Isaac and Jonah are savior-type figures; hence, there is no need to seek a Christ in Christianity. Judaism has had one or more all along.

2. "Miraculous" births vis-à-vis God's visiting Sarah, Rachel, and Hannah.

3. Vicarious Atonement: Sacrifice of Isaac and the driving of the scapegoat into the wilderness (Azazel).

4. Forbidden Marriages (*'arayot*): The necessity of maintaining a high degree of morality for family and Jewish survival. To adopt Christianity would mean endangering the moral life of the community, since Christianity has abrogated the whole Torah, including the moral legislation.

Judaism has all the elements of salvation. The Jew need not graze in strange pastures. This is the basic message of the Scripture lessons for Rosh Ha-Shanah and Yom Kippur.

NOTES

[1] *Megillah* 31a (Soncino translation).

[2] Though the biblical passage does not specifically mention Rosh Ha-Shanah (it is the first day of the seventh month), the rabbis interpreted these verses as referring to the New Year.

[3] *R.H.* 16a (Soncino translation).

[4] Rachel is mentioned in the *haftarah* (Jer. 31:15).

[5] *R.H.* 11a (Soncino translation).

[6] *Meg.* 30b.

[7] *Meg.* 31a

[8] Idelsohn, A.Z., *Jewish Liturgy and Its Development*, Henry Holt and Co., 1932, p. 230.

[9] *Ibid.*, p. 233.

[10] Petuchowski, Jacob J., *Prayerbook Reform in Europe*, WUPJ, 1968, pp. XI, XII.

THE TORAH AND HAFTARAH READINGS FOR THE HIGH HOLY DAYS

[11] Pilchik, Ely, "Innovation in the Selection of Torah Readings for the Holy Days," *CCAR Journal*, No. 16, Jan., 1957, p. 46.

[12] Levey, Samson, R., "The Best Kept Secret of the Rabbinic Tradition," *Judaism*, Fall, 1972, p. 463.

[13] Spiegel, Shalom, *The Last Trial*, Schocken Brooks, New York, 1967, pp. XIII, XIV.

[14] *Ibid.*, p. 30.

[15] *Ibid.*, p. 45.

[16] *Gen. Rabba* 56:5.

[17] *Gen. Rabba* 56:3. I am grateful to Rabbi Ronald Brown for bringing this Midrash to my attention.

[18] Ginzberg, Louis, *The Legends of the Jews*, JPS (1945), Vol. IV, p. 310.

[19] *Columbia Encyclopedia*, 3rd ed., 1963, *s.* "Mary," p. 1320.

[20] From the *piyyutim* of the Rosh Ha-Shanah service.

[21] *Ibid.*

[22] Finesinger, Sol B., "The Shofar," *HUCA* (VIII-IX), 1931-32, pp. 193-228.

[23] *Ibid.*, p. 216.

[24] Jer. 31:20.

[25] Idelsohn, *op. cit.*, p. 233.

[26] Galatians 3:24-25; 4:18.

[27] Orlinsky, Harry M., "The so-called 'Servant of the Lord' and 'Suffering Servant' in Second Isaiah," Supplements to *Vetus Testamentum*, Vol. XIV, Leiden, E. J. Brill, 1967, p. 10.

(This is part of a paper submitted in fulfillment of the minor for the D.H.L. I am thankful to Professor Stanley Dreyfus for suggesting this topic to me and for his invaluable help in the preparation of this paper.)

Gate of Repentance: A Review-Essay

Eric L. Friedland

Gate of Repentance, by John D. Rayner and Chaim Stern, London: Union of Liberal and Progressive Synagogues, 1973–5733, 500 pages.

PRAYER, LITURGY OR RITUAL are hardly the all-absorbing, burning issues they once were. Yet liturgical creativity has hardly been snuffed out. The last few years have seen the appearance of the Conservative *Mahzor for Rosh Hashanah and Yom Kippur,* edited by the craftsmaster Jules Harlow, and the much-lionized Reform *New Union Haggadah.* The Central Conference of American Rabbis has recently brought out its revamped *Union Prayer Book,* renamed *Gates of Prayer.* Others, official or nonconformist, in print or oral, are still in the making. Our English counterparts have made their contribution with the winsome and graceful matching volumes, *Service of the Heart,* for the weekday, the Sabbath and the Festivals, and *Gate of Repentance* (henceforth to be referred to, if disconcertingly, as GOR), for the High Holy Days. Both of the lastnamed prayerbooks are reaching these shores in much altered shape under the Reform movement in the United States. The books may be said to act simultaneously as a harbinger of what the new American Reform liturgy will bring and as partial evidence of where it is today theologically. The rite under review, GOR, is truly admirable in many respects, beginning with its attractive and compact format. It is marked by a fluent, proportionate and lucid style, a fresh religious candor, a revived but unconstricting appreciation for tradition, and an unshy love for Israel. The authors, John Rayner and Chaim Stern, drew upon earlier models, transformed them, fitted them in new settings, so that the end result is uniquely and patently theirs.

Two influences that loom large in the present High Holy Day manual are the *Union Prayer Book* (UPB) II and the *Liberal Jewish Prayberook* (LJPB; London, rev. 1937), the latter by

ERIC I. FRIEDLAND is Associate Professor of Judaics, Wright State University, Dayton, Ohio.

Israel I. Mattuck (1883-1954). The ground plan began chiefly with these, attended by significant changes, to be sure. Key sections, like the highly meditative Memorial Service on Yom Kippur (In GOR minus the haunting, slightly theatrical tone, as struck in the choral refrain, "O, what is man, the child or dust? What is man?"; with the *yizkor* prayer and *el malé rahamim* both restored) and Ne'ilah (going all the way back to David Einhorn's German version in his *'Olat Tamid*), are all clear borrowings from the UPB and LJPB, now not quite as elevated or melodramatic.

The imprint of Mattuck can be recognized in a number of instances, here happily for the good (as the elder compiler could on occasion advance rather whimsical, unconventional arrangements). Among the less eccentric features from Mattuck continued, or expanded upon, in GOR may be reckoned the free use of material from the Psalms, the retention of the entire Book of Jonah for reading during the Afternoon Service (a somewhat unusual procedure in Reform prayerbooks), the enrichment of the customary text with extraliturgical and not infrequently non-Jewish pieces (in the case of GOR, for example, poems by Rilke, Madame Blavatsky, Shelley, and an item by Karl Jaspers, to be produced below, are taken in), and the inclusion of ample illuminating notes at the end of the volume. Strictly speaking, one of the prayerbooks to embody the category Jakob J. Petuchowski tellingly labels "Independent Reform," GOR departs from this very category by incorporating a Musaf for Yom Kippur (though none for Rosh Hashanah). The only comparable rites from this side of the Atlantic to reserve an Additional Service solely for the most solemn of days are Leo Merzbacher's *Order of Prayer*, II (New York, 1863) and Adolph Huebsch's German-language *Gebete für den öffentlichen Gottesdienst*, II (New York, 1875).

It is to be noted that generally Musaf and Minḥah, under Independent Reform, dexterously coalesced into a single service, as done for the first time in Einhorn's *'Olat Tamid* and afterwards adopted in the UPB. Whereas the Amidah for Musaf in Mattuck's prayerbook, GOR's antecedent, amounted to a downright deformation, to the extent of utilizing only the last two benedictions, together with the Priestly Blessing, the revision in GOR takes us by pleasant surprise with a trim digest of the Amidah for the Additional Service, in the manner of the ancient Amidah-extracts, as the *Havinenu* for the weekday and *Magen Avot* for Friday night. (Incidentally, unlike either the UPB or the LJPB,

ERIC L. FRIEDLAND

the GOR does furnish an Amidah that is substantially intact for the Afternoon Service on Yom Kippur.) The creators of GOR do seem now and then to feel constrained to compress, in order to allow time for their rewrite of Mattuck's novel, if effusive, section on the meaning of Jewish history, touched off by the Avodah (emphasizing, in the long-standing Reform view, Israel as God's priest-people bringing atonement and reconciliation to mankind). GOR passes on and elaborates Mattuck's original scheme by taking into account, in a sensitive and moving fashion, the Holocaust and the rebirth of the State of Israel as signposts in a still-unfinished historical drama of salvation.

A debt is owed still another liturgical trailblazer that has not inconsiderably affected contemporary expectations of what a Jewish service of worship should consist of: the Reconstructionist two-volume Maḥzor, first issued in 1948. An important example of GOR's prudent borrowing is its use of the Reconstructionist grand, and very up-to-date, opening to the Avodah — indeed, the long history of Jewish liturgical productivity attests to the proliferation of poetical reworkings of the preamble to the Avodah proper — with a portrayal of humanity's emergence out of a teeming primeval cosmos. Though here slightly worked over for stylistic improvement, Eugene Kohn's Reconstructionist equivalent to the medieval prefatory *Amitz Koaḥ* (Ashkenazic) and *Attah Konanta* (Sephardic) still has its capacity to move the worshipper of the latter half of the twentieth century. Rayner and Stern did well to embrace Kohn's re-creation.

What can be detected from the way the borrowings were made is a reanimated respect in GOR for liturgical form, without that prayerbook's being classified among those *siddurim* that come under the rubric of Petuchowski's "Reform from Within." Fortunately, however, elasticity, innovation and contemporaneity are by no means lost thereby. Hebrew accompanies virtually every text, irrespective of whether the sacred tongue or the vernacular is employed in the actual service. Home observance is accorded full attention. The hitherto absent *Birkat Ha-Mazon* and *Havdalah,* with startlingly detailed instructions exceptional even in traditional *maḥzorim,* occupy a prominent position in the present volume. By the way, the *Ha-Mavdil* poem for the end of Rosh Hashanah has the appropriate refrain *'shanah tovah!'* in place of the familiar *'shavu'a tov.'* These restorations in GOR make up a healthy corrective to an almost anarchic shapelessness under Mattuck's sway — which, it must be confessed, did have its bright, expansive moments — without suppressing the compilers' literary inspiration, creative instincts and religious quest.

Instances of liturgical inventiveness and fresh spiritual perspectives abound. The labors of others, olden and modern, serve as springboards for the authors' own ruminations and endeavors. To Chaim Stern credit is due for some of his poetic outpourings included in this manual, as this one from the beginning of the Rosh Hashanah Eve Service:

> We are weak, and the task seems hopeless,
> until we remember that we are not alone.
> There is a grace that every dawn renews,
> a loveliness making every daybreak fresh.
> We will endure, we will prevail, we shall see
> the soul restored to joy,
> the hand returned to strength,
> the will regain its force.
> We shall ride with hope — we, the children of
> him who crowded the heavens with stars,
> endowed the earth with glory,
> and filled our souls with wonder.

The *Viddui* ("confessional") comes to life with its full alphabetical complement (as against the former three-word formula similar to the one found in Daniel 9:5 and, to my knowledge, first employed by David Einhorn); and so does a longer '*Al Ḥet* with a harder-hitting and more plain-spoken selection of verses from the traditional Ashkenazic litany of sins than the generalized and near-innocuous ones encountered in the UPB (and thence in the LJPB) turns up in the GOR. The novelty lies in a new supplementary all-English '*Al Ḥet* which follows that is probing and disarmingly frank. The worshipper can no longer hide behind the supposed impertinence of the charges levelled: the language is today's. The conscience is once more prodded. The passage deserves to be quoted *in toto*.

> We sin against You when we sin against ourselves.
>   For our failures of truth, O Lord, we ask forgiveness.
> For passing judgment without knowledge of the facts;
>   and for distorting facts to fit our theories.
> For deceiving ourselves and others with half-truths;
>   and for pretending to emotions we do not feel.
> For using the sins of others to excuse our own;
>   and for denying our responsibility for our own misfortunes.

ERIC L. FRIEDLAND

> For condemning in our children the faults we tolerate in
>   ourselves;
>   and for condemning in our parents the faults we tolerate in
>   ourselves.
> For nurturing racial prejudice;
>   and for denying its existence.
>
> We sin against You when we sin against ourselves.
>   For our failures of love, O Lord, we ask forgiveness.
> For confusing love with lust;
>   and for pursuing fleeting pleasure at the cost of lasting hurt.
> For using others as a means to gratify our desires;
>   and as stepping-stones to further our ambitions.
> For taking advantage of people weaker than ourselves;
>   and treating with condescension those whom we suppose to be
>   inferior to us.
> For withholding love to control those we claim to love;
>   and shunting aside those whose age is an embarrassment to us.
> For hiding from others behind an armour of mistrust;
>   and for the cynicism which eats away our faith in the possibility
>   of unselfish love.
>
> We sin against You when we sin against ourselves.
>   For our failures of justice, O Lord, we ask forgiveness.
> For keeping the poor in the chains of poverty;
>   and turning a deaf ear to the cry of the oppressed.
> For using violence to maintain our power;
>   and for using violence to bring about change.
> For waging aggressive war;
>   and for the sin of appeasing aggressors.
> For poisoning the air, and polluting land and sea;
>   and for all the evil means we employ to accomplish good ends.
>
>   *All*
> For all these sins, O forgiving God, teach us to forgive ourselves,
>   and help us to overcome them.

Another equally pointed *Viddui*, pitched in a somewhat different key, comes into view on pages 354–356.

It is clear from the foregoing that the penitential character of the Day of Atonement is nowise lost or slighted; nonetheless, concern and regret for past misdeeds and resolution to amend do not serve as the solitary focus of the day's worship. Another motif, up till the present time not all the paramount, asserts itself with greater urgency, qualifying the former primarily introspective cast of the day: the Jews' collective self-affirmation as a people (cf. p. viii). Religio-ethnic self-definition and group rein-forcement are underscored in the main to a degree hitherto unknown in twentieth-century Reform prayerbooks. Yom Kippur now cries for the reunion of the whole House of Israel. Recon-structionism, the Columbus Platform of 1937, the revival of the Jewish state, the resurgence of ethnic awareness in our time doubtless conduced in stages to the significant change of mood noticeable in GOR. The current condition of the Jewish com-munity, especially in lands of relative equality and ease, a high rate of assimilation, intermarriage, intensifying secularization, forces the High Holy Day synagogue-goers to consider in imme-diate, concrete terms whither they are tending *qua* people. This consideration, couched liturgically and pressingly, is most likely unprecedented. Aḥad Haam's foreboding of servitude amid free-dom finds indirect expression here. The recovery of the entire *Tzur Yisrael* ("O Rock of Israel, redeem . . .") before the Morning Amidah in place of the previous mutilated Reform version and the reproduction elsewhere of Jeremiah 31:31–34 point out this new-found preoccupation with the survival, unity and health of the Jewish people.

Zion has come to figure more and more prominently in Reform rites, long known for expurgating the all but ubiquitous references in the classical Siddur to the return to and restoration of Israel's historic abode. The GOR goes beyond merely conforming with this "Zionizing" trend—a turn already discernible in the earlier SOH (1967), where prayers on behalf of the State of Israel are offered up and a section on that beleaguered republic is included in the division of the prayerbook devoted to special themes—by admitting in GOR, within a special reading during Musaf on the significance of Jewish history, a not inconsiderable part that dilates on the wonder of Israel's rooting itself once more on its ancient soil. Some six pages focus on this theme with relevant passages from Scripture, among them Ezekiel's familiar chapter on the dry bones resurrected (i.e. the people of Israel *redivivus*) and buoyant and thrilling verses from Deutero-Isaiah. The ex-ultant, proud tone in the preceding passages in no way entails dropping classical Reform's stress on the universalist side of Judaism. Our editors make sure of that, for one, by adhering to Mattuck's original *heilsgeschichtlich* scheme and bringing the whole section to an end that is world-encompassing in the prophetic and messianic sense. For a clincher, they artfully enlist an epigram by Karl Jaspers:

ERIC L. FRIEDLAND

> This is the vision of a great and noble life;
> to endure ambiguity and to make light shine through it;
> to stand fast in uncertainty;
> to prove capable of unlimited love and hope —

and, from other parts of the traditional Maḥzor, the universalist *Ve-Yeetayu, Melokh 'Al Kol Ha-Olam* and the *Alenu* (the first paragraph supranationally emended). The relocation of the last-named prayer arrests the reader's attention — and not altogether inappropriately — as the *Alenu* normally leads the way to the Avodah. When the overall design and nationale are understood, the almost drastic rearrangement can be respected.

The prayerbook under discussion unquestionably constitutes a marked and gratifying improvement over the ones prevailing before now. Given the varied aims underlying the creation of GOR and the huge nature of the task, it is almost inevitable that criticisms, chiefly of the technical sort, would have to be made. To start with, none of the *Birkhot Ha-Shaḥar,* or Preliminary Blessings, have their terminating clauses, the ḥatimah (the closing *barukh attah . . .*), even though most of the same ones did in the prior companion volume SOH. No explanation for the omission is forthcoming either in the preface or in the footnotes. Unlike prayerbooks subsumed under the category of Independent Reform, GOR interposes a Kaddish, of the "non-mourning" variety, between the different services on Yom Kippur, specifically between the Morning Service and the Additional Service, between the Additional Service and the Afternoon one. What makes this Kaddish unusual is that it is not the wonted Kaddish *titkabbel* but a *Ḥatzi*-Kaddish, which, of course, is a good deal shorter. A question might be raised: why bother at all even with this half-measure? It is noteworthy, nevertheless, that for the interval between Minḥah and the Memorial Service, the authors introduce, after the pattern of older German Liberal *maḥzorim,* a lofty and lilting *piyyut* by Judah Halevi inspired by the Kaddish in place of the expected transitional, "inter-service" Kaddish, possibly since the Mourner's Kaddish is subsequently recited in full during the Yizkor Service. Then, the last Kaddish for the day in GOR is the traditional *Ḥatzi*-Kaddish chanted before the Amidah of the Concluding Service. Interestingly, many American Reform synagogues of the last century insisted on a Kaddish of this "non-mourning" type just for this one case, during Ne'ilah. A precursor of the UPB, the aforementioned A. Huebsch's *Gebete,* has it; so several decades later did a special edition of the UPB itself, designed for those temples which wanted that Kaddish with its yearning and triumphant melody.

A more serious comment might be added on the probably unintended examples of sexism scattered throughout GOR. To cite a single instance, the phrase in the spirited "Partisans' Song" that reads *undzer gevure* is rendered as 'our manhood' (p. 304). What of the valiant Hannah Senesh, whose "Blessed is the Match" has a place in this volume (pp. 307–308)?

Just a year before the London-based Union of Liberal and Progressive Synagogues issued its GOR, the Rabbinical Assembly of America (Conservative) published its *Maḥzor for Rosh Hashanah and Yom Kippur* (New York, 1972) in a striking format. The editor is the discriminating and masterly Jules Harlow. Although there is no mistaking which is the more traditional and which the more radical, the convergences between GOR and the Harlow work are dramatic and numerous, all the more so perhaps since the begetters of the separate rites did not confer with each other in the preparation of their respective prayerbooks. A few comparisons will bear out the astonishing parallelisms and, in not a few cases, actual duplication in conviction, taste and form. Both share:

1. the martyred Hillel Zeitlin's poem of religious longing ('One hint of Your eternal Presence/And I am refreshed with the dew of youth') (Harlow, pp. 44–45; GOR, p. 51);
2. a scansion of the *illu finu* paragraph ('though our mouths overflow with song as the sea ...') from *Nishmat* in verse (Harlow, p. 103; GOR, p. 53), to which the Hebrew so easily lends itself;
3. the use of the stately Psalm 103 (Harlow, pp. 388–391; GOR, pp. 135–137), meet and right for a Yom Kippur service but long missing in the Ashkenazic rite, though at hand in the Sephardic one all along;
4. *Elleh Ezkerah* (the rabbinically-derived account of the Ten Martyrs), abbreviated and joined with an updated martyrology (Harlow, pp. 554–569; GOR, pp. 287–304; the nearness of the survivors to the horrible events of the Holocaust may well explain the divergence in length and detail in this portion of the service);
5. the same passage from the Apocryphal Ben Sira (Ecclus. 50:5 ff.) eulogizing the High Priest during the Avodah (Harlow, pp. 612–613; GOR, p. 275);
6. the highly ethical Leviticus 19 either as a replacement (GOR,

ERIC L. FRIEDLAND

pp. 338–340) or as a possible alternative (Harlow, pp. 628–
631) to the traditional lesson, Lev. 18, with its formidable list
of prohibited sexual relations, for reading during Minḥah;

7. a Memorial Service that is treated as an independent, self-
contained service in its own right (Harlow, pp. 684–694;
GOR, pp. 365–379), appearing directly before Ne'ilah, according to well-established Reform usage;

8. the Sephardic Ne'ilah hymn, *El Nora 'Alilah* (Harlow,
pp. 720–721 – with a misspelled *she'at* instead of *sha'at*; GOR,
pp. 405–406), an oldtime favorite in Reform and Liberal
prayerbooks of the last century;

9. a translation of *Ashamnu* in alphabetic acrostic after the model
of the original (Harlow, p. 461 and others; GOR, p. 215; both
having "xenophobic" for "x," and the British one "we have
forgotten Zion" for 'z'; and

10. poignant questioning of God for His silence (somewhat muted
in Harlow's *Elleh Ezkerah* and more pronounced in GOR, as
on pp. 298–300).

The enumeration above may be faulted for not mentioning the
many fitting prose and poetic selections of European, American
and Israeli writers, apart from the prayerbook compilers themselves, that bestow on GOR – and the new Conservative Maḥzor,
too – immediacy, appositeness and much appeal.

   In sum, what we see in the High Holy Day prayerbook out of
London is a high level of literary maturity combined with extraordinary theological frankness and integrity, both byproducts of
Diaspora Jews' acculturation and sophistication in abidingly
liberal and hospitable lands of their habitation, and a bracing
presentday response to an ancient tradition that constantly re-
news itself. We shall be under obligation for a long time to Rabbis
John Rayner and Chaim Stern for empowering us to sound
that response.

———————

Historical Notes on the American Reform High Holy Day Liturgy

Eric L. Friedland

Both the High Holy Day *Gates of Repentance (Sha'arei Teshuva)*[1] and *Gates of Understanding (Sha'arei Bina) II*,[2] its commentary, have been with us for a little while, enough for us to have a feel for them. Both, as all of the liturgical works in the *Gates* series, represent a watershed in the steady evolution of Reform Jewish worship. They are a helpful gauge by which we can measure the extent and depth of Jewish theological and ethnic commitment in Reform Jewry and its spiritual leadership. The movement's High Holy Day prayerbook may be its clearest statement, if only because of its highly concentrated character and religious intensity. This comes out equally in the handbook explaining the Reform *machzor*'s layout, text, and rationale, the clear and useful *Gates of Understanding II*.

Doubtless because of limits of space, of intended audience, and possibly of resources, the editors did not spend much time in showing the vicissitudes of certain prayers in Reform liturgy. The details of the development in Reform and other non-Orthodox forms of prayer are in themselves instructive and quite respectable, and deserve no less than the traditional forms to be reverently and proudly recorded for posterity. Tracing the kaleidoscopic mutations of the classical *siddur* and *machzor* as exemplified in the American non-Orthodox rites can be quite an edifying exercise. The Reform rite in the United States has a rich, variegated background that is waiting to be fully chronicled.

In the few pages that follow I would like to discuss some of the ways in which certain prayers or sections of the liturgy for the *Yamim Nora'im* came to be the way they are. From time to time some of my own personal reactions will be shared with the reader.

ERIC L. FRIEDLAND is the Harriet Sanders Professor of Judaic Studies at United Theological Seminary/University of Dayton/Wright State University in Dayton, Ohio.

ERIC L. FRIEDLAND

Let me mention a couple of slip-ups at the start, so that we may get on with the exploration into the background of some of the revised texts in *Gates of Repentance* and *Gates of Understanding II* and see how and why they came to be the way we now know them. In a work on such a scale as the new commentary on the Reform *machzor*, one cannot totally keep from committing oversights or always prevent an occasional error from creeping in.

In note 71 on page 172, in the sentence beginning, "Unlike the British *Liberal Jewish Prayer Book*[3] and *Gate of Repentance*[4] (p. 29), which place this passage *Meloch al kol ha-olam* in the *Kedushat Hayom* ... we keep it in its traditional place...," there is a snafu. The traditional place happens to be *Kedushat Hayom*; the British Liberal prayerbooks went their own way by putting the passage in question in the *Kedushat Hashem* section instead.

With regard to note 64 of *Gates of Understanding II*, on the previous page, in the emendation introduced by Chaim Stern and John Rayner in *Gate of Repentance* (and subsequently taken over by the American *Gates of Repentance*), the second of the *Uvechen* paragraphs in the High Holy Day *Amida* that stands out in relation to all the prior editions of the *Union Prayer Book II* has not as much to do with "and cause the light of redemption to dawn for all who dwell on earth" as with Stern's and Rayner's restoration of the traditional clause "fill Your land with gladness and Your city with joy." By contrast, a literal translation of the old *Union Prayer Book*'s non-particularist Hebrew rewrite of the traditional text would read something like "joy to all who dwell on earth and the sprouting of [messianic] might for those who proclaim the unity of Your name." Retaining Reform's universalism and leaving the Davidic Messiah out of the picture, Rayner and Stern now recall Jerusalem, to a large extent in the language of the classical *machzor*.

In continuity with the antecedent editions of the *Union Prayer Book II*, the *Gates of Repentance* concludes the day-long Yom Kippur services, after the last blast on the *shofar* and before *Havdala*,[5] with an apt benediction:

And now, at the close of this day's service, we implore You, O Lord our God:

Let the year upon which we have entered be for us, for Israel, and for all the world,

A year of blessing and prosperity.

Amen.

HISTORICAL NOTES ON THE HIGH HOLY DAY LITURGY

A year of salvation and comfort.

Amen.

A year of peace and contentment, of joy and of spiritual welfare.

Amen.

A year of virtue and of reverence for God.

Amen.

A year that finds the hearts of parents united with the hearts of their children.

Amen.

A year of Your pardon and favor.

Amen.

Adonai yishmor tsetecha uvo-echa me-ata ve-ad olam.

May the Lord bless your going and your coming from this time forth and for ever.

Amen.

It provides the right touch. The benediction is actually an adaptation of the entreaty uttered by the High Priest as he quitted the Holy of Holies on this solemn day — with Psalm 121:8 tacked on. Because it went unused in its proper place during the *Avoda* in the *Union Prayer Book*, inasmuch as it did not seem timed just so, the 1894 compilers settled upon relocating it at the end of Yom Kippur services and prefacing it with "And now we implore Thee once more, O Lord, our God, at the close of this day's service, in the words of the high-priest of yore: / Let the year..." A word of explanation in *Gates of Understanding II* about this transfer would have been welcomed and doubtless have evoked interest.

The *Kaddish* and Related Items

In line with the *Gates of Prayer*'s reclamation of a form of the *Kaddish* other than the Mourner's *Kaddish*, namely the Half-*Kaddish* before the *Barechu* in the Evening and Morning Services,

ERIC L. FRIEDLAND

Gates of Repentance carries on by reinstalling the *Chatzi Kaddish* before the *Amida* during the *Ne'ila*.

Although the *Union Prayer Book* has always had a tender hymn on this spot, many a Reform temple reserved the right to have the *Chatzi Kaddish* chanted before the last *Amida* for the day, probably because of its special pleading and moving melody. The Union of American Hebrew Congregations produced decades ago a recording, *Selected Liturgical Music for the High Holy Days,* in which Cantor Frederick Lechner of New York's Central Synagogue at the time and a choir sang this *Chatzi Kaddish.* In the Hebrew/German rite[6] prepared by Adolph Huebsch (1830-84) when the New York congregation bore its older name, Ahawath Chesed, the only *Chatzi Kaddish* to appear *at all* is the one before the *Amida* during *Ne'ila.*

It is good to be reminded that the *Kaddish* acts as more than a prayer on behalf of the departed. Both *Gates of Prayer* and *Gates of Repentance* go a long way toward correcting a popular misapprehension, like as not, aided and abetted by the former editions of the *Union Prayer Book* which used the *Kaddish* solely as a prayer for the deceased.

My reservation has to do with labeling, in the *Gates* prayerbooks, the *Chatzi Kaddish* in English as the "Reader's *Kaddish,*" even though it is that, in addition to serving as a pause between one unit of Jewish worship and another. It is, however, admittedly strange calling this type of *Kaddish* a "Half-*Kaddish,*" as is commonly done and as if it were somehow worth a half a mass or some such thing. The Sephardim have the good judgment to refer to it as *Kaddish Le'eila,* which may be a solution to the oddity of using a numerical fraction for the name of a prayer. As for the designation of "Reader's *Kaddish,*" it, strictly speaking, applies to the *Kaddish Titkabel* (so called because of the extra paragraph inserted, starting with the word *Titkabel*), also tagged as *Kaddish Shalem.*

Gates of Repentance is the very first *Union Prayer Book* to have a *Kaddish Shalem,* though it is hard to ascertain just what the grounds are for reintroducing it on Yom Kippur, right before the final crowning *Shema.* Is it perhaps because people are accustomed to hearing a *Kaddish* spoken minutes before a service is over; or is it a way of letting the worshiping throng know that there is even another category of *Kaddish* with its specific request that our "divine Parent accept the prayers and supplications" (*Titkabel tzelotehon uva'utehon. . .*) intoned all this day? It is interesting that the *Union Prayer Book*'s principal archetype, *Olath Tamid,* by David Einhorn,[7] had only one other *Kaddish* of

HISTORICAL NOTES ON THE HIGH HOLY DAY LITURGY

the non-mourning variety, a *Kaddish Titkabel* doing its duty as a kind of hiatus between the Morning and Afternoon Services.[8]

In *Gates of Understanding II*, Lawrence Hoffman shares the view that an affinity exists between the *Kaddish* and the Lord's Prayer because both are eschatologically-oriented.[9] In what was originally his doctoral dissertation on the evolution of the *Kaddish*, the later American Sephardic Rabbi David de Sola Pool declared the *Paternoster* "the twin sister of the Kaddish."[10] I would offer for consideration the alternative theory that the most celebrated prayer credited to Jesus corresponds more closely to the *Tefila Ketzara* or any of those private prayers composed by rabbinic Sages for their own personal use.[11] In addition to looking forward to God's kingdom, the *Kaddish*, as a doxology, raptly heaps praises on God, which the Lord's Prayer does not. Like the rabbinic *Tefila Ketzara*, the Lord's Prayer does petition God to fulfill one's personal needs ("Give us this day our daily bread").

One of the outstanding preachers of his day, the radical Reform Rabbi Joseph Krauskopf (1858-1923), tinkered with the *Kaddish* itself — by substituting in Hebrew and in English biblical verses pertaining more directly to the themes of death and immortality[12] — but this drastic liturgical overhaul was to last only during his rabbinic tenure at Keneseth Israel in Philadelphia. It is remarkable, too, that his *Kaddish* was the longest Hebrew prayer of any in his entire exceptional ritual. Incidentally, until little under a decade ago it was not all that unusual to hear in British Reform (as opposed to Liberal) synagogues the *Kaddish* recited wholly in Hebrew rather than in Aramaic.[13] Now only the customary *Kaddish* is recited, and the Hebrew *Kaddish*, the British Reformers' or Krauskopf's, linguistically faultless as either one was, is no more than a passing curiosity. Though enjoying unwonted staying power in non-Orthodox prayerbooks for nearly two centuries, the *Kaddish* with the innovatory paragraph *Al Yisra'el ve'al tzadikaya* (freely paraphrased in the old *Union Prayer Book* as "The departed whom we now remember have entered into the peace of life eternal. . .") is all but passé. In the *Gates of Prayer* and *Gates of Repentance*, the Mourner's *Kaddish* is nowadays exactly the same as the Orthodox one.

There is a natural conservative tendency when it comes to rites associated with death, but even here changes in another direction can be detected. The changing circumstances of the Memorial Service on Yom Kippur echo the evolving conceptions of death and afterdeath. The last stanza of the perdurable *piyut* sung on Kol Nidrei night, "*Ya'aleh Tachanuneinu*" ("Unto You with contrite spirits"), is rendered in *Petach Teshuva* as

ERIC L. FRIEDLAND

May our supplications find You
In the quiet of the eve,
And Your hand with each new morning
Send us succour and reprieve:
That Your love and mercy guide us
When our earthly home we leave.

A comparison between the introductions to the *Kaddish* in *Gates
of Repentance* with either the older *Union Prayer Book* or *Petach
Teshuva*, too, will reveal a growing American hesitancy to be all
that definitive about life beyond the grave. The British Liberal —
and Reform — prayerbooks have to date not let on any qualms
about the indestructibility of the human soul in the afterlife. Not a
single edition of the *Union Prayer Book II*, including the preliminary 1893 edition, was ever without the calming hymn at the start
of *Ne'ila*, as a rule immediately before the final *Amida* of the day:

The sun goes down, the shadows rise,
The day of God is near its close,
The glowing orb now homeward flies
A gentle breeze foretells repose;
Lord, crown our work before the night;
In the eve let there be light.

While still in clouds the sun delays,
Let us soar up, soar to heaven;
That love may shed its peaceful rays,
New hope unto our souls be given.
O may the parting hour be bright:
In the eve let there be light.

And when our sun of life retreats,
When evening shadows 'round us hover,
Our restless heart no longer beats,
And grave-ward sinks our earthly cover.
We shall behold a glorious sight:
In the eve there shall be light.[14]

The fact that the hymn caught on as it did, even in liberal Conservative rites like Szold's and Jastrow's *Abodath Israel* and its
successor, *Seder Avodah* (where the editor Max D. Klein translated the entire hymn into Hebrew, *Hashemesh Yifneh*[15]), points
to its deep-seated esthetic, theological, and emotional drawing
power. Preempting *Petach Teshuva*'s stylistic adaptation of the
closing stanza with

HISTORICAL NOTES ON THE HIGH HOLY DAY LITURGY

> And when the end of life draws near,
> And darkness threatens to enfold us,
> We shall not be dismayed by fear,
> Our trust in You will still uphold us.
> With You, eternity is bright:
> In the evening there shall be light.

attests American Reform's former certainty about the world-to-come ebbing into a class of pious ambiguity.[16]

Aleinu

Drawing upon his expertise in Rabbinics and Gaonica, Hoffman wrote a fine-tuned essay on the origins of the *Aleinu*.[17] There is, however, scarce a word on the prayer's ups and downs in the American Reform rite.

Although there are basically three Hebrew versions of the *Aleinu* in *Gates of Prayer*, only two of these find their way into *Gates of Repentance*. The missing version is the Stern/Rayner one in *Service of the Heart*[18] and *Petach Teshuva* which has the advantage of striking a happy balance between particularism and universalism without any of the negative language as in the preface of the traditional *Aleinu*.

Since the British revampment is incongruously translated in *Gates of Prayer* (p. 620), here is the fairly literal translation as it appears in the Stern/Rayner rites:

> Let us now praise the Lord of all, the Maker of heaven and earth; for He chose us to make known His unity, and called us to proclaim Him King.
> We bow...

Sound as it is doctrinally and literarily, this emendation really should have been allowed to stand in the English, degenderized, along with the Hebrew.

Unlike *Petach Teshuva*, *Gates of Repentance* provides an *Aleinu* not only at the conclusion of the service, but also one before the triad of *shofar* blasts and another before the *Avoda*. New for a *Union Prayer Book* is the presence in *Gates of Repentance* of an *Aleinu* before the Blowing of the *Shofar* in the three *shofar* sections traditionally found in the *Musaf* for Rosh Hashana.

It is probably not generally known that the time-honored *Union Prayer Book*'s *Aleinu*, happily alive and well in *Gates of Prayer* (p. 617), going back not only to Isaac M. Wise but also to the unjustly neglected Leo Merzbacher (1810-56)[19] in their respective rites, did not always go uncontested.

ERIC L. FRIEDLAND

The provisional 1893 edition of the *Union Prayer Book* had for its regular *Aleinu*, in English,

> It is our duty to render praise and thanksgiving unto the Creator of heaven and earth, who delivered us from the darkness of false belief and sent to us the light of His truth.

which is based on Szold's and Jastrow's High Holy Day Hebrew *Aleinu* (*Aleinu leshabeach . . . le-yotzer bereshit, shebera'anu lichvodo, vehivdilanu min hato'im, vesam chelkenu betorato, vegoralenu ba'avodato. Va'anachnu kore'im* ...). The same 1893 edition's *Aleinu* on the Hebrew side was the Merzbacher/Wise formula that was to become ingrained, via translation, in all subsequent editions of the *Union Prayer Book, Gates of Prayer* included.[20] But the regular all-Hebrew *Aleinu* in the special 1906 edition reads (alongside the standard *Union Prayer Book* English-version: "Let us adore the ever-living God..."!) as follows:

> It is our duty to praise the Lord of all ... who has assigned our portion in His Torah (*shesam chelkenu betorato*) and our lot in His service (*vegoralenu ba'avodato*).
> And we bow...
>   (my translation — E.L.F.)

This version is derived from the rite prepared by Adolph Huebsch for his congregation, the aforementioned Ahawath Chesed. Apparently this same *Aleinu* was still chanted before the *Avoda* at the Central Synagogue at least until a short while ago. In the recording made by the Union of American Hebrew Congregations alluded to earlier, the *Aleinu* is none other than that of Huebsch and the 1906 edition of *Union Prayer Book II*!

It is admittedly a bit of a letdown that nowhere in *Gates of Understanding II* is mention made of kneeling and prostration wherever done, at the supreme moment of the *Aleinu*, either to launch the triple division of the *shofar* blasts or to lead into the *Avoda*. The occurrence of kneeling in the Szold-Jastrow *Abodath Israel* is easy enough to grasp because of that prayerbook's penchant for traditional forms. There not only did the officiants kneel but the congregation was expected to follow suit. The same movements and the same text have held on all the way through Max D. Klein's left-of-center Conservative *Seder Avodah II*. It is hard to verify what the procedure was in some of the earlier American Reform rites as no instructions would be provided. For instance, neither Wise's *Minhag Amerika* nor Merzbacher's *Order of Prayer* stipulated any rubrics. Incidentally, Merzbacher is responsible for coming up with the term "Adoration" for the *Aleinu*. On the Hebrew side of his prayer text he put to use the term *Hishtachavaya* (literally, prostration) for his uncommon title. The question is, for the pre-*Avoda Aleinu* at least, was there actually a *Hishtachavaya*?

Conversely, in his prayerbook, David Einhorn could always be counted on to furnish concrete guidelines as to what was to be said or done by whom and when. For the pre-*Avoda Aleinu* quoted above, Einhorn had the congregation rise, and, at the moment of "*Va'anachnu kore'im*," the *Vorbeter* (cantor or reader) solemnly uttered each word one at a time and the congregation and choir repeated it one by one. Ceremoniously as this *Aleinu* was handled, kneeling was not indicated. This does not, however, mean that Einhorn, with his aptitude for the dramatic, passed up the opportunity for liturgical choreography. Ever since its experimental 1893 volume, every *Union Prayer Book II* has reliably had at the end of *Ne'ila* the well-known "*Va'anachnu kore'im*" verse disengaged from its *Aleinu* matrix just before the climactic *Shema* through "*Adonai, Hu ha-Elohim.*" The stationing of a detached "*Va-anachnu kore-im*" here came from *Olath Tamid*. Its particular solemnity at this point is undeniable. Einhorn heightened its effect by having the rabbi and then the congregation fall on their knees (*unter Kniebeugung*). Apparently his son-in-law and translator, Emil G. Hirsch, thought the better of it and decided against reproducing in English the directive about kneeling.

The Sounding of the *Shofar*

One of the prominent features of worship during the High Holy Day season is of course the Sounding of the *Shofar* (*Teki'at Shofar*).[21] It is no secret that this feature was prodigally enhanced in *Gates of Repentance* at the impetus of *Petach Teshuva*. Basically the framework never ceased to be that of the *Union Prayer Book* harking back to its first regular edition (1894). There the pattern has been to coalesce (1) the traditional *Teki'ot Meyushav* before the Return of the Torah to the Ark and (2) the sequence of the three liturgical major blocks *Malchuyot-Zichronot-Shofarot* with their accompanying *shofar* blasts planted in the *Musaf* Service. What resulted was a set of the *Teki'ot Me'umad* — in other words, the *Malchuyot-Zichronot-Shofarot* complex — somewhat anomalously switched to where the *Teki'ot Meyushav* were to be. It was not until as late as the 1945 edition that the *berachot* before the blowing of the *shofar* were reinstated.

In *Gates of Repentance* the merger of the *Teki'ot Meyushav* and *Teki'ot Me'umad* and its placement after the reading of the *haftara*

ERIC L. FRIEDLAND

remains the same as it always has been, but marking *Gates of Repentance* off from its *Union Prayer Book* forerunners are the reintroduction (1) of the *Aleinu* at the beginning of the aforesaid triadic complex and (2) of the classic Hebrew texts for *Malchuyot-Zichronot-Shofarot*, slightly curtailed, in Service I, and generous helpings from *Petach Teshuva* in Service II.

As might be expected by now, this is not the first time that the Hebrew texts of *Malchuyot-Zichronot-Shofarot* with some abridgement were to turn up in the *Union Prayer Book*. In the 1906 edition mentioned earlier, really in a class by itself, the whole fabric of *Malchuyot-Zichronot-Shofarot* in Hebrew crops up with the *shofar* blessings *after* the close of the *Malchuyot* division, which scheme *Gates of Repentance* was — probably unwittingly — to take up again in 1978. *Union Prayer Book II* has always had a felicitous selection of mostly untapped biblical verses in Hebrew (cf. *Petach Teshuva*'s even more opportune choices repeated in *Gates of Repentance* on pages 210-211, 213-214, and 216).

In the history of American Jewish liturgical change, the problem of handling the two *shofar* services, the *Teki'ot Meyushav* and *Teki'ot Me'umad*, turned out some divergent solutions. Wise's *Minhag Amerika* was pretty traditional insofar as it upheld the distinction between the two services and kept them in their proper places. Its unexampled treatment of *Teki'ot Meyushav* in the Morning Service, however, catches the eye. After a German/ English reading and a choral rendition of the quite appropriate, though previously unused in this context, Psalm 98, and a recitation of the two *shofar* blessings,[22] Wise brings in psalmodic verses (*Adonai melech ... le'olam va'ed*; I Chronicles 16:15; Psalm 98; and, after the last set of *shofar* blasts, Psalm 89:16), adumbrating the themes of *Malchuyot-Zichronot-Shofarot* in the *Musaf* Service. The verses were to be sung in Hebrew by the choir and to alternate with the three sets of notes on the *shofar* thrice-blown. The German instructions for the *Schoferblasen* (*sic!*) indicate that the choral rendition with an assist from the organ was to synchronize with the reader's summoning (*makri*) the notes and the *Ba'al Teki'a*'s sounding them on the *shofar*.

Olath Tamid's treatment of the *Teki'at Shofar* startles by its summariness. Einhorn reserves his paraphrastic *Malchuyot* for the *Tefila* (*Amida*) in his Rosh Hashana Evening Service (as part of *Kedushat Hayom*), *Zichronot* for the one in the Morning Service, and *Shofarot* after the *haftara* and before the sermon, a hymn, and the Return of the Torah to the Ark. His drawn-out forward-looking and universalist paraphrase of *Ata Nigleita* (the *Shofarot* section) culminates in *Teki'a, Teru'a, Teki'a* on cornet and trumpets (*Horn und Trompetenklang*), and that's that!

HISTORICAL NOTES ON THE HIGH HOLY DAY LITURGY

In an effort to close ranks and bridge the very dissimilar Wisean and Einhornian treatments, the editors of the provisional 1893 *Union Prayer Book* adopted *Olath Tamid*'s distribution of *Malchuyot-Zichronot-Shofarot* between the Evening and Morning Services of Rosh Hashana, included Wise's fortunate choice of Psalm 98, shortened Einhorn's marathon paraphrastic *Shofarot*, and drew to a close with Wise's *Teki'ot Meyushav* as described above. By the way, all these latter items were placed *after* the Return of the Scroll. The only differences are that neither of the introductory *shofar* blessings appeared and that each of Wise's three sets of blasts was here done once rather than the accepted three times. Could it be that the arrangers of the preliminary 1893 text rested content with the minimum halachic requirement (Rosh Hashana 4:9)? In any event, one of the subsequent editors of the 1894 version found this resolution wanting and dumped it.

Structurally the British *Petach Teshuva* followed a different tack altogether in that *Teki'ot Meyushav* and *Teki'ot Me'umad*, both trailing behind the Return of the Scroll, are kept. Separating the two are a meditation and *Unetaneh Tokef*, the latter only through the climactic "But repentance, prayer and good deeds annul the severity of the judgment." In their resourceful fashion, Stern and Rayner turned the *Malchuyot* division to the sovereignty of God manifest in creation and reactivated a wonderful *piyut* by Judah Halevi on precisely this theme, "*Elohim, El Mi Amshilecha?*" ("O God, to whom shall we compare You?").[23] As for the *Shofarot* section, they devoted it to the Redemption yet-to-be-realized, the Kingdom-to-Come. Hence the prayer ordinarily anchored in the *Malchuyot* section, *Meloch Al Kol Ha'olam* ("Our God ... may You rule in glory over all the earth..."), is moved, because of its futuristic thrust, to the *Shofarot* section. After the final *shofar* notes are sounded, the hymn "All the World Shall Come to Serve You" is sung, followed by another piece also originally from the traditional *Malchuyot* section, the *Aleinu*. In this sequence not only are we given tighter thematic consistency but also we are artfully led to the high point which also happens to be the concluding portion of the day's worship. No less profitably Stern and Rayner have a similar expectant rearrangement for the ending of their transformed *Avoda*. Thus the *Aleinu* in *Petach Teshuva* comes at the terminus of the *Shofar* Service on Rosh Hashana and of the *Avoda* on Yom Kippur instead of acting conformably to tradition as the preamble to each.

The Sounding of the *Shofar* in *Gates of Repentance* undoubtedly surpasses what prevailed hitherto, in that it recovers the unequalled majesty of the classical Hebrew texts as in Service I and reproduces in large part the fluid prose of two endowed liturgists,

ERIC L. FRIEDLAND

Chaim Stern and John Rayner, for Service II. At first it struck me
as curious that whereas the old *Union Prayer Book* adhered to the
identical number of blasts for *Malchuyot-Zichronot-Shofarot* as in
the traditional Ashkenazic *Machzor* in fulfillment of the minimum
requirement, *Gates of Repentance,* like *Petach Teshuva,* tripled
the number, until I realized the blasts add up to 30, coinciding
exactly with the obligatory *Sheloshim Kolot* according to the
Talmud.[24]

Musaf and *Mincha* in *Gates of Repentance*

With *Gates of Repentance* a full-blown *Mincha* Service for Yom
Kippur is back in place, complete with its Torah Service and
Amida. There is no question that from its very inception the *Union
Prayer Book* has always had an Afternoon Service for Yom
Kippur, which included a Torah Reading, but it could not exactly
be called a *Mincha* per se, if only for the reason that an *Amida*
was lacking. The temporary 1893 edition, however, was outfitted
with not more than the initial Three Benedictions of the *Amida,*
the last of which was the *Kedusha* ordinarily earmarked for
Musaf. By the same token, virtually all the precursors of the
Union Prayer Book, even those that furnished no *Musaf* and/or
Mincha for Sabbaths and Festivals, made a point of accommodat-
ing both, especially for the High Holy Days.

The sole exception was David Einhorn's pace-setting *Olath
Tamid.* Einhorn followed his own bent and carved out something
that was without equal. For Yom Kippur day he turned out only
two *Amidot,* one for the Morning Service and another for the
Concluding Service, each of them, incidentally, technically complete and untruncated. In between, filling in for a separate *Musaf*
and *Mincha,* he deftly fused the two services by bringing in, in
conjunction with a quota of Psalms and *piyutim,* those items
which are trademarks of each service, like *Unetaneh Tokef* (here
foreshortened), an *Avoda,* and the Torah Reading. The only
departure is the Memorial Service which is too added here. Apart
from the unexpected relocation of the Memorial Service *within* the
Afternoon Service, Einhorn's layout has served as the dominant
model for the *Union Prayer Book II* from which the latter did not
stray since its premier 1894 edition.

What then distinguishes the current edition from its predecessors
are (1) the restoration of a full *Mincha* with its own *Amida* and
Torah Service, and (2) the placement of the *Avoda* and Martyrology as parts of a synopsis of Jewish history up to its hoped-for
eschatological conclusion, a *Heilsgeschichte* in a nutshell, so to
speak. As for the *Union Prayer Book*'s inspirational extras, read-

HISTORICAL NOTES ON THE HIGH HOLY DAY LITURGY

ings in poetry and prose, these are generally put in a section entitled "Additional Prayers" — in place of *Musaf* — between the Morning Service and the Afternoon Service. It is the *Avoda* and a kind of multiform disquisition on the "Meaning of Jewish Existence" based thereon that make *Gates of Repentance*'s *Mincha* as long as it is.

As may be recalled, the traditional *Avoda* starts out, in verse and acrostic, with the creation of the world through the singling out of Abraham and his progeny, Israel, to the election of the *Kohanim* from the tribe of Levi for their service of atonement. Pulling out the stops in the way he applies his forceful theology and his daring exegetical originality, Einhorn recast the *Avoda* as the occasion for explaining — passionately and eloquently — the destiny of the Jewish people as *Priestervolk* to the world:

> Not as a sinner, burdened with the penalty of his iniquity, did Israel go forth into the wider world, but his was the mission of the suffering Messiah. Leaving behind him his old home, the temple and its sacrificial cult, the pomp of the sacerdotal services; giving up the symbolism of the age of his preparation for his larger historic duty; he marched forth to found everywhere temples of a truer worship and a deeper knowledge of God and to lead by his self-sacrificing devotion *all mankind* to the spiritual altar of atonement. He was both priest and sacrifice, sent out like the sacrificial goat in the old ritual into the desert taking the sins of all men upon his own shoulders and *carrying them away.*
>
> (Hirsch's translation)

The upshot of the Jewish people's priestly/messianic mission is described in rhapsodic language:

> At last, Thy true sanctuary will arise spanning the wide limits of the earth, and at this, Thy true and only altar, atonement will be wrought not by the sevenfold sprinkling of blood but by the sevenfold rays of Sinai's sun.
>
> (Hirsch's translation)

The *Avoda* in all the editions of the *Union Prayer Book II* stuck closely to Einhorn's text and theology — Jewish missiology, one may call it — with minor changes and much of the expansive language toned down.[25] The immediate predecessor of *Petach Teshuva*, the British *Liberal Jewish Prayer Book II* (1937), edited by the European-born and HUC-trained Israel I. Mattuck (1883-1954), placed the *Avoda* in its Additional — rather than Afternoon — Service and followed it up with a series of scriptural readings (mostly the "Servant of the Lord" passages in Second Isaiah) under the heading "The Meaning of Jewish History,"

ERIC L. FRIEDLAND

winding up on an affirmative note with a repositioned *Aleinu*,
Israel Zangwill's stirring translation of *Veye'etayu*, "All the World
Shall Come to Serve Thee," and future-oriented biblical passages
along with entreaties on behalf of the Jewish people and of all
humankind.

It took the vision, learning, and artistry of Chaim Stern and
John D. Rayner to refashion Mattuck's *Avoda* and sequel into a
thing of impressive scope, movement, spirituality, and beauty.
They succeeded in marshalling here, among other features, the
Martyrology, modern poems about the Shoah, allusions to Zion
reborn, the Deutero-Isaianic Suffering Servant, and other scriptural passages in a way that is not one whit overdone. All the
component parts hang together harmoniously.

Under a similar caption, "From Creation to Redemption," *Gates
of Repentance* had the good fortune and sense to embrace Stern's
and Rayner's *Avoda* as a story of God's pilgrim people that
marches on.

Gates of Repentance's Piyutim

In a somewhat incidental fashion Hoffman provides a tidy, well-
grounded summary on the development of the *piyut*.[26] The ways
medieval liturgical poems have been selected and handled in the
various Reform prayerbooks are a tale unto itself.

It is encouraging to see some of the old familiar Ashkenazic
piyutim stage a comeback.

Since its beginnings the *Union Prayer Book II* held no more
than, say, a half-dozen Ashkenazic liturgical poems for its Yom
Kippur services, with such perennials as *Ya'aleh* and *Unetaneh
Tokef*. In its special 1906 edition the *Union Prayer Book* was
given rein with its Hebrew inserts numbering some additional
Ashkenazic lyrical favorites. These included the anonymous
alphabetic acrostic "*Ata Hu Eloheinu*" ("Thou art our God in
heaven and earth") and Meshullam ben Kalonymos' "*Imeru l-
Elohim*" ("Say of God") and "*Ma'aseh Eloheinu*" ("Great are the
works of our God"), the latter two abbreviated and all three left
untranslated. There is an unquestioned felt piety in the Ashkenazic
pieces revived by *Gates of Repentance*, "*Omnam Ken*" ("Yes, it is
true," pp. 376-377), "*Ki Hineh Kachomer*" ("As a clay in the
hand of the potter," pp. 381-382), and "*Le-El Orech Din*" ("Now
all acclaim You king," pp. 401-402).

The fact remains, nonetheless, that the *piyutim* in *Gates of
Repentance* are substantially Sephardic-derived, most of them
mediated by the standard-bearer Hamburg *Gebetbuch*[27] through its
several 19th-century American liturgical heirs. Spanish Jewry's

HISTORICAL NOTES ON THE HIGH HOLY DAY LITURGY

medieval poet laureate Judah Halevi's "*Yah Shimcha, Aromimcha*" ("The Lord is Your name," pp. 471-474) and standby "*Mi Yiteneni*" ("O that I might be a servant unto Thee," pp. 395-396) and pieces by others like "*Malki Mikedem*" ("O Sovereign Source of salvation," pp. 396-398, which is really either Italian or Greek, as Stern informs us), "*Ata Konanta*" ("Author of life," pp. 410-411; the acrostic prelude to the *Avoda*), "*El Nora Alila*" ("God of awesome deeds," pp. 508-509), and "*Beterem Shechakim Va'arakim*" ("The Lord will reign," p. 510) found their way into the Reform rite from the Sephardic liturgy. The route taken by the acrostic "*Pitechu Lanu Sha'arei Tzedek*" ("Open for us the gates of righteousness," pp. 517-518), a new revival, is just as oblique. It came by way of the Conservative *machzor* edited by Jules Harlow,[28] ultimately originating in the Sephardic *Kaddish Titkabel*, spun out specifically for Yom Kippur. A more apt choice could scarcely have been made: the last of a whole string of gates mentioned are *sha'arei teshuva*, the Hebrew for "the gates of repentance"!

Interestingly enough, little under a century ago the independent prayerbook creator, Joseph Krauskopf, finished his Yom Kippur services with this very Sephardic *Kaddish* insert as a parting benediction:

Minister:
(*Facing the Congregation.*)

Te'anu berachamim min hashamayim.

May God in mercy hear your prayer;
And answer your supplication.
With the opening of heaven's portals
To receive the earth-sustaining sun
May He also open unto you
The gates of light and of love,
The gates of knowledge and of truth,
The gates of atonement and of mercy,
The gates of help and of support,
The gates of peace and of plenty.
May He remove from your midst
Hatred and strife, envy and discord,
And grant you the noble wishes of your heart,
Now and for evermore. Amen

Choir:

Amen. - Hallelujah.

ERIC L. FRIEDLAND

Conclusion

The foregoing notes on *Gates of Repentance* and *Gates of Understanding* form only a digressive sketch of how aspects of the American Reform liturgy have taken shape, how internal and external influences have had their play, and how modernity continually interacts with tradition, often in surprising directions.

The more we come to know of ourselves as humans by rediscovering our proximate and distant past, the more secure and full our identities become. The more links with our liturgical past we establish, the more discriminating, mature, and lasting are our future efforts in the area of worship likely to be.

An only-slightly-varnished mirror of who and where we were and are inwardly, the prayerbook examined in all of its multifarious stages and endless dimensions can illumine our path as we plot our way onward. In a sense, it is very much a *shomer she'erit am kadosh.*

NOTES

[1] Chaim Stern, ed., *Gates of Repentance (Sha'arei Teshuva): The New Union Prayerbook for the Days of Awe* (New York: Central Conference of American Rabbis, 5738/1978).

[2] Lawrence A. Hoffman, *Gates of Understanding II (Sha'arei Bina 2): Appreciating the Days of Awe* (New York: Central Conference of American Rabbis, 5744-1984).

[3] Israel I. Mattuck, ed., *Liberal Jewish Prayer Book II: Services for the Day of Memorial (Rosh Hashanah) and the Day of Atonement* (London: Union of Liberal and Progressive Synagogues, 1937).

[4] John D. Rayner and Chaim Stern, eds., *Gate of Repentance (Petach Teshuva): Services for the High Holydays* (London: Union of Liberal and Progressive Synagogues, 5733/1973). So as not to confuse the British *Gate of Repentance* with the American *Gates of Repentance*, I shall hereafter refer to the former by its becoming Hebrew title, *Petach Teshuva.*

[5] The last two items are later additions, the terminating *Teki'a Gedola* in the 1922 edition and *Havdala* in *Gates of Repentance.*

[6] Adolph Huebsch, ed., *Gebete fuer die Oeffentlichen Gottesdienst der Tempelgemeinde Ahawath Chesed [Seder Tefila leRosh haShana veYom haKipurim]* (New York, 5635/1875).

[7] David Einhorn, ed., *Gebetbuch fuer Israelitische Reform-Gemeinden [Olath Tamid]* (Baltimore, 1858).

[8] By contrast, Isaac M. Wise's *Minhag Amerika* (Cincinnati, 1857 — like Benjamin Szold's and Marcus Jastrow's *Abodath Israel* (Philadelphia, 1873, — always had all types of *Kaddish*, barring the *Kaddish Derabbanan* and the special funeral one, *Kaddish Itchadata.*

HISTORICAL NOTES ON THE HIGH HOLY DAY LITURGY

[9] *Gates of Understanding II*, p. 47.

[10] David de Sola Pool, *The Kaddish* (New York: Union of Sephardic Congregations, 1964), p. viii.

[11] Berachot 16b-17a; cf. Claude G. Montefiore and Herbert Loewe, *A Rabbinic Anthology* (Cleveland and New York: Meridian Books; Philadelphia: Jewish Publication Society of American, 1963), pp. 360-363.

[12] Joseph Krauskopf, *The Service Manual* (Philadelphia, 1892), p. 38.

[13] Ministers of the West London Synagogue, *Forms of Prayer for Jewish Worship [Seder haTefilot]*, 6th ed. (Oxford: The University Press, 1931), vol. I, p. 10.

[14] Although neither *The Hamburg Temple Hymnal* [=Hamburg Templegemeinde, *Allgemeines Israelitisches Gesangbuch*] (Hamburg, 1833) nor any of the works of the prolific hymnographer/liturgist Leopold Stein has the German original, Benjamin Szold's *Abodath Israel* (Baltimore, 1863) does — for all that, betraying no clue as to who wrote it.

[15] Max D. Klein, ed., *Seder Avodah: Service Book for Rosh Hashanah and Yom Kippur* (Philadelphia: Press of Maurice Jacobs, 1960), p. 808.

[16] A more detailed study on the subject of American Jews' changing views regarding life beyond the grave as reflected in the *Yizkor* Service may be found in my "The Atonement Memorial Service in the American *Mahzor*," in the *Hebrew Union College Annual* LV (1984), pp. 243-282.

[17] *Gates of Understanding II*, pp. 42-46.

[18] John D. Rayner and Chaim Stern, ed., *Service of The Heart [Avodat haLev]: Weekday, Sabbath and Festival Prayers for Home and Synagogue* (London: Union of Liberal and Progressive Synagogues, 5728/1967).

[19] Leo Merzbacher, ed., *The Order of Prayer for Divine Service [Seder Tefila], II, Prayers for the Day of Atonement* (New York, 1855).

[20] The Hebrew of the same was to show up in the *Union Prayer Book II* only for the *Aleinu* before the *Avoda*. Now of course it materializes in all the *Gates* prayerbooks as one of two or three versions of the Adoration in Hebrew.

It is of more than passing interest that Einhorn's pre-*Avoda Aleinu* left no trace whatsoever in any edition of the *Union Prayer Book II*. Perhaps it was considered too unfamiliar even to be considered, consistent though it be with Einhorn's theology:

> It is meet for us to worship before the Lord of the universe, to announce the greatness of its Creator who appointed the seed of Abraham to be a blessing unto all the families of the earth. And we bow down... (Emil G. Hirsch, trans., Dr. David Einhorn's *Olath Tamid, Book of Prayers for Jewish Congregations* [Chicago, 1896].)

[21] The traditional *Machzor* has two *shofar* services, one after the Torah Reading (*Teki'ot Meyushav*) and another, a threefold arrangement (*Malchuyot-Zichronot-Shofarot*; *Teki'ot Me'umad*; or *Teki'ata deRav*), during *Musaf*. Max Arzt explains briefly the reasons for the separate services in his *Justice and Mercy: Commentary on the Liturgy of the New Year and the Day of Atonement* (New York, Chicago, and San Francisco: Holt, Rinehart and Winston), p. 152. Although the Ashkenazic custom is for all to

ERIC L. FRIEDLAND

rise each time the *shofar* is blown, the Sephardim *sit* during the *Teki'ot Meyushav* and stand for the ones during *Musaf.*

[22] The first *beracha* is revised "Karaitically" *"vetzivanu lishmor et yom teru'a"* ("and commanded us to observe the Day of the Blowing of the Shofar"). The British Reform *Forms of Prayer* of the West London Synagogue had, for a long time but not now, also in Karaitic style, *"vetzivanu lehashmia kol shofar"* rather than the rabbinic *"vetzivanu lishmoa kol shofar."* While the Torah prescribes *sounding* the *shofar,* the Sages of the Talmud were the ones who made a *mitzvah* of *listening* to its sounds.

[23] Halevi's lofty poem appeared in Huebsch's *Gebete fuer die oeffentlichen Gottesdienst* as an introduction to the *Kedusha* during the *Amida* of the Afternoon Service. The poem's 22nd line has Isaiah 6:3 ("Holy, holy, holy..."), the central verse of the *Kedusha. Petach Teshuva*'s predecessor, the *Liberal Jewish Prayer Book II* (1937), placed the poem before the *Barechu* on Rosh Hashana morning. The poem in its entirety may be found in Hayyim (Jefim) Schirmann, *Hashira Ha'ivrit BiSfarad UveProvence,* I (Jerusalem: Mosad Bialik; Tel Aviv: Dvir, 5719/1959), pp. 532-536.

[24] Rosh Hashana 33b and 34b.

[25] Compare the long Einhorn-derived penultimate prayer on pages 518-522 in *Gates of Repentance* with his German original, which covers over ten pages!

[26] *Gates of Understanding II*, p. 77.

[27] S. J. Fraenkel and M.J. Bresselau, ed., *Ordnung der Oeffentlichen Andacht fuer die Sabbath-und Festtage des Ganzen Jahres [Seder ha-Avoda].* Nach dem Gebrauche des Neuen-Tempel-Vereins in Hamburg (Hamburg, 1819).

[28] Jules Harlow, ed., *Mahzor for Rosh Hashanah and Yom Kippur: A Prayer Book for the Days of Awe* (New York: The Rabbinical Assembly, 1973), p. 724.

The Penitent's Hour

Martin W. Levy

The open ark yawns, the melody tugs
let all our vows on this *Kol Nidrei*
be null, I plead, tongue stuck
the calf-stained parchment scents all
untended sins, naked before You.

Triumphant in silver, the scroll speaks
invisibly, who is fit for this task?
Repentance rings true for another's turn.
Lips mumble pregnant tales
a tortured veil over failures
the lions of Judah unmoved.
The silvered words: I am your Creator,
author of freedom, absolver.

Mid-afternoon, once Mother whispered
apples and honey will keep you
her voice pungent with Parisian scents
lemon squeezed fingers and faint sweat
pickled herring juice slathered on *challah*
promises of raisin *kugel* and sweet *strudel.*

Alone before the oak-stained ark
a silver *yad* points down,
cancelled oaths are Your domain
mine the public patina, magnified
and sanctified they cry
filmed eyes blind to Your trust.
The voice returns, walk humbly, try again.
Gold threaded mantels haunt me
Be there this hour in my prayer.

MARTIN W. LEVY is Rabbi of Temple B'nai Israel in Galveston, Texas.

Yamim Nora'im: The Traditional Liturgy and *Gates of Repentance*

Leo Trepp

The current *Gates of Repentance* (*GoR*) is of great value and spirituality; it serves well, and will do so for many years to come. The thoughts I offer are the result of successful experimentations. I invite my colleagues to experiment on their own, if they are so inclined, and to offer their results when a new revision of the book will be in the making, which, I expect, will be long after my lifetime.

The changes will not materially extend the length of the service. They are basically concerned with its organization. They rest on the traditional *machzor*, because in it the service has a unity that, on Rosh Hashana, unfolds in a highly dramatic crescendo, and, on Yom Kippur, gives clear articulation to each of the Tefillot.

Rosh Hashana

Ma'ariv

Ma'ariv proclaims the theme of the day (Ps. 81:4-5). In it the dual character of Rosh Hashana is proclaimed. Rosh Hashana is Yom Tov, "*Yom Chagenu,*" but equally day of the Shofar, of judgment. *Ma'ariv* is transition from weekday to holiday mood. It is anticipation of the morrow. But now we are to experience fully the joy of the feast.[1]

This may have been one of the reasons that *Avinu Malkenu* was not included in the traditional service. If this be so, then there is wisdom and psychological insight in that omission. The festive mood is not to be disturbed. The penitential character will be revealed tomorrow; it is held in abeyance.[2]

LEO TREPP lives in Napa, California, and teaches one semester annually at the University of Mainz, where he is University Professor of Jewish Studies. He is the author of several volumes, including *The Complete Book of Jewish Observance* (New York: Summit, 1980).

LEO TREPP

Shacharit: The Ascent

Shacharit is gradual ascent. It opens with the daily *Berachot* and the Sabbath "Verses of Song."

Nishmat: The King is Seated — The Equality of Men and Women

With *Nishmat* it moves toward Rosh Hashana. The "bailiff" calls out: "*Ha-Melech Yoshev!*"[3] "The Sovereign is seated on the judgment seat." The hour of judgment has arrived. The congregation, in response, gives acknowledgment (Ps. 35:1) and sings:

בפי יׁשרים תתלׁומם
ובדברי צדיקים תתברך
ובלשון חסידים תתקדׁש
ובקרב קדושים תתהלל

This arrangement of the four lauds, found in ancient *mach-zorim*, transforms the response into a statement of great significance, namely the equality of men and women in our worship. The acrostic reveals that man and woman — Yitzchak and Rivkah — are equals and, complementing each other, make praise possible. Actually the action — the verb — rests on the woman, as it did in the lives of Isaac and Rebecca. This is one of the few instances in the traditional liturgy where the equality of men and women finds expression and therefore deserves emphasis.

Amida and Avinu Malkenu

Through the *Amida*, and its "*Kedushat ha-Yom*" *beracha*, we have become fully attuned to the character of the day and are ready to give expression to our feelings aroused by it. Therefore, on the Pilgrimage Festivals, *Hallel* follows the *Amida* and brings *Shacharit* to its joyful climax. Correspondingly, on the *Yamim Nora'im*, *Avinu Malkenu* takes this place.[4]

By its position as by its content, *Avinu Malkenu* burns into our consciousness that we stand in judgment. *Avinu Malkenu* is also the last direct personal plea that will be uttered on Rosh Hashana; the rest is affirmation and praise. This climactic character of *Avinu Malkenu* is reduced if the *Unetaneh Tokef* precedes it, as in *GoR*. It might therefore be postponed. Instead, *Avinu Malkenu* might be included in *Shacharit*, with which it forms a unit.

YAMIM NORA'IM AND *GATES OF REPENTANCE*

The Great Fugue

The service, from now on, unfolds as in a great fugue. The same themes are introduced again and again in ever changing variations to show their richness and plumb their depth.

Torah Reading: The Divine Message — The Themes

Aware of the awesomeness of the day the congregation is ready to receive the divine message.

The Torah reading tells of every human being's ultimate confrontation with the call of God. Abraham hears the commanding voice; he responds with "*hineni.*" He does not know the outcome of the test. Ideally, the contemporary Jew is to forget about the "happy ending" and suffer with our forefather the agonies of trial, for we too may expect trials, the outcome of which is uncertain. God may demand of the Jew the complete surrender of his or her life, and every Jew must be prepared and ready for it. Strengthened by the resolution of Abraham's test, the worshiper may trust in God's mercy, expressed in the plea of *Avinu Malkenu.*

The reading of the *Akeda* is therefore deeply meaningful. The *Haftara* complements it. It reveals the sensitivity of a woman. Eli, the priest, does not understand the silent outpouring of the heart before God; Hannah, the woman, has to teach him. She has a much deeper insight into the meaning of communion with God. For her, offering a son does not mean surrendering his life, as it does for Abraham, but it means dedicating him to the service of God and his people. Only as men and women jointly find their way to God, will God be found and God's will understood.

Since the scriptural text, used as *Haftara* in the traditional *machzor*, offers one of the few occasions of a woman's prayer, Hannah's hymn of thanksgiving in I Samuel 2 deserves to be added. It reveals a woman's view of God who, as judge, is full of compassion, is protector of the downtrodden, and redeemer of the oppressed. At the same time these verses introduce the themes of *Malchuyot* (I Sam. 2:1-2), *Zichronot* (3-9), and *Shofarot* (10).

Torah reading and *Haftara* have prepared us, subliminally as it were, for *Malchuyot, Zichronot,* and *Shofarot,* doing so in a sequence that corresponds to the human condition. God has to take note of us, to *remember* us, in order that we come into life and grow up. God took note of Sarah, and Isaac was born (Gen. 21:1ff); of Hannah, and gave her a son, Samuel (I Sam. 1). God then demands of us that we affirm the divine sovereignty through our lives, as did Abraham (Gen. 22:1ff) and as Hannah pledged the fruit of her womb to God (I Sam. 1:11-12). God then grants us

LEO TREPP

redemption. Abraham is blessed and through him all the nations of the earth will ultimately find *redemption* (Gen. 22:15-18). This idea, according to the Midrash, is connected with the Shofar (Gen. 22:13). Samuel becomes the leader and rescuer of his people.[5]

The equality of men and women has thus been made manifest. Abraham may be more heroic; Hannah is profoundly more sensitive. Only as both are recognized as equal leaders can the meaning of the *Yamim Nora'im* be understood and realized. The alternate *Haftara* may therefore be omitted.

The Torah Reading of the Alternate Service

The Torah reading of the alternate service is in tune with Rosh Hashana as "birthday of the world." An additional relationship emphasizing judgment and forgiveness is established through the Midrash that holds that on this day, the first of Tishri, Adam was created, sinned, was judged, and was pardoned.[6]

Here, however, the alternative *Haftara* (Jer. 31:1-19) should be chosen and the first one omitted. (The first one, Isa. 55:6-13, is traditionally recited on fast days, which Rosh Hashana is not.)

The Torah reading — in contrast to the first service — has not prepared us for *Malchuyot*, *Zichronot*, and *Shofarot*. The *Haftara* does so now. Its emphasis lies on redemption, the theme of *Shofarot*, and on remembrance, the theme of *Zichronot*. It begins with redemption (Jer. 31:1-13) and shifts to remembrance (verses 14-19), including a verse that is actually one of the *Zichronot* selections (verse 19). God's sovereignty, the divine power to shape history, undergirds the prophecy. It might then be desirable to include verse 19 in the selections of *Zichronot*.

Additionally, the *Haftara* corresponds to the first *Haftara* and extends it. In the first it was Hannah, now it is Rachel, whose plea brings redemption to the people. In both cases divine remembrance and redemption are the result of a woman's plea.

Teki'ot Meyushavot

The *Teki'ot* after the Torah reading reinforce the messages and reveal our readiness to respond to them. *Teki'a* is the call to attention. It is God's call to Abraham. *Shevarim* is the human response, the readiness to break with the past. It is Abraham's road to Mt. Moriah. *Teru'a* is the whimpering of our contrite heart, aware of our fractured life. This contrasts with Abraham's absolute surrender. The final *Teki'a* signifies the partnership God has established with us; it reveals our desire to move in new directions and God's approval and gracious acceptance of our resolve. It is God's blessing given to Abraham and Hannah, God's pledge of redemption given to Abraham and Rachel.

These *Teki'ot* do not belong to *Malchuyot, Zichronot,* and *Shofarot,* and were added later in antiquity. Originally, there were only the *Teki'ot* connected with *Malchuyot, Zichronot,* and *Shofarot,* and they were included in *Shacharit.* The Romans suspected in the early sounding of the horn a call to rebellion and attacked the Jews. The three special sections with their *Teki'ot* were therefore transferred to *Musaf.* Sounding the Shofar at a later hour convinced the Romans that the Jews "merely followed their custom" (J. Rosh Hashana 4:5; B. Rosh Hashana 32b).

The custom of the later sounding of the Shofar has remained. By this time the people had come to hear the Torah and the synagogue was filled to capacity. To accommodate the elderly and sick, additional *Teki'ot* after the Torah reading were introduced. Frail and sickly people could now go home immediately after hearing the Shofar. During the sounding the people could also remain seated. These *Teki'ot* are therefore called "*meyushavot.*"[7]

By placing the *Teki'ot* outside the context of *Malchuyot, Zichronot,* and *Shofarot,* an unexpected result was attained: wordless *kavana.* Nowhere else do we find it. Changing times and conditions are thereby permitted to enter the contemplation and meditation of the worshiper. It is dynamic rest, silent word.

Allow me to suggest that these *Teki'ot* be introduced again. The congregation stands while the *Berachot* are sung, then is seated and with closed eyes listens to the sounds. The listeners reflect on the Shofar's sounds as interpretation of the word of Torah that is still on the reader's desk, each person for himself or herself, each generation, world-wide, according to its needs.

Teki'ot as Bridge

These *Teki'ot* are therefore a symphonic bridge. They link Torah as the word of God with the following human response. We shall also see that they can form the frame for the entire ensuing service. The worshiper, as a listener to a symphony, may not be consciously aware of the progression but is nevertheless led onward in mind and emotion as themes are touched upon to be repeated and developed later.

The Amida: Avot and Gevurot — Exposition of the Themes

In a few words, the themes of sovereignty, remembrance, and redemption are introduced.

In *Avot*, God is "the supreme God," i.e., the absolute Sovereign. God "*remembers* the faithfulness of the ancestors unto the children." God "brings *redemption* to their children's children."

In *Gevurot*, God is mighty through time and space; sustaining the living through everlasting divine remembrance, God makes salvation to sprout.

Unetaneh Tokef as Variation

Unetaneh Tokef may now be understood as a development of these themes. Several variations appear and lead onward.

The first variation

Unetaneh Tokef opens with a proclamation of God's tremendous majesty. It moves to God's *remembrance* of all creatures in judgment: "deeds long forgotten" are recalled. It climaxes in proclaiming God's *saving grace* in response to our repentance, prayer, and charity. They *ward off* the harshness of the decree, a divine act of rescue.

The second variation

Only two themes now are introduced in reversed order: We remind God of our human condition, our weakness ("man is dust"); and, ultimately, we proclaim God Sovereign ("but you are the King").

Unetaneh Tokef as Ascent to God

The Leit-motifs

Unetaneh Tokef is preparation to *Malchuyot, Zichronot*, and *Shofarot*. This can be recognized by observing its "leit-motifs."

Malchuyot opens with "*Aleinu*" ("the throne of God's glory is in heaven above and on the earth beneath"). *Unetaneh Tokef* opens with the leit-motif of God's Kingship ("on this day Your Kingship is exalted").

Shofarot ends with the *Beracha*: "Sound the great Shofar for our redemption." *Unetaneh Tokef* alludes to it: "The great Shofar is sounded."

Zichronot has Rav's meditation: "on this day the fate of nations is in the balance — for war and peace, for famine and plenty. So too with every single creature: life and death are in the balance" (based on M. Rosh Hashana 1:2). *Unetaneh Tokef* states: "You muster ... every soul ... decreeing its destiny."

Finally, *Shofarot* proclaims: "You revealed Yourself as our King." *Unetaneh Tokef* brings this motif: "But You are King, the everlasting God." It is now the sound of liberation.

By referring twice to *Shofarot, Unetaneh Tokef* succeeds in creating a counterpoint. The Shofar sound that terrifies even the angels is ultimately the Shofar of liberation and redemption.

The Two Levels of Ascent

The First Level: From *Unetaneh Tokef* to *Kedusha* —
Our Individual Lives

The Stages

We begin by proclaiming the awesome greatness of God. God sits in judgment. All of creation is gripped by fear; we appeal for God's mercy. This appeal moves through three stages.

The first stage leads to "*Teshuva, Tefila, Tzedaka.*" These do not wipe out sin and their consequences; they merely mitigate their harshness, "*roa hagezera*" (see B. Berachot 17a; M. Avot 4:13,19).

The second stage, "*ki keshimcha,*" proclaims that *teshuva* leads to the immediate embrace by God; the human sins and their consequences are completely obliterated. "*Im tashuv miyad tekablo.*"

The third stage (omitted in *GoR*) proclaims that God will pardon even those that are unworthy, for this is God's name. As Israel — fighter for God — is called by God's name, Israel calls upon *God* to sanctify *the divine* name by showing compassion with the people hallowed to sanctify the name of the Eternal.[8]

It is a dramatic crescendo leading from total submission to daring affirmation of our claim on God. We are God's people, pledged to God and calling on God to live up to the divine pledge made to us. We are absolutely God's own. This knowledge permits us now to join the angelic chorus in the *Kedusha.*[9]

Kedusha, God's Kingship

The contrapuntal development is completed. In the beginning the angelic host, the universe, shared with Israel the terror of the day of judgment; now Israel leads this chorus of heaven and earth ("all things to the end of time") in joyful sanctification of God. We proclaim God's holiness and Kingship in unison.

LEO TREPP

This concludes the first ascent. The introduction in *GoR* which speaks of Rabbi Amnon should be omitted. (As a son of the age-old Jewish community of Mainz this grieves me, but appears inescapable.) We know now that the hymn originated in the Byzantine Empire, as we have found a version of it in the Geniza fragments. Our version found its form through Kalonymus ben Meshullam at Mainz, who never claimed to have created it. Most likely the hymn came from the East to Lucca, Italy, home of the Kalonymus family, and was brought by them to Germany.[10]

Transition to the Second Level: *Uvechen Ten Pachdecha*

Kedusha as Bridge

Now *Kedusha*, in which our first ascent has found its culmination, becomes the starting point for the second ascent. According to ancient Palestinian rite, the *Malchuyot* verses were incorporated into *Kedusha*.

The concluding section *"uvechen ten pachdecha ... vetimloch ata"* was originally the summation of *Malchuyot*. It has become a part of every *Kedusha* of the *Yamim Nora'im*.[11]

Uvechen Ten Pachdecha: A New Transitional Variation

Uvechen Ten Pachdecha leads us from our individual course through history to the course of history itself that will be the theme of *Malchuyot, Zichronot,* and *Shofarot.* The first paragraph alludes to God's sovereignty: "Yours is the *majesty.*" The second paragraph voices the plea that God may *remember* us: "Grant honor to Your people, hope to those who seek You." The third paragraph brings the *redemption* "when the rule of tyranny will pass from the earth, and You alone shall have dominion."

The Second Level of Ascent: Through History

Malchuyot, Zichronot, and *Shofarot* as Variations on Basic Jewish Themes

Creation, Revelation, Redemption

We can see in *Malchuyot-Zichronot-Shofarot* an ascent from creation to revelation and redemption. God is the *Creator* and therefore Sovereign. We now understand why *Malchuyot* was combined with *Kedushat ha-Yom*, the sanctification of "the world's birthday."

God is aware of all creatures. Their actions stand before the Presence. God is, therefore, ever-present. *Revelation* is ongoing. In the sound of the Shofar, the Eternal will bring *redemption* to the eternal people and all humanity.

God, Humanity, and History

We can see here a call to historical awareness. The significance of Judaism lies in its historical consciousness. History calls for an initiator; otherwise it is but a sequence of incidents. It calls for a goal; otherwise it is but a series of episodes. For those on the road, a *remembrance* of things past must serve as a guide for the tasks ahead; otherwise, there can be no ethical progress.

The initiator of history giving it scope is God, the Sovereign. This is proclaimed in *Malchuyot.* The road rests on God's and our remembrance whence we came and where we are going. This is *Zichronot.* The end is the redemptive moment, when humanity, by the sound of the Shofar, will find everlasting liberty. This is *Shofarot.*[12]

The Themes Are Fully Developed by the Whole "Orchestra"

Aleinu — The Exposition: The Congregation Kneels

Before we enter the road marked out for us, we anticipate its goal. This is *Aleinu.* Israel, as humanity's vanguard, anticipates the day when the whole world will join it in adoration and pledge of loyalty to God.

To lead us beyond the climax of the *Kedusha,* a higher point has to be found and it is, indeed, introduced: the congregation bends its knee to God. This dramatic moment should be restored, at least for rabbi and cantor. Christians kneel; Muslims kneel and prostrate themselves daily. At least on these days, we should also kneel. It is dramatic and it is meaningful.[13]

The Teki'ot Me'umadot

Each of the three special sections, *Malchuyot-Zichronot-Shofarot,* are accentuated by Shofar sounds, indicating that we have reached the fullness of the development.[14]

At each of the three blasts after *Malchuyot-Zichronot-Shofarot,* the congregation stands to commit itself to the work of universal redemption entrusted to it.

The road has been traversed. The congregation is blessed with Aaron's blessing and voices its hope for peace, the ultimate redemption of the world.

Aleinu as Recapitulation

The service ends with *Aleinu,* which now serves as a summation of our progress. The whole service has now been framed by it, its unity established.

LEO TREPP

Shofar as Recapitulation

And now, at the end, while the congregation stands, the entire sequence of the Shofar sounds could be repeated. The second *Aleinu* and Shofar thereby constitute a "recapitulation" of the symphonic themes; they frame of the whole service.[15]

Yom Kippur

The Yom Kippur service lacks the dramatic progression of Rosh Hashana. It centers around one subject, *Selicha*, which it takes up in ever new variations. Nevertheless each of the Yom Kippur *Tefilot* has a theme. *Ma'ariv* is overture. *Shacharit* centers on our pleas for *Selicha*. *Musaf* brings the remembrance of *Avoda*, the service of the high priest in the Temple. *Mincha* is dedicated to Jewish martyrdom, and *Ne'ila* brings the last fervent outcry for forgiveness before the gates are closed. From it we take assurance that God has forgiven.

The only *machzor* in which these themes are truly articulated is that of the western Ashkenasic rite.

Ma'ariv

No longer do we enter in a weekday spirit; days of penitence have preceded the day.

Ya'aleh

"*Ya'aleh*" is really "overture." We are given the order of the whole day's service. We come with contrite spirit in the evening; on the morrow we shall offer our *Selicha* at *Shacharit*; in *Avoda* we shall review the ancient form of purification and identify ourselves with its *Viddui*; at *Mincha* we speak of those who gave their all for God's sake; and at *Ne'ila* we shall end the day in awed jubilation.

Ya'aleh is a "variation" of "*Ya'aleh veyavo*" in the *Amida*. Would it be desirable to include it as theme before the Yom Kippur *Ya'aleh*?

Avinu Malkenu

On this evening we speak the *Avinu Malkenu*. It is the climax of our confessions and our pleas for forgiveness. *Avinu Malkenu* at *Ma'ariv* sets this night apart from all other nights of the year.

Adon Olam

As conclusion of the service, *Adon Olam* might be appropriate.[16] Its theme recapitulates the ideas of God's sovereignty, providence, and deliverance and thus forms a link to Rosh Hashana. At the same time it links *Ma'ariv* to the worship of the morrow.

Shacharit

By opening *Shacharit* with "*Adon Olam*" the service commences where it ended the night before. The unity of the whole day's worship is emphasized.

The Theme of Shacharit Is Selicha

"During the morning hours God judges the world, but, seeing the world's plight moves from the judgment seat to the seat of compassion" (B. Avoda Zara 3b). This inspires our pleas at *Shacharit* and might be emphasized by adding some excerpts from the traditional *Selichot*.[17] There exist magnificent poems, some by our greatest medieval masters. Above all, many *Selichot* are relevant for us as Holocaust descendants. They deserve to be reexamined.

Unetaneh Tokef could be omitted. *Avinu Malkenu* would again be the climax of *Shacharit*.

Torah Reading

The reading, as chosen by *GoR*, emphasizes the unity of the people: men, women, children, the "*ger.*" They all form a union of equals under the covenant that binds them to God and, therefore, to each other. Theirs is the choice between good and evil, and they bear the consequences of this choice: life or death.

The *Haftara*, that conforms to the traditional *machzor*, outlines our tasks under the covenant in concrete detail. They lie in the field of social justice and human compassion. The selections are appropriate. The relationship between Torah portion and *Haftara* is well established. The thoughts expressed will be further extended in the Torah reading chosen for *Mincha*. A link, unifying the readings of the day, is established.

LEO TREPP

Musaf

The Theme of Musaf is "Avoda"

Gates of Repentance has a section called *"Tefilot Nosafot,"* "Additional Prayers." It uses a derivation of the term *"Musaf."* I believe the term *"Musaf"* could therefore be restored.

Actually *Gates of Repentance* has *Musaf* but calls it *Mincha* and omits the *Mincha* service. But both *Musaf* and *Mincha* can have their individual themes.[18] *Musaf* in *GoR* would therefore include elements of the present *Mincha*.

The Development of *Musaf*

Musaf on Yom Kippur corresponds to the *Malchuyot-Zichronot-Shofarot* service, the traditional *Musaf* of Rosh Hashana. Like it, it constitutes the core service of the day. Like it, it belongs in the morning service.

The intentional parallel development can be recognized by the inclusion of two sections that actually relate to Rosh Hashana — namely, *Unetaneh Tokef* and *Aleinu*. They are nevertheless included.[19]

Lacking the dramatic sounding of the Shofar, *Musaf* calls for distinguished liturgical music, especially in its high point, the *"Avoda,"* toward which the entire service builds. *Musaf* should open with the Half-*Kaddish*, one of the most beautiful "virtuoso" compositions for the *Yamim Nora'im*. This opening also announces that a very significant service is about to begin. The dramatic unfolding, although much simpler than on Rosh Hashana, evolves through the first berachot to *Unetaneh Tokef* and the full antiphonic *Kedusha*, as we find it at *Shacharit. Kedushat ha-Yom* follows (pages 308-316).

The *Avoda*

The *Avoda* begins with *Aleinu* and the people kneel. It continues with *"Ata konanta,"*[20] and leads to the account of the Temple service (pp. 421-424).

At the confessions of the High Priest, the response of the people *"vehakohanim"* could be repeated three times, or only once as at present. Each time, however, the people kneel and prostrate themselves. It is a highly dramatic moment in an otherwise long service that lacks drama. It also elevates Yom Kippur over Rosh Hashana, when we kneel only once.

The *Avoda* moves to our own duties and failings (pp. 424-425), followed by "*Al Chet*" (p. 404-405), and the plea "Infinite Presence, teach us gentleness" (p. 403). The importance of the synagogue is emphasized: "The Second Temple" (p. 425 bottom-426) leading directly into "*Retze.*"

Conclusion

The *Amida* ends with the concluding *Berachot* (pp. 406-408), including the Aaronidic blessing and with "*Hayom te'ametzenu*" (p. 357) that was omitted at the end of *Shacharit*. "*Eleh Ezkera,*" including "The Ten Martyrs," could be omitted here and *Musaf* concluded.

Mincha

The Torah Reading

The Torah reading as chosen by *GoR* links itself organically to the *Haftara* of the morning and reinforces it. It tells us what we must do to become holy. The message of the Torah heard in the morning and that of the afternoon reading are complementary. The societal obligations, imposed on Jews by Isaiah in the morning *Haftara*, are extended in the afternoon Torah reading, just completed.

The *Haftara* reveals that they relate not merely to fellow Jews, but extend to all humanity. Every human being is "your neighbor."[21] For this reason, Jonah was sent to Nineveh.

At the same time the *Haftara* leads to the next part of the service. In many ways Jonah mirrors the fate of the Jewish people in the pursuit of its task: exiled into the world; at times denying its heritage, but affirming it proudly under pressure; suffering in the belly of its enemies; obstinate but compelled to carry out its mission; often less faithful to God than non-Jews, but ultimately risking its life for its message.

Pivotal for Jonah's transformation is his prayer and meditation in the belly of the fish. It is a personal outcry as the floods surround him, as he has descended to the uttermost depths of suffering. It is *teshuva* out of which assurance of redemption grows and swells into thanksgiving to God. At no time does the prophet argue with God regarding the fate decreed for him. Jonah's spirit forecasts the spirit of the Jewish people through endless periods of persecution and martyrdom.

The *Haftara* is therefore an affirmation of our tasks. Jonah's prayer, framed in singular form, calls every individual to account.

LEO TREPP

At the same time, the *Haftara* is prologue to *Mincha*. It sets its mood.

In *GoR*, Jonah's prayer is included in the Hebrew text, but omitted in the translation. Its importance should earn it a place in the translation as well.

Mincha and Yizkor

The Theme of Mincha is Martyrdom

As clearly recognizable in the western Ashkenasic *machzor*, this is the time to remember Jewish suffering and martyrdom. The introductory *Berachot* of the *Amida* might open the service, as they do now in *GoR*.

Excerpts from Selichot Might Follow

The traditional *Selichot* might be examined for possible introduction: "O God, how much have I been harried ever since my youth" (David ben Samuel Ha-Levi); "The voice that whimpers, it is Jacob's voice" (Kalonymus ben Judah); "O God, do not stand moot at my blood" (David ben Meshullam). Here the persecutions during the Crusades are depicted in graphic details, and the words acquire new relevance for us.

The Ten Martyrs

This leads to the story of the Ten Martyrs in the *selicha*, "*Eleh Ezkera*." This *selicha* has a preface that is omitted in *GoR* but might well find a place in it. It is of mystical character and has a deep theological significance. It offers the reason for our trials.

> Rabbi Yishmael purified himself, spoke the holy Name of God, rose up to the heavenly heights and asked of the man [angel] ... who answered him: "Accept it, you blameless and beloved ones, for I heard it from behind the curtain [from God] that you have been elected for that."

Thus did our ancestors answer the question, "How could God do that?" and the post-Holocaust generation has been given a guide. It was neither guilt, nor the absence of God, according to the ancients, but God's unfathomable will. I believe that the kabbalistic element need not concern us, as the study of Kabbala has become widespread. To emphasize the heroism of Jewish *women*, the story of Miriam bat Tanchum and her seven sons might be considered (B. Gittin 57b), to be followed by the story of the 400 boys and girls captured by the enemy to be disgraced. The girls set the example of *Kiddush ha-Shem*, inspiring the boys to follow it (B. Gittin 57b, preceding the previous selection). The same unconditional surrender to God was demonstrated in the self-sacrifice of the Jewish girls at Warsaw during the Nazi times. Their memory might therefore be evoked. These selections would reveal both the heroism of Jewish women as our role models and the vitality of the sacrificial spirit of Judaism throughout the ages.[22]

The section might end with the words of Nelly Sachs, "World, why have you taken our soft mothers from us and the fathers who say: My child, you are like me! We orphans are like no one in this world any more! O world! We accuse you![23]

The *Selicha* is traditionally followed by another one: "To this day, how many thousands of thousands have given their lives for the sanctification of Your Name."

These *selichot* can serve as introduction to the Remembrance of the Holocaust Martyrs that was previously omitted. In the spirit of the preceding *selichot* the words need a much stronger thrust. They are much too soft and polished. As a survivor, I feel disappointed by them; to our children, they may fail to convey the fury of the events.

Mincha has directly led the worshiper to the *Memorial Service.*

Ne'ila

Our fervor reaches its ultimate height. *Ne'ila* has two themes: "Open for us the gates" is symbolic of the climactic character of this hour.

In connection with it, the whole period of penitence flashes by the worshiper's mind. Will our prayers be accepted? The traditional *Ne'ila* therefore recalls the prayers during the entire span by including the opening verses of all the concluding *selichot* (*pizmonim*) recited during the entire period. It is a résumé, a plea before God: "We have been standing before You throughout all this period, and this is what we have said," leading up to the outcry of Rabbenu Gershom: "From one exile to the next." These selections should be available to worshipers and congregations that wish to use them.

Of the "Additional Prayers," the selection "As clay in the hand of the potter" (*GoR*, S. 381) may be suggested. It rests on Jeremiah 18:6 and, at the same time, reveals a subtle humor, as does a scherzo in a symphony. "You are the potter, and if we, Your creation, leak, it is the potter's fault" (see B. Sukka 52b).

LEO TREPP

Avinu Malkenu — Affirmation of Faith

We reach the culmination of the service, *Avinu Malkenu* and "*Shema.*" The concluding meditation may precede or follow the *Avinu Malkenu.*

The Last Teki'a

The Shofar sound that follows symbolizes our liberation from the enslavement to our sins and gives the call to action.[24]

Conclusion

I believe that the suggestions I have made may possibly add to the drama of Rosh Hashana, revealing the meaning in an organic sequence of prayers. They will also articulate the unity, as well as the individual character, of the *Tefilot* of Yom Kippur.

I would welcome the critique of my colleagues.[25]

NOTES

[1] *Ma'ariv* on Rosh Hashana was short. Many had fasted on that day and were to be returned to their home and meal quickly. See Elie Munk, *Die Welt der Gebete*, vol. 2 (Frankfurt: Hermon Verlag 1938), p. 190.

[2] If the members meet for *Kiddush* after the service, where they greet acquaintances they have not seen for a long time, there is reason not to disturb the joyfulness of the evening.

[3] At Mainz, where I worshiped in my youth, this is the version for the *Yamim Nora'im*, instead of "*hayoshev.*"

[4] *Hallel* would be inappropriate today. "They who stand in judgment should sing praises?" (B. Berachot 32b).

[5] See *Midrash Tanchuma*: Vayera, par. 23 (end); *Pesikta de-Rav Kahana*, Piska 23:10. The order is reversed, as *Zichronot* is *followed* by *Malchuyot*; for the reason of this arrangement, see note 12 below.

[6] *Pesikta de-Rav Kahana*, Piska 23:1.

[7] I remember that at Mainz, where I attended services in my youth, the rabbi, calling out the sounds, was seated.

[8] Choni, invoking God's holy Name, asks God to bring rain to the people, simply because they need it. The question whether they are worthy is not raised (M. Ta'anit 3:8).

[9] The introductory call to *Unetaneh Tokef* "*Uvechen lecha ta'aleh kedusha,*" as found in the traditional *machzor*, emphasizes the unitary character of the hymn and indicates that it constitutes an ascent. It might be introduced.

[10] See Eric Werner, *The Sacred Bridge* (London: D. Dobson, and New York: Columbia University, 1959), p. 253, and Joseph Heinemann, *Prayer in the Talmud* (Berlin and New York: Walter de Gruyter, 1977), p. 241, note 54.

[11] When Halacha ruled, according to Rabbi Akiba, that *Malchuyot* be included in "*Kedushat Ha-Yom*" and be followed by Shofar sounds, "*Kedushat Ha-Shem*" became the bridge. Had it remained in *Kedushat Ha-Shem* there would follow a *Beracha* without the concluding Shofar sounds. A dramatic sequence would have been interrupted, a clear indication that the sequence constitutes an organically unfolding unit. See the debate between R. Yohanan ben Nuri and Rabbi Akiba about the placement of *Malchuyot* and the sounding of the Shofar (M. Rosh Hashana 4:2; B. Rosh Hashana 32a). The Halacha follows Rabbi Akiba.

[12] Halacha reflects this idea. *Malchuyot-Zichronot-Shofarot* are based on the verse of Torah: "On your joyous occasions ... you shall *sound* the trumpets ... they shall be a *reminder* of you before the Lord, your God: *I, the Lord, am your God*" (Num. 10:10-11). This would mean that *Shofarot* was to open the sections, followed by *Zichronot* and ending with *Malchuyot*. The Rabbis however ruled: "First accept God's sovereignty over yourselves, then appeal to God that God remember you, and finally let this remembrance culminate in your freedom" (*Machzor Vitry* [Berlin: Mekitze Nirdamim, 1893], p. 346); see also B. Rosh Hashana 32a.

[13] Mordecai Kaplan said to me once that in honesty we should either leave out the words "*kore'im*" or kneel whenever we speak them.

[14] There was precedent for the second and third *beracha*. On days of public fasting to plea for rain, *Zichronot* and *Shofarot* were added to the *Amida* and after each the priests sounded the Shofar (M. Ta'anit 2:1-5). The Shofar sound after *Malchuyot*, whose eulogy actually proclaims the sanctity of the day, was later added by the rabbis. It emphasizes the importance of the day and reveals the coherence of the three *berachot*. ("Rabbi Yose ben Judah ruled: 'whenever *Zichronot* is mentioned, *Malchuyot* goes with it'" [B. Rosh Hashana 32a].) On fast days the people brought the Ark, covered with ashes, into the city square. Then, in prayer, heard the sound of the Shofar. We have bent the knee to God before the open Ark and now hear the Shofar. The theme is now fully developed.

[15] Additionally, people like to listen to the Shofar tones and we are given an opportunity to honor various members by permitting them to sound the Shofar.

[16] It was composed for Yom Kippur and in some congregations (Worms) is sung only on this evening. See Ismar Elbogen, *Der jüdische Gottesdienst in seiner geschichtlichen Entwicklung* (Hildesheim: Olms, 1962), pp. 88f.

[17] The *selichot* literature has been unjustly neglected, perhaps because the number of *selichot* was always optional, depending on the length of the day, or because they are sometimes written in difficult medieval Hebrew and contain allusions to midrashim that are no longer identifiable by the average worshiper.

[18] *Musaf* originated with the *Anshei Ma'amad* in the Temple, who repeated the morning prayer, perhaps with some additional pleas for their people,

LEO TREPP

who had sent them. It was ruled by the Amoraim that *Musaf* had to bring something new. By speaking of the sacrifices, something new had been added (J. Berachot 4:6).Throughout the year it will be difficult to find "something new" except the sacrifices. On Yom Kippur there is the narration of "*Avoda*." Since *GoR* introduces "*mechaye hametim*," giving it the meaning of revival of nature, there may be a possibility of introducing *Musaf* with its special character of Yom Kippur.

[19] The Western Ashkenazic rite actually replaces *Unetaneh Tokef* by another *piyut*, but leaves *Aleinu*, for which there was a precedent, since *Aleinu* was also transferred into the daily service. The traditional service prepares the worshiper for the *Musaf Avoda* by the Torah selection (Lev. 16:1-34) in which the ordinance of the *Avoda* is read.

[20] *GoR* uses the oldest of the *Avoda piyutim*, composed by Yose ben Yose (Palestine, 7th century) and also used by Amram and the Sephardim (see Elbogen, op. cit. pp. 216-217). The Ashkenazim have instead "*Amitz Koach*," written by Meshullam ben Kalonymus of Mainz. The choice of *GoR* not only goes back to the earliest version but may have as its purposes to express our linkage to the land of Israel and all groups of Jewry. This might be pointed out at the beginning. The middle sections (pp. 411-420) could be omitted or abbreviated, depending on the available time.

[21] "*Rea*," the neighbor, includes the new-Jew, even according to Samson Raphael Hirsch who writes: "carry love in your heart toward your non-Jewish brother, as your Torah teaches you" (*Neunzehn Briefe über Judentum* [Berlin: Welt Verlag, 1919], pp. 91f, 15th Letter).

[22] See *Mahzor for Rosh Hashana and Yom Kippur* (New York: The Rabbinical Assembly, 1972), p. 561.

[23] Nelly Sachs, *O The Chimneys* (Philadelphia: Jewish Publication Society, 1968), p. 31.

[24] It is a reminder of the Year of the Jubilee, when, at the sound of the Shofar, all slaves were liberated (Lev. 25; 8ff). Our liberation from sin and its consequences is related to the liberation of the slaves who lived in a kind of limbo between Rosh Hashana and Yom Kippur. Their toil ceased on Rosh Hashana but their freedom was granted on Yom Kippur (B. Rosh Hashana 8b; *Machzor Vitry*, p. 395). We have, ever since Rosh Hashana and up to this moment, existed in an equal state of uncertainty.

[25] I have tried to emphasize the role of women, but have not been able to give consideration to gender equality in the *machzor* text, an essential task of great difficulty. It entails the adjustment not only of the English, but, in honesty, of the Hebrew text as well.

Dreams and Promises
for the New Year

Martin W. Levy

Dear demons: shield me from Elul's amber face
'tekiah's' wail disturbs the dust
of sins known and recounted.
God's hamsa wrestles its prey
gnarled feet stumble, approaching
a lover whose cheek glistens, scarred.
The ram's horn awakens slumberers
who spit out work promises
layered with sweat and bile.
The steam from a worn tallis drenches
the pray-er, drowning his syllables.

Wash the dirt from riverbank's greed
summer spreads of honey, apples, figs
ripen and spoil, pungent sins bathe us.
Vows evaporate, concealed
deceit runs deep.
The leather straps singe my arm
and strangle those half-hearted amens.

Last year's spirits dance
and drip cold cream tears,
under the moon's mattress
a 'shevarim' crackles
awake!

Yom Kippur Worship:
A Missing Center?

Herbert Bronstein

"Our world rests on three pediments" (*Avot* I.2). The rabbinate of Rabbi Dreyfus, our cherished friend, is solidly and creatively based on three fundaments. First, much to the benefit of our widest world (*Olam*), he has served as an active and productive congregational rabbi, preacher, and teacher of "*Amchah*." Second, he is a fine scholar-academician of learning and integrity, and, third, continuously, a servant of the Central Conference of American Rabbis. In this respect, we have worked together on liturgical projects to which he contributed indefatigably of his learning, his meticulous care, and his unflagging energy. In all these he has been both passionate and principled and, at the same time, not without a perceptive and incisive sense of humor. My hope is that he will not find too many mistakes in the essay I have submitted in his honor.

What is the most important element in Yom Kippur worship? Most Jews would answer: "The *Kol Nidrei*," without, despite all available interpretations, having a very clear answer as to why. This is a people's verdict, of considerable weight in the emergence of liturgies. But the *Kol Nidrei* is a late element in the worship of Yom Kippur. Opposed by the Geonim of Babylonia, it did not find general acceptance until about 1000 C.E. Some knowledgeable Jews might cite as critical to Yom Kippur worship the texts of the *Vidui* (Confession).

A central element, however, of Yom Kippur worship as it emerged in antiquity is missing today from most non-Orthodox Jewish worship, or has been so "re-done" as to be present in name only. I am referring to the *Avodah* texts of the middle section (*Emtzai*)

HERBERT BRONSTEIN (C57) is senior scholar of North Shore Congregation Israel, Glencoe, Illinois.

HERBERT BRONSTEIN

of the *Musaf* ("additional service") of Yom Kippur day. The *Avodah* (which itself, of course, means "service") refers, in this context, to rites critical for atonement and spiritual renewal as they took place in the ancient Jerusalem Temple on the Day of Atonement. In various Orthodox liturgies, Ashkenazic or Sephardic, the texts of the *Avodah* have resulted from a process of accumulation of various liturgical "pieces" over the course of many centuries. There is an *Avodah* service in Reform Jewish liturgies, as well, but since there is no *Musaf* or "Additional Service" in the standard Reform liturgies, a reworking of the *Avodah* has been shifted to the afternoon or *Minḥah* service of Yom Kippur day. The elimination of the *Musaf* service from Reform Jewish worship as early as the late nineteenth century is, of course, understandable in the light of Reform's constant and consistent opposition, from its beginnings, to prayers for the future restoration of the priestly sacrificial cult of the Jerusalem Temple.

The various *maḥzorim*, high holy day prayer books standard in Conservative Judaism, beginning with a prayer book edited by Morris Silverman once in extensive use in the middle of the twentieth century, have also continued to manifest discomfort with references to the ancient Temple sacrificial cult. One finds frequent insertions of interpretive passages justifying references to sacrifices as reminiscences of ancient piety or as a metaphoric connection with the land of Israel and Jerusalem or with the spirit of self-giving. As if in embarrassment, the sacrificial texts, which are printed in the original Hebrew, are often not translated into English.

The *Gates of Repentance* endeavors to restore an *Avodah* in some way to its original core meaning. However, the Reform version of *Avodah*, though quite lengthy, has been semantically reduced and vitiated to what has been termed by our colleague Lawrence Hoffman, in his *Gates of Understanding*, as "a photo album" of Jewish historical experience. As a result, the original core meaning of a text central to Yom Kippur worship—which, as we shall see, could have very significant application today—has been lost.

Not, certainly, as an argument for the retention of prayers to restore sacrifices (!) but in behalf of the preservation of the design of our liturgy in its *transformation* or *transvaluation* of the motif of sacrifice, some words must be said of sacrifice as foundational to Jewish liturgy—perhaps to all Jewish and Christian liturgies. Whatever the various interpretations or trans-valuations of sacrifice as a religious institution, all of what we used to call the "High" or, better, "Axial"

YOM KIPPUR WORSHIP

religions take their forms from reinterpretations of prior archaic cosmologies and cosmogonic cults involving complex sacrifice, which emerged in ancient river valley agricultural systems. In these, at temple sites considered to be both the center of the world and the nexus and axis between the physical world and the spiritual realm of the gods, on sacred days, particularly the New Year, rites were performed reiterating the creation of the world. These rites functioned, in ancient worldviews, to renew the ordered cycle of existence and ensure perenniality, and so the material well-being as well as the social structure of a given society.[1] Echoes of these ideas, morally transformed, reverberate in Rosh Hashanah liturgy to this day. The spirit of sacrifice has been retained in many religions as foundational in another sense: the discipline of self-transcendence (central to the various axial religions) in identification with God or a metaphysical reality beyond the individual self. With this in mind we can return to our subject: the central part of the *Musaf* or additional service of Yom Kippur, the *Avodah*.

At the risk of treading on very familiar ground, we state again that the *Musaf* is a repetition on holy days of the second main component of Jewish worship, the *Tfilah* or "Prayer" *par excellence* of Jewish worship. The *Tfilah* was understood in early rabbinic times as a replacement, as it were, or "stand-in" for sacrifice and was statutorily recited at the times (morning and afternoon) when sacrifices were once offered in the Jerusalem Temple.[2]

Every *Tfilah* or *Amidah* ("Standing Prayer") is made up of three parts:

1. Three initial prayers of praise of God regularly recited in every service. In each of these the focus is on God, the God of faith, God's redemptive powers in the realm of the physical and the metaphysical, and God's Holiness.

2. An intermediate section, which varies according to the nature of the day, such as the Sabbath or specific holy days, each with its divinely ordained observances, which, including prayer, constitute Israel's service to God.

3. Three culminating prayers for acceptance of the worship, voicing thanksgiving, and affirming peace the ultimate expression of redemption, "the seal of all blessings."

It is my opinion that however textually different the ancient statutory liturgies, designed by ancient sages and developed over the centuries, they all share a deep structure that is both motif and narra-

HERBERT BRONSTEIN

tive, a movement from God (above, #1), through the service performed by the people of Israel (above, #2), to the culmination of redemption (above, #3). This is true in terms of deep structures of both of the two basic sections of the daily, Sabbath, and holy day prayers (*Sh'ma* and its Blessings and *Tfilah*). It is also true of the regular Grace after Meals (*Birkat Hamazon*).

Whether on the Sabbath or on Pilgrimage Festivals or on the High Holy Days, then, the middle blessings of the *Tfilah* or *Amidah* focus on the service of that particular day itself. This middle section is, in fact, called the "Sanctification of the Day (*Q'dushat Hayom*)." It encapsulates the central theme of the day and its observance, including, during the *Musaf* especially, Torah texts that prescribe the sacrificial service of that particular day in the ancient Temple.

In the case of Yom Kippur, the middle section of the *Musaf* is comprised of a reiteration, ultimately derived from various texts of the Mishnah, describing the sacrificial service of that day in the ancient Temple.

Now, in order to emphasize the centrality of the *Avodah* we must go into this section of the liturgy in greater detail. In a typical traditional liturgy today, allowing room for a variety of *piyyutim* (special poems or hymns), the following is, then, the order of the middle section of the *Tefilah Amidah* of the additional service on Yom Kippur. First, there is a general opening framework similar to those of other holy days in which are voiced characteristic motifs such as the chosenness of the people of Israel, and acknowledgment that God gave holy days to the Jewish people, in this case, Yom Kippur for forgiveness of sins and atonement with God through the Temple service. The introductory prayer, as is typical of other holy days as well, acknowledges that we are no longer able to perform the sacrifice and to find atonement with God through sacrifice at the Jerusalem Temple because of our sins for which we have been exiled from the Land. This is followed, in traditional liturgies, by a prayer for the restoration of the Temple and its rites. Appropriately, a reference to the particular sacrifices of the day assigned by Scripture is included.

The distinctive core section, as it has emerged over the centuries, of the *Avodah* proper is preceded by three liturgical "frames." The first of these is the *Alenu* (repeated from the Rosh Hashanah service). That is that great summation of the Judaic world outlook beginning with praise of the transcendent Creator of the Universe and emphasizing the particular calling of the Jewish people to serve with God in the repair of the world and the struggle against idolatry toward

YOM KIPPUR WORSHIP

the day when all will serve God in a redeemed world and God universally acknowledged as Sovereign. A second framing prayer is a supplication to God emphasizing that care must be taken in this service, and pleading that the Divine Presence be with the utterances of the leaders of the worship (*Heyeh Im Pipiyot*). Since the ancient sacrificial rites required an exacting care and order to preserve and regenerate the order of the world, this prayer parallels the incumbency on the High Priest of old to perform the sacrificial service with exactitude, utter concentration, and devotion. This point deserves reiteration: Since the actual sacrifices are not, cannot, and would not be performed today, the essential central portion of the *Avodah* must be, rather, a verbal recapitulation, better, a mentally mimetic reenactment of the "original" rite of Yom Kippur that took place in ancient days. The third "frame-prayer" is *Aḥilah L'el*, an appeal by the leader of the service for Divine strength to support his weaknesses.

Following these framing prayers, the core of the middle section of the *Musaf*, the *Avodah*, is constituted traditionally by a grand *piyyut*, a liturgical poem that, however different in various rites, follows the same ideational plan or design motif. In the Ashkenazic liturgies this poem is almost always *Amitz Koaḥ*, a multiple alphabetic acrostic written almost certainly by Meshulam ben Kalonymos of Lucca and Mainz (tenth century). In Sephardic liturgies, the *piyyut* is regularly *Atah Konantah*, considerably simpler but also an acrostic, traced back to the Middle Ages in Burgundy and Savoy, and preserved in north Italian communities as well.[3] These two great *piyyutim* differ in text but share the same design motifs and narrative scheme and both are alphabetical acrostics—which is itself also noteworthy. The inclusion of the entire alphabet is meant to signal the endeavor to communicate an encompassing wholeness, a sense of *completion*, which, in this case, is quite important beyond serving as a mere literary device.

Again, whether by design or through unconscious processes derived from constant association with Judaic textual sources, the story-line or narrative structure as found in all statutory liturgies of Judaism moves *from* God's creation of the world *through* Jewish covenant service *to* the culmination of redemption. In this case, it is the *Avodah* section of Yom Kippur that represents Israel's covenant service of God in the move from God through Israel's service that is required for the atonement necessary for a redemptive culmination. Referencing biblical and rabbinic texts (the latter from *Mishnah*

HERBERT BRONSTEIN

Yoma), the *Avodah-Piyyut* progresses from the Creation, through Noah and the patriarchs, to the tribe of Levi (*Nota bene*), and to the High Priest, who performs the *Avodah* service at the symbolic center of the world, where, after considerable preparation and sacrifices, he recites the *Sh'ma* in the Holy of Holies, pronouncing the Ineffable Name of God while those in attendance prostrate themselves, proclaiming the praise of the Name of the glory of God's kingdom forever and ever. Following this the High Priest says the culminating words of the text: "You shall be purified." With the necessary sacrifices and the ritual of the scapegoat and prayers of the High Priest, then, the atonement rites performed for any deviations from religious norms that threaten the order of the world are completed. Thus the moral order of the world is renewed, atonement achieved, and the well-being, on all levels, of people and land assured.

The sense of completion and wholeness is celebrated at this point in various liturgies with *piyyutim* that express wholeness, perfection, and glory, such as *Mareh HaKohen* ("The Appearance of the Priest") and *Ashrei Ayin* ("Fortunate the Eye that Beheld These Things"). But instead of the sense of culmination that we expect at this point in the service, what follows instead in traditional liturgies are texts expressing abrupt and calamitous disruption represented by the destruction of the Temple, the violent ending of any possibility of this, Israel's service, the *Avodah*, as performed in the Temple in ancient days. We must recall that Jerusalem, the Temple, more particularly the Holy of Holies, in ancient consciousness, at the center of the center of the world was considered to be the connecting place between heaven and earth, the place from which the order of the world was to be maintained. The destruction of the Temple implies that the center is broken. In ancient religious consciousness, with the center broken, the harmony of the cosmos and the moral order of the world could not be maintained. The basic design motif, from Creation through Israel's service (symbolized by the service in the Temple) to Redemption is disrupted. Accordingly, at this point, in many traditional liturgies, there are texts that represent not only calamity, but utter lack, emptiness, and religious impotence: "There is no Temple, there is no altar, there is no altar fire, there are no vessels, there are no implements," and so forth, and so forth.

A traditional liturgical motif not entirely acceptable to our theological views and historic consciousness also appears again at this point: "Because of our sins we were exiled from our land." Nevertheless we find also a strong suggestion, even guidance, to us in our

YOM KIPPUR WORSHIP

own liturgical work in the replacement of sacrifice in the traditional liturgy with prayers for forgiveness (*slihot*) and confession (*vidui*). These substitute for the *Avodah* rites of old. They are now our service, and not actual sacrifices.

But more telling is the fact that this is the point at which a fatefully tragic dimension of Israel's service to God appears in the *Avodah*: *Qiddush HaShem*, martyrdom. On the way to redemption, in the implied view of traditional liturgy, this is Israel's ultimate sacrificial service to God. Sacrifice is, as we have noted, foundational to the classical "High" religions representing as it does utter self-transcendence in identification with God; and martyrdom is the ultimate act of self-transcendence. For many Jews over the centuries this remained the ultimate atoning service of redemption. In itself this is not so strange in the context of the theme of the overall sense of self-transcendence in Judaism. Self-transcendence, after all, is basic to the Judaic affirmation of faith, the *Sh'ma*, and indeed to all true service of the Divine: love and devotion to God *with all our being, nothing held back*. This motif is evident in Akiva's reference, on the brink of his own martyrdom, to the *Sh'ma*. Teaching to the last, he tells those assembled that he has never completely been able to understand—and, more important—never been able to perform the *mitzvah* mentioned in the *Sh'ma*, to love and serve God with all one's heart, with all one's soul, with all one's being. Now he understands and is able to do so, through giving his all to God.

Thus, in the traditional *Avodah* liturgy, is the appearance of the classic *piyyut* of martyrdom, the *Eilah Ezkerah*, depicting the torture and death of ten rabbis under the empire of Rome. Other subsequent martyrologies have accumulated in the liturgy during the course of the centuries that accord with the same pattern. In the *Avodah* service, then, a simple statement of the pattern would be: from God's creation of the world and establishment of the priesthood and Temple and Temple worship, to maintain and renew the order of the world through Israel's covenant service of God (symbolic of the performance of the *mitzvot*), leading in covenant partnership with God, to redemption. With the destruction of the Temple, martyrdom is also a service-role assigned to Israel leading to atonement and redemption. While we would not wish to center this pattern, or even espouse this view, we would want liturgically to interpret the reasons for the destruction of the Temple, based on sources in our tradition that point to ways of service required of us now. Various sub-motifs are found in ancient rabbinic discourse that interpret the

HERBERT BRONSTEIN

meaning of this disruption and are of considerable liturgical interest today. Recalling that the Temple was symbolically the focus of the maintenance and restoration of world order, it is well known that the rabbis taught that the First Temple was destroyed because of the three cardinal sins of idolatry, murder, and lust, and the Second Temple was destroyed because of gratuitous hostility, petty contention, and meaningless hatred (*B. Yoma* 9b). There is much for us to say, liturgically, of the idolatries, violence, and hate on the wider scene from which we and the world suffer in our day, as well as the narcissism and focus on self as opposed to the self-transcending service to God in the various modalities that *can* lead to redemption.

In these respects a comment is in order about which I spoke in the process of preparing the Reform Haggadah, when I employed the term, many years ago, "creative retrieval." I mean the retrieval from our own traditional sources and our own roots, from the design of our own liturgy, of meaningful elements relevant to our own time. From another perspective, I have also used the term borrowed from Gabriel Marcel, "resourcement." This is meant to imply that our own tradition itself has the resources for an approach to our world in our time and with our needs, which demands that we put ourselves back into the essential meaning of those sources. This process also is the source of our own spiritual renewal. In no place in our liturgical heritage are the possibilities clearer than in accumulated texts of the *Avodah* of Yom Kippur, but far more, in its design.

Among us, various ways can be discovered to accomplish this purpose, ways that are appropriate and consonant with the basic liturgical pattern I have described. We can use the traditional *Avodah* service text as Torah study on Yom Kippur or in preparation for the high holy days, teaching the transvaluation of sacrifice begun explicitly by our early rabbis into deeds of mercy, repentance, and prayer. But it is important, to begin with, that we come to some understanding of the basic pattern, lest through *amaratzus* or flippancy, or heedless self-arrogation, the structures of our spirituality with its magnificent patterns relapse into desuetude or into the banal.

Beyond the image of the Jerusalem of the altar, the Jerusalem of the priests and the sacrificial rites, is the ancient human symbol of "the Center" from which and toward which broken harmonies could be restored, fire rekindled against the harsh brutality and cold indifference of a disordered world, a spark preserved to renew the light of the world. Yes, the First Temple, according to rabbinic liter-

YOM KIPPUR WORSHIP

ature, the symbolic center of order, was destroyed because of idolatry, lust, and murder. The second Temple, in the same sources fell because of baseless hate, gratuitous trivial jealousies, and petty meanness. But, through our modern historic consciousness we know that the temples were destroyed by the battering of the boundless greed of arrogant power, the monstrous wreckings by Babylon and Rome. In our own time, we have witnessed "the place," existentially, of sanctity desecrated, the altar fire scattered, the words of ordering prayer lost in whirlwinds of the destruction of European Jewry along with so much of its spirituality, the "Ritual" abandoned, forgotten, and nearly lost. The destruction of the Jerusalem Temple can symbolize for Jewry a fissure of tragedy in the wholeness of life, revolving spheres broken from the moral orbit, vessels of holiness and light shattered and the throne of glory cracked, all images from our past including the image of the thrusting out from God's presence from the world.

Despite the destruction of the Temple, nevertheless our people went on to transvalue and reinterpret the meaning of the ancient Yom Kippur service. Our liturgies, too, must serve for the ordering prayer of the priests, the restoring vision of the prophets, the preserving doctrines of the sages, at the altar, the center, the place of light thrice holy from above in our synagogues, our places of worship, where Torah is taught and lived. This is the ideal meaning of the *Avodah* service. In our age particularly it is important that we recover and preserve it.

Notes

1. M. Eliade, *Patterns in Comparative Religion* (Lincoln: University of Nebraska, 1996), pp. 367–409 and T.H. Gaster, *Thespis* (New York: Harper, 1961) pp. 37–49, 61–103.

2. See for example, *B.T. Sota* 32b, *Song R* 5:2; *B.T. Berachot* 32b; *B.T. B.M.* 59a. See also *B.T. Berachot* 26b; *Y.T. Berachot* 4:17b.

3. Cf. J. Rosenberg, *Qovetz*, Berlin, 1856; I. Elbogen (Jewish Publication Society, 1993), p. 239.

Additional
Discussion Questions

On *Un'taneh Tokef*

1. Margaret Moers Wenig, "The Poetry and the Power of Paradox,"
    CCAR Journal, Spring 2009.
    In the case of *Un'taneh Tokef*, is there justification for removing or
    editing the text of the liturgy? Why or why not, and if yes, what
    is that justification? How can the complex poetic structure and
    use of imagery in this *piyut* bring our prayers to a new level?
    What are your thoughts on the inclusion of an unabridged ver-
    sion of the *piyut* in the Reform *machzor*?

2. Daniel Plotkin, "Giving Meaning to Our Days: Reimagining
    Un'taneh Tokef—A Survey of Selected Sermons," *CCAR Journal*,
    Spring 2009.
    With which of these sermons do you identify the most? Which
    present the greatest challenge to your beliefs? Explain your re-
    sponses. How do current events influence our interpretations of
    the liturgy?

On *Kol Nidrei*

Read the transcript of the end-of-call discussion between Rabbis
Prinz, Zimmerman, Zecher, and Spicehandler, which includes their
personal experiences and memories of *Kol Nidrei*. How do they use
the liturgy of *Kol Nidrei* to help bring comfort during times of difficult economic realities? What are their views on the importance of
consulting both other clergy and laypeople when making liturgical
decisions? What else do you find interesting about their comments,
and why?

On Other Parts of Yamim Noraim Liturgy

1. Bernard M. Zlotowitz, "The Torah and Haftarah Readings for
    the High Holy Days," *CCAR Journal*, Fall 1975.
    What connections can you make between the Torah and haf-
    tarah readings and the themes of the Yamim Noraim? What im-
    plications does the theory that these readings serve as a polemic
    against Christianity have for our communities?

2. Leo Trepp, *Yamim Nora'im*: The Traditional Liturgy and *Gates of Repentance,"* CCAR *Journal,* Summer 1991.
   What themes of the liturgy do the textual changes and creative ideas in this article highlight? How might you incorporate some of these ideas into your services?

3. Herbert Bronstein, "Yom Kippur Worship: A Missing Center?" *CCAR Journal,* Summer 2004.
   How is the Yom Kippur *Avodah* service a relevant piece of liturgy for our time? In what other areas of worship or Jewish practice might you utilize "creative retrieval" or "resourcement"?

On the Reform Jewish Approach to High Holy Day Liturgy

1. Eric L. Friedland, *"Gate of Repentance*: A Review-Essay," *CCAR Journal,* Winter 1977.
   How does this review of *Gate of Repentance,* the *machzor* of the London-based Union of Liberal and Progressive Synagogues, contribute to our understanding of the development of our High Holy Day liturgy?

2. Eric L. Friedland, "Historical Notes on the American Reform High Holy Day Liturgy" *Journal of Reform Judaism,* Summer 1988.
   How does the author's commentary on *Gates of Repentance* shed light on the context and intention of the decisions made by the editors of the *machzor?* What do you see as the "next step" for the liturgical pieces that he discussed in his article over twenty years ago?

On God Imagery, Language, and Theology

1. Joel Mosbacher, "Searching for God in the 7th Grade," *CCAR Journal,* Spring 2009.
   In your experience, what best facilitates the spiritual expression of your congregation? In what areas might you want to encourage theological development? How can the Yamim Noraim serve as an opportunity for spiritual exploration, expansion, and education?

2. Nancy Flam, "The Angels Proclaim It, But Can We? 'The Whole Earth is Full of God's Glory,'" *CCAR Journal,* Spring 2009.
   According to Rabbi Flam's expanded definition of *din,* what manifestations of *din* have you witnessed in the past year, and how can you respond to them with *rachamim?* What opportunities can you provide for the practice of mindfulness during services or through other programs?

3. Yoel H. Kahn, "Wrestling with God's Image in the High Holy Day Liturgy," *CCAR Journal*, Spring 2009.

   How do you respond when you feel torn between the historical value of the liturgy and a personal objection to its message? Can a piece of liturgy be spiritually meaningful even if its message is problematic? Why or why not? What is your response to the idea presented in this essay of searching for countertexts, rather than "fixing" the liturgy itself?

Poetry for the High Holy Days

1. Martin W. Levy, "Dreams and Promises for the New Year," *CCAR Journal*, Summer/Fall 1995.

   Which images in this poem express the condition in which we enter the month of Elul? Who are the "demons" in the beginning of the poem? What is the role of the shofar in this poem?

2. Ephraim M. Rosenzweig, "Rosh Hashanah Morning," *CCAR Journal*, Summer 1973.

   What is the role of faith in the story of the *Akeidah*? How does this compare to the role that you see faith playing in your life? In the lives of those in your congregation?

3. Martin W. Levy, "The Penitent's Hour," *Journal of Reform Judaism*, Summer 1989.

   What mood does this poem express regarding the moment of *Kol Nidrei*? Which aspects of the *Kol Nidrei* experience that are highlighted in the imagery of this poem resonate most strongly with you, and why? What thoughts and emotions do you experience when standing before the open ark on *Kol Nidrei*, and what effect do these have on you?

Suggestions for Further Reading

Agnon, Shmuel Yosef. *Days of Awe: A Treasury of Jewish Wisdom for Reflection, Repentance, and Renewal on the High Holy Days*. New York: Schocken Books, 1975.

Elbogen, Ismar. *Jewish Liturgy*. Philadelphia: Jewish Publication Society, 1993.

Elkins, Dov Peretz. *Rosh Hashanah Readings: Inspiration, Information and Contemplation*. Northvale, NJ: Jason Aronson, 1992.

Elkins, Dov Peretz. *Yom Kippur Readings: Inspiration, Information and Contemplation*. Northvale, NJ: Jason Aronson, 1992.

Gershon, Stuart Weinberg. *Kol Nidrei: Its Origin, Development & Significance*. Northvale, NJ: Jason Aronson, 1994.

Goodman, Philip. *The Rosh Hashanah Anthology*. Philadelphia: Jewish Publication Society, 1992.

Goodman, Philip. *The Yom Kippur Anthology*. Philadelphia: Jewish Publication Society, 1992.

Hammer, Reuven. *Entering the High Holy Days: A Guide to the Origins, Themes, and Prayers*. Philadelphia: Jewish Publication Society, 2005.

Hoffman, Lawrence A. *Gates of Understanding 2 (Sha'are Binah): Appreciating the Days of Awe*. New York: CCAR Press, 1983.

Kates, Judith A., and Gail Twersky Reimer. *Beginning Anew*. New York: Touchstone, 1997.

Levy, Benjamin. *A Faithful Heart: Preparing for the High Holy Days*. New York: URJ Press, 2001.

Olitzky, Kerry M., and Rachel T. Sabath. *Preparing Your Heart for the High Holy Days*. Philadelphia: Jewish Publication Society, 1996.

Spiegel, Shalom. *The Last Trial*. Woodstock, VT: Jewish Lights Publishing, 1993.

CPSIA information can be obtained at www.ICGtesting.com
Printed in the USA
BVOW05s1921090114

341259BV00004B/8/P

9 780881 231298